Stories from small museums

Manchester University Press

Stories from small museums

Fiona Candlin, Toby Butler, and Jake Watts

Manchester University Press

Copyright © Fiona Candlin, Toby Butler, and Jake Watts 2022

The right of Fiona Candlin, Toby Butler, and Jake Watts to be identified as the authors of this work has been asserted by them in accordance with the Copyright, Designs and Patents Act 1988.

Published by Manchester University Press
Oxford Road, Manchester M13 9PL

www.manchesteruniversitypress.co.uk

British Library Cataloguing-in-Publication Data
A catalogue record for this book is available from the British Library

ISBN 978 1 5261 6686 9 hardback

ISBN 978 1 5261 6688 3 paperback

First published 2022

The publisher has no responsibility for the persistence or accuracy of URLs for any external or third-party internet websites referred to in this book, and does not guarantee that any content on such websites is, or will remain, accurate or appropriate.

Typeset
by Sunrise Setting Ltd, Brixham
Printed in Great Britain
by CPI Group (UK) Ltd, Croydon

Contents

List of figures

Every effort has been made to obtain permission to reproduce copyright material, and the publisher will be pleased to be informed of any errors or omissions for correction in future editions.

List of figures

List of figures

Acknowledgements

Stories from small museums was written as part of the Mapping Museums project, which was generously funded by the Arts and Humanities Research Council (AHRC). We are indebted to them for their support, as we are to our colleagues in the research team: Alexandra Poulovassilis, Andrea Ballatore, Jamie Larkin, Val Katerinchuk, and Mark Liebenrood. Our research was made possible by their prior work in data collection, the design and production of a database, and data analysis. We would also like to thank Irina Zigar for her last-minute research assistance.

We are indebted to the founders and volunteers in all the museums that we visited, who are too numerous to mention individually. They very generously shared their histories and experiences with us, showed us around their collections, and patiently educated us on the differences between trains and locomotives, the structure of the British Army, and the history of their villages and towns, among other topics. We are especially grateful to the people who allowed us to feature them and their museums in this book, for checking and rechecking relevant sections of the book, and for letting us use their photographs. Thank you, too, to Julian Farrance and Kelsey Loveless from the National Army Museum, Paul Evans at the Army Museums Ogilby Trust, and David Harrigan from the Lincolnshire Aviation Network for their expert insight on regimental museums and military aviation museums. Any errors are our responsibility.

Meredith Carroll at Manchester University Press offered support and direction for the book, and Alun Richards helped steer it to completion. Matt Cook read the first complete draft and the later version of the introduction, Lianne McTavish and an anonymous reviewer wrote reader's reports, and Andy Flinn read the final draft. Their comments were encouraging and challenging in equal measure and helped shape the finished text. Thank you for being such good critical friends. We

Acknowledgements

are also grateful to Aoife Monks and Carolyn Burdett, who worked out the title, and Paul Morgans, who prepared the images for print.

We are grateful to our families and friends. Fiona Candlin would like to thank Alex Candlin, Greg Candlin, Kieron Corless, Jo Morra, Liz Orton, and Peg Rawes for their practical help and intellectual companionship. Toby Butler would like to thank his wife, Liz, for holding the fort while he was away interviewing for long periods. Jake Watts would like to thank his partner, Ryan, for all his support, and his parents, Mick and Julie, for their constant encouragement.

0 km 100

Laidhay Croft

Gairloch Museum

SCOTLAND

Black Watch Museum

Scottish Vintage Bus Museum

Edinburgh

Museum of Free Derry

Whitehead Railway Museum

NORTHERN IRELAND

Belfast

Royal Irish Fusiliers Regimental Museum

Nidderdale Museum

Museum of North Craven Life

Ingrow Loco

Peace Museum

Museum of Rail Travel

British Commercial Vehicle Museum

Manchester

Museum of Transport

RAF Ingham Heritage Centre

Metheringham Airfield Visitor Centre

National Waterways Museum

WALES

ENGLAND

Suffolk Regimental Museum

Brynmawr and District Museum

Aldbourne Heritage Centre

Museum of Asian Music

Purfleet Military Heritage Centre

Criterion Heritage Centre

Tŷ Ebbw Fach Heritage Centre

London

Cardiff

Kent & Sharpshooters Yeomanry Museum

Shipwreck Museum

Bakelite Museum

Adjutants General Corps Museum

Horsepower: The Museum of the King's Royal Hussars

Perranzabuloe Museum

Charlestown Shipwreck & Heritage Centre

King Edward Mine Museum

Introduction

Founding stories, finding stories

It was midsummer, the sun was shining intermittently, and I was sitting in the garden at the Bakelite Museum with the founder and curator, Patrick Cook, a small slight man with a large moustache, well turned out in a vintage tweed suit. Our conversation proceeded in fits and starts as Patrick went to make and serve afternoon tea for visitors or paused to answer questions about the collection. In one of the lulls I took the chance to ask how he first established the museum. He replied, 'It's a very long story, Fiona.' 'Start at the beginning,' I suggested. 'Is there a beginning?' he queried. After further prompting he said, 'The question has different answers. I adapt to the listener and their expectations – so I can give you the

Figure 0.1 Patrick Cook at the Bakelite Museum, Somerset

1

simplistic version.' Patrick was being contrary, which is not unusual, and in offering 'the simplistic version' he was gently mocking my academic status. Nonetheless, he was making important points: there is no clear starting point for a museum, or for that matter anything else, and there are always different ways of presenting and accounting for the same project.[1]

Patrick had established the only Bakelite museum in the UK and possibly the world, but he was certainly not alone in setting up a small museum. Since the 1960s, tens of thousands of people in the UK have collected millions of objects and launched museums on all manner of subjects. Museums of cartoons, fairgrounds, golf, tomatoes, vacuum cleaners, sewing machines, and sci-fi have opened, as have museums of rural life, belief and identity, transport, war and

Figure 0.2 Exhibition at the Cartoon Museum, London

conflict, and local history. These new small independent museums, or micromuseums, as I refer to them here for the sake of brevity, now account for over half of all the museums in the UK. They are not eccentric exceptions or curious anomalies. In terms of numbers, they easily dominate the sector, as they do elsewhere in the world.[2]

Stories from small museums asks what prompted the boom in the number of micromuseums. Who exactly opened the new museums and why did they want to do so? What kinds of museums did they open? Where did the objects come from and where were they housed? Who paid for these spaces and things, and who did the work? And what were the wider circumstances of the new micromuseums? How was it possible that people could open so many museums?

To answer these questions, Toby Butler and I travelled across the UK to talk to the museums' founders. They told us all manner of stories about lobbying local landowners and councils, unexpected donations, builders who worked for cost, learning how to mend roofs or lay bricks, organising coffee mornings, favours called in, volunteering – of generally taking a do-it-yourself approach. The founders also told us about the objects and places that they valued or loved, communities and identities that had been lost or that they were attempting to build, people they had known, family histories, friendship, belonging and not-belonging, and the pleasures of working together.

Figure 0.3 Neil Cole, the Museum of Classic Sci-fi, Northumberland

The people whom we met talked about what was happening in their villages and towns, homes, and workplaces. In almost all cases, their narratives were closely interwoven with some of the major social, political, and economic shifts of the late twentieth century, which Jake Watts then researched in more detail. Changes to the structure of the Armed Forces emerged as an important factor in the boom, as did the modernisation of the railways, industrialisation and de-industrialisation, the reorganisation of local government, tourism, and second homes, among many other factors. The growing number of micromuseums was intimately linked to national and international, as well as to local, histories.

Patrick gave numerous reasons why he started the Bakelite Museum. As a teenager, he and his brother had constructed a natural history museum in the kitchen at home, and they had planned on opening a fully fledged museum as adults; he loved the material and the way it was styled; the smell of Bakelite had a Proustian quality, because it reminded him of his grandmother's house; and he had used Bakelite to construct installations when he was an art student in London in the 1970s. He said he preferred it because it was a reviled material and, he added, it was readily available in the flea markets of the time.[3]

In this Introduction I begin with the same question I asked Patrick and many other museum founders – how did it get started? I situate the book in relation to the Mapping Museums project, of which this book forms part, and outline what we mean by a museum. I then introduce the heritage debates that were contemporaneous with the museums boom and explain how the Mapping Museums research verified some aspects of the heritage debates and challenged others, particularly those arguments that linked the expansion of the museum sector to de-industrialisation. I outline the historian Raphael Samuel's argument that micromuseums are a form of unofficial history and consider its validity. My narrative is intended to provide the empirical evidence and framework that underpin our research, demonstrate how our central questions arose, and explain its relationship to literature on the topic.

I then move on to the second question that we commonly ask museum founders – what happened next? This proves to have a lengthy answer. I outline why we decided to conduct oral histories, how we planned that research, whom we judged to be a museum founder, and how we inadvertently produced a rather optimistic account of the museums boom. I discuss the importance of visiting museums in person and draw attention to the gender and ethnicity of our narrators, noting how we address that subject within the text as a whole. I close by discussing the construction of oral history narratives, and by outlining the scope and structure of the book.

Mapping Museums

For me, *Stories from small museums* began in a bed and breakfast in Norfolk in south-east England in the summer of 2014. I had noticed that academic debates on museum history, practice, and theory almost invariably concentrated on national or large independent museums and that small independent museums generally fell beneath the scholarly radar.[4] I wanted to work out if and how the dominant debates in museum studies would change if academics studied the Vintage Wireless and Television Museum in London or the Dartmoor Prison Museum, rather than the British Museum or the Bilbao Guggenheim, and so I started visiting micromuseums across the UK.[5]

In the course of conducting that research I spent a good deal of time wandering around the UK, hence my visit to Norfolk. I would arrive at a collection of buttons or bicycles only for the curator or a visitor to recommend another interesting museum in the locality. The next set of incumbents would then send me on to a further destination – a museum of shells, gas production, or Victorian science. Few were ever mentioned in the guidebooks I'd bought or on the websites I'd consulted, and I kept searching for a comprehensive list of museums to help me plan ahead. As I investigated, I began to realise that there was no such list. There were numerous surveys, but there was nothing that included all the museums in the UK. Arts Council England only collected information on accredited museums – in other words, those certified as having attained professional benchmarks; the Museums Association only gathered information on their members; and other organisations only listed the museums in their remit, be it in Wales, regiments, or universities. Many museums, and especially small museums, were neither accredited nor members of an association, and were generally overlooked elsewhere.[6]

At first the lack of information seemed little more than an inconvenience. Slowly, however, I began to realise that it limited our collective understanding of the museum sector. If we were unable to track which museums were open at a given time, where they were, their size, governance, and the subjects they covered, then how could we get a grasp of the sector as a whole? The lack of coherent information also stymied historical investigation. Although scholars knew that the number of museums had sharply increased in the late twentieth century, it was not clear exactly when they had opened, where, or what had happened to them. Had the new museums even remained open? As the situation stood, it was impossible to assess if and how the sector had changed.

Sitting in my Norfolk bed and breakfast, looking out at the pancake-flat fields, I realised that I wanted to combine the study of individual micromuseums with a recent history of the museum sector. And for that I needed a list – or, better still, a database – that would enable me to search, analyse, and visually plot information about museums over time. Clearly, it was work for more than one person and it was well beyond my own skill set, so on returning to London I started contacting fellow academics for advice. Eventually, and more through serendipity than calculation, I met Alexandra Poulovassilis, professor in computer science, director of Birkbeck Knowledge Lab, and a specialist in complex systems with considerable experience of developing joint projects with arts and humanities researchers. She agreed to collaborate. Together we applied for and were awarded an Arts and Humanities Research Council grant for a multi- and inter-disciplinary project called 'Mapping Museums: the history and geography of the UK independent sector 1960–2020'. This book is the last output from that research.

To cut a long and complex story very short, we worked with a team of researchers to gather information on all the museums that had been open in the UK since 1960, we designed and built a database, and we analysed the data.[7] We took 1960 as the starting point for our research, partly because a large survey of museums had been conducted that year, and partly because we wanted to have a view of the sector before the boom occurred, which was generally assumed to be at some point in the 1970s or 1980s. It took us four years to collect data, develop the website and database, analyse the data, and write a report: research that was made publicly available online in 2020.[8]

So what did we discover? The data was extensive, and I will discuss some aspects of our findings in the sections that follow, but I want to highlight a few points from the outset.[9] It showed that there had undoubtedly been a massive expansion in the number of museums. There were around 1,000 museums open in the UK in 1960, with another 3,000 museums opening in the years that followed, not all of which survived. Most of these new museums were small, which we defined as having fewer than 10,000 visitors per year, although in many cases they only attracted audiences in the hundreds, and by far the majority of the new venues were independent in that they did not receive core funding from the state. In 1960, the museum sector had been roughly equally split between government-funded and independent museums, but by 2017, when we ran our analyses, the independent museums accounted for over 70% of the total.[10] By that point around half of all museums in the UK were both small and independent. When size and governance are combined, they are the biggest single group of museums in the UK.

What is a museum?

At this point I want to pause and explain exactly what we mean by a museum. The Mapping Museums research team spent the first two years of the project agonising about definitions of museums and criteria. Our deliberations and decisions had a direct impact on what was listed in the database and thereby on our analysis.

The obvious way to decide which museums to include in the database was to use a definition. The issue was, which one? Our research covered sixty years. During that time the UK Museums Association had introduced the first official definition of museums, and they had revised or replaced those terms on four subsequent occasions.[11] While there were some commonalities across all five versions – they all stipulated that a museum collects objects or material evidence – other aspects of the definitions had changed. For instance, the first version, introduced in 1971, included museums that were inaccessible to the general public, such as specialist medical museums, whereas the terms adopted in 1977 stipulated that a museum must provide access to the public.

To complicate matters further, definitions vary geographically within the UK. The English, Northern Irish, Scottish, and Welsh governments all have separate bodies with responsibility for museums, and Scotland opted to follow the code set by the International Council for Museums (ICOM), because unlike the Museums Association definition it recognises intangible heritage. The ICOM definition was rewritten in 2007 and again in 2019, although the new terms were deemed so ideologically laden, aspirational, or vague that twenty-four national committees wrote to express their dissent.[12] As of 2021 the terms had not been ratified, and it is likely that another formulation will take its place, giving some indication of both the contested nature of definitions and the level of difficulty involved in devising them. Thus, no single definition covered the period and geographic area encompassed within our study.

More importantly, using an ICOM or Museums Association definition would impose a professional framework on our research and narrow our field of study. All the definitions specify that museums are institutions, and in ICOM's case 'permanent institutions'. They also stipulate that museums have specific forms of governance. When the ICOM definition was temporarily introduced, in 1977, it required museums to be organised on a not-for-profit basis, as it still does, and since 1998 the Museums Association has stated that museums are necessarily held in public trust. Thus, in these models, any organisation that is informally established (for instance, in rooms in private houses or workplaces) or has fragile

7

premises (such as sheds) or is financially insecure is disqualified, as are museums that are privately owned, run on commercial lines, or put together by a group on an ad hoc basis.[13]

We decided to develop our own criteria for which venues to include in the database. In most cases it is relatively straightforward to decide if something is a museum or not: it looks like a museum, is called a museum, and performs museum-like activities. However, some organisations occupy a conceptual grey area. If a town hall has an extensive collection of portraits and silverware on display in its main function room, could that be considered a museum? Are the historical displays in the foyer of a corporate headquarters a museum, or the curated paintings in hospital corridors? What about historic buildings that have a few objects on display, or a diorama that indicates how the windmill or croft was once used and occupied? How about art galleries with no collections? We needed a rubric to guide our decisions, and we wanted our criteria to be as inclusive as possible while still being usable.

At first, we wondered about simply including any organisation that called itself a museum. The problem with this is that nomenclature is no guide to identity. In the 1980s and 1990s numerous heritage centres and visitor centres were established, some of which were information centres or had exhibitions that consisted only of wall texts, while others fitted the most conventional requirements for a museum in that they collected, safeguarded, researched, and interpreted collections, making them accessible to the public. Or museums had names like The Box, The Land of Lost Content, Morayvia, Sick to Death, and Enginuity.

Eventually, we decided that for the purposes of our study, museums would have a collection, care for objects in the long term, and that at least some of those objects would be on display. They also had to have a public orientation and occupy demarcated space. The first criteria – having a collection – is a conventional one, but to the best of our knowledge even museums that focus on intangible heritage – for instance, Mythstories Museum in Shropshire – are accompanied by some kind of object-based exhibition, in Mythstories' case the books and props used in storytelling. Caring for objects in the long term gave us a rationale for excluding art galleries without collections, which otherwise fulfil every museum function, while the element of display helped us distinguish between museums and types of organisation that collected or stored but did not prioritise the exhibition of objects – for instance, some archives.

We chose the term 'public orientation' rather than 'access', because some places are technically accessible but do not welcome visitors – for instance, historic houses that are required by law to let people see specified works of art or items of furniture. Conversely, some small museums may be quite inaccessible because lack of staff or funding prevents them from opening for more than a few days a year, or by appointment only. However, as long as those openings were publicised, happened on a regular basis (say, the last Sunday afternoon in the month), and visitors were actively welcomed, then we listed the museum in our database. Lastly, stipulating that museums should have a demarcated space or threshold was a means of differentiating them from collections that are dispersed throughout a building and have a primarily decorative function, as is often the case in town halls and businesses.

We did not include pop-up, online, or mobile museums, although these are deserving of more analysis. This was partly out of a pragmatic need to limit the scope of the study but mainly because we were interested in the relationship between museum development and location. We wanted to know whether numbers of museums had risen more in some places than others, whether there were links between the types of museum that opened and where they opened, and if and how museums were embedded in their local areas. Pop-up and mobile museums move from site to site, and online museums are not located as such, and so they did not fit the scope of our research or indeed the criteria we eventually established. We also excluded archives, libraries, and places of worship unless they had an artefact collection and accompanying displays in a separate museum space, although this was often a difficult distinction to draw.[14]

There will always be different ways to demarcate the museum sector, and none of them are set in stone. Our approach produced a more expansive account of the museum sector than recent surveys have allowed. Our version includes small, ad hoc, commercial, and private museums, as well as museums that are not members of the Museums Association or accredited by Arts Council England, and that are too modest to be featured in guidebooks.

The heritage debates revised

During the 1980s and 1990s the expansion of the museum sector was the subject of intense and often vitriolic debate. A wide range of journalists, academics, and commentators made strong claims about the rising number of museums in the UK and elsewhere. These polemic exchanges became known as the heritage debates and they continued to be cited well into the new millennium. Writing in 2018, Anna Woodham pointed out that textbooks and anthologies on heritage invariably start with a chapter on the debates, and indeed her own essay on the subject opens the anthology *Heritage and Museum Studies*.[15] Woodham and other academics have argued against or rethought certain aspects of the heritage debates, particularly notions of nostalgia, but there has been no overall reassessment of the increased number of museums in the UK or of the factors that underpinned the expansion of the sector.[16] The fact that the number of museums in the UK tripled inside two or three decades, and that the profile of the museum sector drastically changed, has been accepted rather than investigated.

A key reason for the lack of attention has been the absence of longitudinal data and so, for the first time, the Mapping Museums project has made it possible to rethink the expansion of the UK museum sector on an evidential basis. In this section I outline the main arguments made during the heritage debates, paying particular attention to accounts that address why the number of museums increased so dramatically, commenting on their validity in light of our new data.

The heritage debates were focused on independent museums, the commercialisation of the past, nostalgic representations of history, and how the past was mobilised in the present for ideological ends. One of the key arguments was that the emergence of the new independent museums in the UK was linked to the near-collapse of the UK manufacturing base, especially after the Conservative government came to power in 1979. In his book *The Heritage Industry: Britain in a Climate of Decline*, Robert Hewison concentrated on The Way We Were at Wigan

Figure 0.4 Schoolchildren on a day trip to The Way We Were, Wigan Pier, Lancashire, 1986

Figure 0.5 Schoolchildren in costume at the fish stall diorama at The Way We Were, Wigan Pier, 1996

Pier in Lancashire and on Beamish: Museum of the North to argue that heritage was being expected to replace the 'real industry upon which this country's economy depends'. The Way We Were concentrated on the local coal-mining industry and its associated ways of life, using living actors to add detail to diorama displays, while Beamish reinstalled houses and buildings from across the North East to create streets and scenes of industry. Hewison wrote that 'instead of manufacturing goods, we are manufacturing heritage', and while the real world of industrial manufacturing decays, 'redundant and obsolete machinery flourishes – in museums'.[17] For Hewison, the new museums presented an ersatz, sanitised, and highly commercialised version of history that allowed visitors to avoid the vicissitudes of the present and indulge in nostalgic visions of a past that never was.

The sociologist John Urry took a much more measured stance. He noted that rapid de-industrialisation had created a profound sense of loss, both of certain kinds of technology and of the social life associated with them, and he observed a correlative and 'remarkable increase in interest in the real lives of industrial/mining workers', especially in the north of England.[18] For him, this provided a context for the development of museum culture, especially for museums of the recent industrial past. He also noted that many of the now redundant industries had been located in the inner cities, and that their premises were now available for other uses, the museums occupying the sites that industry left behind. Other authors explored similar themes. Bob West looked at how controversial job training schemes introduced to alleviate unemployment had provided cheap labour for the complex of industrial museums at Ironbridge Gorge in Telford, and Bella Dicks wrote about the Big Pit in Wales, where ex-miners were being hired to take visitors around the heritage sites where they had once worked.[19]

Only a few academics or journalists ever contested the post-industrial narrative of the expanding museum sector. One of them was the historian Raphael Samuel, whose work provides a touchstone for various aspects of this study. He argued that most industrial museums had their origins in the 1950s and 1960s, which was a time of full employment, and that they were motivated by pride in industry, not by its passing. For him, the attempt to preserve the first steel-framed building as a heritage site connected the achievements of the past to the skyscrapers of the present and to the buildings of the future.[20]

Unlike his contemporaries, Samuel did not concentrate on museums of industry and manufacture. Instead, he wrote about a diverse range of museums and suggested that the expansion of the museum sector occurred in the countryside as well as in urban areas. John Corner and Sylvia Harvey made a similar argument, but these lines of thought were not pursued by later academics, and it is noticeable that the association between de-industrialisation and the new museums retained much greater traction.[21] For instance, writing in 2011, the sociologist and museums specialist Gordon Fyfe commented that 'new museums were invented to recover the material culture of an old industrial working-class heritage' as traditional class politics waned and a post-industrial society emerged in the UK.[22]

There were some precise and analytical discussions during the heritage debates, Bob West's examination of state-funded labour at Ironbridge Gorge and Patrick Wright's book *On Living in An Old Country* being cases in point.[23] However, most of the arguments relied on assertion and counter-assertion and as a whole the heritage debates suffered from a lack of evidence. There was a general assumption that the boom was largely due to the rise of museums relating to industry and manufacture, but no-one established that was the case. The argument concerning de-industrialisation also implicitly (and sometimes explicitly) located the museums in areas of recent de-industrialisation, such as South Wales and the north of England (other industrial areas, such as the Scottish borders, were not mentioned) and, again, no-one seems to have checked whether the new museums were actually concentrated in these locations. Although the commentators did not have access to the kind of longitudinal data that the Mapping Museums project generated, there was certainly enough available information to indicate that any equation between the museums boom and de-industrialisation was hasty at best.[24]

Our study produced firm information with respect to the heritage debates. During the 1980s and 1990s commentators made rather excited declarations that museums were opening at the rate of one a fortnight, and then one a week, or even three a week, and that the number of museums had doubled or even tripled in the space of two decades.[25] That turned out to be mostly correct. Just short of a hundred museums opened in 1974 and the same again in 1986, averaging out at just less than two a week, and high numbers of new museums opened in the intervening period. Notably, though, the boom did not abruptly end. Even if the heritage debates began to lessen in intensity, the sector continued to grow through the 1990s, albeit at a more gradual pace, and only began to decrease in size after 2015, when for the first time the number of museum closures began to outstrip that of the openings.

Some of the claims made in the debates were not substantiated by our data. While the number of museums devoted to industry and manufacturing had quickly increased – from nine in 1960 to around 140 by the year 2000 – many other subjects underwent similar or even greater expansion; for instance, the number of transport museums rose from fourteen to over 220 in the same period. And in terms of total numbers, industry and manufacture was only in eighth place, with local history being far and away the most common subject for a museum. By 2000, there were over 700 local history museums in the UK, and they accounted for almost one quarter of all UK museums. Buildings took second place (in our categorisation these were mainly large historic houses), followed by war and conflict. Other subjects, including sea and seafaring, belief and identity, and leisure and sport, were not so numerous and did not grow quite so dramatically, but nonetheless became commonplace, gaining between 80 and 100 new museums apiece. Museums focusing on new subjects were also founded, including museums of communications, food and drink, and utilities. In short, the range of subjects covered by museums in the UK diversified rather than just developing in one principal area.

Likewise, the geography of the museums boom was brought into question. Commentators had located the museums boom in the post-industrial north, but almost one third of the total number of the UK's museums were and are in the south of England. The North West and particularly the North East have comparatively low numbers of museums.[26] Thus, while some museums may have been founded in response to industrial decline and provided ways of dealing with a correlative sense of loss, this narrative does not account for all or even most of the museums that opened during this period. It is possible, as John Urry implied, that museums devoted to other subjects, to teddy bears or to the postal service, were able to open because they found accommodation in buildings left empty by the recent process of de-industrialisation, but, again, that interpretation does not explain the huge rise in numbers in the south of England or the Highlands.

The Mapping Museums data also challenged some aspects of Raphael Samuel's argument. He pinpointed the expansion in the number of museums as being during the 1950s and 1960s, a time of full employment, and hence construed them as being largely celebratory. Although the number of museums was growing in the 1960s, the largest increase occurred in years that were marked by recession and unemployment. In other respects, though, Samuel's account of the boom was closer to the mark than that of his contemporaries. He certainly recognised that the vast majority of the new museums were small enterprises, not the large independent museums that attracted tens of thousands of visitors every year and which were the focus of some of the heritage debaters' ire. Samuel also spotted that there was a range of subject-matter, and that many of the new museums were located in small towns and the countryside and not only in the cities (although only a relatively small proportion of the museums that opened in these rural areas were explicitly focused on rural industry).

There was a real ambition to the heritage debates that can be easily overlooked. Commentators were drawing connections between individual museums and society at large, and they were attempting to explain a rapid shift in the cultural landscape. Museums were treated as a means of grasping and commenting on wider cultural and social change, and in this book we follow that lead. Even so, questioning the evidence is not just an exercise in nitpicking. Rather, the explanations as to why the museums boom occurred and what it signified in broader cultural and social terms rested on a series of assertions that were not verified. The argument that the wave of museums indicated an epidemic of nostalgia or, less pejoratively, that they were a response to loss was made on the basis that they related to industries that were waning or defunct. In light of the Mapping Museums data, that position is harder to maintain.

Raphael Samuel's unofficial histories

Unlike his peers, Raphael Samuel approved of the boom in museums and saw them as evidence of popular engagement with history. In *Theatres of Memory*, published in 1994, Samuel argued that official academic models of history were hierarchical and limited in scope, not least because they ignored popular engagement with history and how it was embedded in the activities and practices of everyday life. People not only learned history at school but from television dramas, romantic novels, children's storybooks, the discoveries of metal detectorists, historical re-enactments, and the songs, place names, legends, and myths of popular memory. Samuel referred to these kinds of activity as 'unofficial history'. For him, history was a popular activity as much as a narrow profession and its practitioners were legion. In a line that is regularly quoted, he wrote that history 'is a social form of knowledge, the work in any given instance, of a thousand different hands'.[27]

Samuel explicitly tied the museums boom to the foundation of small museums, not to large entrepreneurial or commercial ventures. He observed that 'one of the most remarkable additions to the ranks of Britain's memory-keepers – or notable recent augmentation of them – would be the multiplication of do-it-yourself curators and mini-museums. Business houses, goaded into action by an enthusiast on the staff ... have incorporated these into the machineries of self-presentation, putting up display cases in the reception area', and individual collectors had turned their homes into 'miniature historical shrines'.[28] For Samuel, the growing number of these 'mini-museums' was a form of unofficial history and indicated a vivid engagement with the past. People who thought otherwise were merely 'heritage baiters', metropolitan snobs who were envious of the popularity that accrued to new museums and heritage projects.[29]

Samuel's account of micromuseums is compelling because it offered a far more inclusive model of museums than that more usually proposed. At the time, the notion of museums representing and reproducing official culture and established canons was gaining widespread acceptance, perhaps most notably through the work of Pierre Bourdieu and Alain Darbel. Their book *The Love of Art*, published in English in 1990, used data from a large-scale research project to show that museum visitors tended to be better educated than the norm and that exhibitions were legible only to those who already had the requisite cultural capital. Those people who did not have access to the dominant cultural codes had no way to navigate exhibitions or to make them comprehensible and thus were effectively excluded from museum visiting.[30] In contrast, Samuel saw museums as being the work of the people.

At the risk of being marked down as a heritage baiter, I want to consider Samuel's position with more care, particularly because it has such a strong bearing on how micromuseums were and might be conceived. Speaking in 1989, the historian Patrick Wright noted that the heritage debates rarely included any input from the people who were involved in setting up and running the new museums.[31]

Perhaps unexpectedly, given his stress on popular engagement, Samuel was no exception. He tended to write about the overarching significance of micromuseums rather than actually engage with the people who set them up. The founders remained unnamed and were mobilised as instances of 'the people', but they could quite easily have been museum professionals or extremely wealthy collectors, or others who were closely connected to the official circuits of culture. Who the founders were mattered in this analysis.

On a related point, it is noticeable that the heritage debates rarely paid detailed attention to the mechanics of funding and labour, with Bob West being a notable exception. The work involved in gathering together millions of objects, finding the spaces to display them, and otherwise establishing a museum remains more or less invisible. Re-reading the heritage debates, it can seem as if museums simply appeared in huge numbers one morning: the spontaneous physical manifestation of nostalgia and loss or of popular historical engagement. Like other authors, Samuel did not investigate the process by which micromuseums were established or ask where the objects came from. Instead, he assumed an identifiable division between the institutions of official history and unofficial mini-museums, which may not have been the case. Again, it is important to know where things came from, the origins of resources, and who was supporting which venues.

Lastly, Samuel elided unofficial history, popular engagement with history, and democratic participation. He characterised micromuseums as being unofficial because they were set up by the people (whoever they are) and not by established institutions (there is also a lack of detail about which institutions, other than universities, are allied with official history, although presumably large established museums would form part of this group). Founded by the people, micromuseums are presumed to be democratic. This formulation ignores the possibility that the people may have created museums that replicated or echoed the forms and content of official culture, or indeed that the museums that Samuel valorised may have had conservative content, or that their founding groups may have been exclusionary.

The idea of a divide between official and unofficial modes of culture has continuing resonance. Writing in 2006, Laurajane Smith made a strong and influential argument for the existence of the authorised heritage discourse (AHD), which takes its cue from the grand narratives of nation and class, technical expertise, and the aesthetic judgement of the ruling classes. The AHD naturalises assumptions about what heritage is and how it should be used, treated, and valued. While Smith recognises that cultural institutions have often worked with wider constituencies, she also points out that such efforts 'tend to be assimilationist and top-down rather than bottom-up substantive challenges to the AHD'.[32] For Smith, the emphasis on community participation can be a means of including people in a pre-existing and established notion of heritage, rather than recognising variation and difference in forms of culture. People either have to join in with official versions of culture or (from an authorised perspective) are understood to miss out and to be more or less without culture.

In 2012, Smith collaborated with Paul Shackel and Gary Campbell to co-edit the book *Heritage, Labour and the Working Classes*. They comment that the AHD deifies the great and the good, the beautiful and old, the comfortable and consensual, and that it ignores and disdains people who are not associated with the economic and cultural elite. Industrial heritage makes an appearance in such forums but it is usually devoid of any sense of struggle or of working-class experience. However, they suggest that once heritage is conceived in its broadest sense, as a cultural process, rather than a set of things and sites, then alternative forms of heritage that may sit outside or are excluded by the AHD come into view. Their volume accordingly assesses and celebrates the ways that working-class heritage presents alternatives or stands in opposition to dominant modes of heritage; in effect, the book covers unauthorised heritage.[33]

The academics involved in 'Understanding Everyday Participation – Articulating Cultural Values', a five-year, large grant project that ended in 2017, make similar points. They argue that there was an official framework for cultural participation in the UK, which they usefully defined 'as the largely formal and traditional practices, venues and institutions funded by government'.[34] For Andrew Miles and Lisanne Gibson, this notion of cultural engagement was narrowly defined and overly focused on a very limited set of activities and organisations, and so they set out to reassess participation in relation to the wider realm of culture. Research by one of their colleagues, Mark Taylor, found that while only 8.7% of UK citizens regularly attended events that came under the umbrella of official culture (audiences that tended to be White, well educated, and well off), most of the population were actively engaged in activities such as gardening, darts, going to the pub, crafts and hobbies, sport, and reading for pleasure.[35] Other researchers in the team conducted long-term analyses of cultural activities that took place outside publicly funded venues, including archery, swimming, and dancing, examining their significance for a wide variety of participants.[36]

Authors working on micromuseums tend to make a similar distinction between official and unofficial, authorised and unauthorised forms of history, heritage, or culture, myself included. My previous book, *Micromuseology*, portrayed micromuseums as operating entirely outside the circuits of public funding and policy, and of being entities quite separate from local authority and national museums, or the large commercially oriented independent museums: indeed, that was central to their appeal. It was this project that took me to the Bakelite Museum, and I wrote about individuals and families opening museums in their homes, sheds, barns, shops, and storage facilities. Although I engaged closely with debates in museum studies, I remained close to Samuel in presenting micromuseums as an alternative to the vicissitudes of conventional museums.[37] That position is also echoed in other work on micromuseums. For instance, in their essay 'No Small Matter: Micromuseums as Critical Institutions', the Canadian scholars Helen Gregory and Kirsty Robinson define micromuseums as 'tiny (usually one room) institutions that are run by individuals or small groups' and 'that do not participate in government funding programs or seek private sponsorships'.[38]

While perspectives and priorities vary between these studies, they implicitly or explicitly recognise a division between official and unofficial spheres. I now have two issues with this position. First, I wonder about the traffic between the official and unofficial zones. There has been a little work done on how official museums are sites of popular engagement, and a few authors have explored the ways in which audiences disrupt or reinvent protocols, but the scarcity of scholarship on micromuseums means there is no detailed research on how unofficial venues might be supported by official forms of culture.[39] Second, I suspect that the division is easier to maintain with respect to particular kinds of activity or venture.[40] In my book I focused on museums that were relatively uncommon, preferring the quirky and the idiosyncratic, or, in studying museums of Irish Republicanism, the radical; Gregory and Robinson similarly concentrated on artist-led micromuseums that counter museum norms. While I remain sure that some museums do function outside of, and offer alternatives to, mainstream institutions, it may be easier to make that case when focusing on unusual or artist-led venues. The situation of transport, war and conflict, or local history museums, among others, might be more complicated.

Samuel's discussion about popular engagement also has strong echoes in contemporary literature. The assumption that popular – or, to use contemporary language, community – projects are necessarily positive for all concerned is still common. Elizabeth Crooke has observed that it is 'a hoorah word that has encouraged warm feelings but not much analysis', and taken issue with that position.[41] Her work on museums in Northern Ireland showed that the codes that define insiders also create outsiders. Community museums can involve exclusion as much as unity, a point that Lianne McTavish has also explored in her discussion of Indigenous and pioneer museums in Canada.[42] It is important to follow their lead and to try to ascertain whether the UK boom was an example of democratic museum-making and if it can be neatly aligned with unofficial histories.

Planning the research

Analysing the heritage debates, particularly in relation to the new Mapping Museums data, raised a whole series of questions. If the late-twentieth-century expansion of the UK museum sector was not a direct result of de-industrialisation, or not solely so, then what other factor or factors had underpinned the rise in the number of museums? Why had so many societies, community groups, and trusts decided to open their own museums? Who exactly founded micromuseums? How were the resources required to open museums mobilised? To what extent could their foundation be considered a form of popular engagement in history? Do micromuseums really stand outside the circuits of unofficial history? While the data provided a picture of the UK museum sector and how it had changed over the last sixty years, it could not address these wider questions. We needed another approach if we were going to find out more.

We knew that the boom had been driven by the foundation of small independent museums and so we decided to concentrate our attention on them, hence the focus of this book. However, researching micromuseums and to a lesser degree medium-size independent museums is difficult because so few keep records of their own histories. Gairloch Museum on the north-east coast of Scotland has a small collection of newspaper clippings and photographs relating to its early years, and the current curator had recorded a conversation with one of the founders shortly before she died. Likewise, Ingrow Loco, a railway museum in West Yorkshire, had numerous photographs of its predecessor organisation, Dinting Railway Centre, and recordings of the founding group remembering its closure. But though these resources are extremely useful, they are not common. In some cases founders write short histories of their organisations, usually on a significant anniversary of its opening, and, again, these are invaluable to researchers, but it is not always easy to establish which museums have produced such documents.[43] We drew heavily on these materials when we found them, but taken in isolation they were not going to answer our questions.

Another option was to use additional data sources to help us analyse our findings. We had already integrated the Office of National Statistics information on social deprivation and geodemographic profiles into the database. We could have added further data on income distribution, property prices, public funding, the rise and fall of particular industries, or the development of motorways (Raphael Samuel thought that the rising number of museums was directly linked to car ownership, and indeed I touch on this point in Chapters 1 and 3). A preliminary analysis showed a correlation between the rising numbers of museums and rising gross national income, and further work could have informed our understanding of the factors that underpinned the boom. However, it would have done little to establish why people chose to open museums or to develop our conceptualisation of micromuseums. As a top-down model, it also risked treating museums as a symptom of larger economic forces, an approach that was singularly inappropriate for analysing a museums movement that is driven from below. Thus, we came to the conclusion that the best way to investigate a largely undocumented history, and to do so while taking account of the perspectives of the people involved, was through oral history.

It was at this point in the project that Toby Butler and Jake Watts joined the team and the three of us started working together. We began by using the Mapping Museums database and analysis to set the parameters of the oral history research. It showed that the boom had peaked in the 1970s and 1980s, that the museum sector had continued to slowly expand well into the twenty-first century, and that the four most common subjects among independent museums were local history, buildings, transport, and war and conflict. We decided to concentrate our interviews in museums that had been founded in those decades and in those subject areas, although we decided not to investigate museums of buildings as they have quite different founders and origin stories to other kinds of museum (plus the owners often resisted their classification as museums).[44]

These criteria established, we duly selected museums that fitted our categories, choosing organisations from across the regions. It was important that the museums that we visited were not clustered in particular types of locale; for instance, we did not want to inadvertently focus on museums in university towns, deprived seaside towns, or remote rural areas.[45] However, we did decide to over-represent museums in areas with diverse populations, because we were keen to see if motivations for opening museums, particularly local history museums, varied depending on the ethnicity of the inhabitants. All told, we chose around forty museums as the focus for the research.

Defining founders

The next step was to decide exactly who the founders were and who we should try to interview.

In the popular literature, small independent museums are generally portrayed as being founded by an individual who has established their own large collection and opened it to the public. This does sometimes happen, and indeed Patrick Cook, who founded the Bakelite Museum, is a case in point. Museums are also launched by siblings, such as the brothers Roman and Max Piekarski, who opened Cuckooland in Cheshire, which houses a huge collection of Black Forest cuckoo clocks; or by married couples, such as Mike and Carol Deer, who spent years gradually filling their attic, garage, and shed with vintage computers, video games, and small electronic devices until they eventually decided to open the Micro Museum in Kent. These museums are almost invariably privately owned and they tend to focus on smaller collectable objects.

Museums of transport, war and conflict, and local history are much more likely to be set up by groups or societies than by individual collectors or a couple, although there is some variation within the individual subject categories. Car museums are regularly privately owned, but railway museums, which are far more plentiful, are almost always a collective enterprise; similarly, military museums may be privately owned, but there are far fewer in number than museums established by a regiment or a special interest group. Privately owned local history museums are almost unheard of. Eileen Burgess, one of the co-founders of Nidderdale Museum, a local history museum in North Yorkshire, told us that she could not remember who had first thought of opening a museum, whether it had been her or her friend Muriel Swires. For her, the point was irrelevant: it had been a group effort. Now in her early eighties, she was reluctant to take any particular credit. As she put it, 'you're only talking to me because I'm the last woman standing'.

In her study of gender in nineteenth- and early-twentieth-century museums, Kate Hill took an expansive view of who was a 'museum-maker'. Rather than just concentrating on museum directors and curators, she included junior assistants, researchers, educators, cleaners, caretakers, secretaries, and donors.[46] Here we take a similar approach, and see each museum as having multiple founders. How the groups initially come together, who they include, and how they function is a point of enquiry for the book as a whole.

The issue of who counts as a founder is also complicated by the time it takes to open a museum. For instance, when Jamie Larkin was compiling the Mapping Museums data in 2017, he spoke to Esther Mann, the curator of the Army Music Museum, to check exactly when it had opened. She said that the museum had been established as a trust in the 1960s and 'became more public in the 1980s'. But, she added, 'if we are being honest, it really only became open to the public in the last five years'.[47] It had taken six decades to emerge as a fully fledged museum. Although this is an extreme example, it is common for museums to evolve over years: they may begin with open days or special events, or the site might be open to the public but there is no museum as such. In consequence, the people who are involved at the beginning are not always the people who oversee its launch, if there is one. We duly conceived of opening as a process, not a moment, and decided to interview accordingly. Although we prioritised members of the original founding groups, we were also interested in meeting staff and volunteers who joined at a later stage.

Visiting micromuseums

Toby started the interviews in the autumn of 2018, setting off from his home in Kent to meet the founders whom he had contacted. His journey followed the narrow roads that hug the coast of Scotland to Thurso, the most northerly town on mainland Britain, and took him by air from Penzance on the southernmost tip of mainland England to the Isles of Scilly. He went east to military aviation museums in the Lincolnshire fens and west to Wales, where he visited a clutch of local history museums in the Valleys that were at the heart of the Industrial Revolution. He visited regimental museums in the Home Counties, railway museums in the Midlands, and when he needed to test hypotheses or interview techniques, he diverged to visit museums that covered different subjects, including shipwrecks, computing, mining, and flower arranging.

Later in the process, I also visited the museums that were likely to feature in this book, conducting follow-up interviews where required. At first this seemed like something of a luxury; after all, Toby had written detailed descriptions of the museums and taken photographs of the sites and exhibits. In principle, I could have relied on his prior research for my writing and just made phone calls or sent emails to check on any missing details. However, even a couple of visits proved that I needed to get a sense of the context of the museums in order to write the book. It mattered whether a museum was on the side of a hill or the valley floor, in a pretty village or an empty high street. For example, when Toby had asked Elizabeth Cameron, one of the founders of the Laidhay Croft Museum, why she had wanted to open and run a museum, she replied that she liked meeting people. This comment was regularly repeated elsewhere and to me it seemed somewhat bland. That changed when I visited the museum. By this point the pandemic had begun. I decided that the safest way to travel was to use my campervan, and so before I set off to Laidhay I tried to book a place at a local campsite. It was full, as campsites so often were during this period, and I asked the owner if there was anywhere else close by. 'This is Caithness,' she retorted, 'there is nothing close by.' I ended up staying in a farmer's field, looking out over the North Sea, and that night I could hear the seals singing. In the morning, I drove along the winding coast road to the village of Dunbeath, which has a population of 129 people, my ancient campervan slowing the traffic as it crawled up the steep slopes. Laidhay is a mile or so further along and comprises a farmhouse and an eighteenth-century longhouse. Elizabeth and her husband bought the site in 1968, and almost immediately she began working with a local heritage group to open the croft as a museum, which she ran in

Figure 0.6 Elizabeth Cameron outside Laidhay Croft

Figure 0.7 Laidhay Croft Museum, Caithness

addition to working on the farm and raising her two sons, Ewen and Stewart. There are no other homes close by.

The croft was closed on the day that I visited, but other motorists spotted my van in the carpark and stopped to see if they could come in. It quickly became clear that Elizabeth was a natural host and tour guide – welcoming, interested, engaging, kind, and very sociable. Within a minute or two she had discovered that one man was a carpenter and so showed him the barn, which has arched beams made from ship timbers washed up on the beach. A woman visitor arrived and explained that she was tracing her family, the MacBeths, who had originated from the next village. Elizabeth said, 'You may have cousins there still,' and told her stories about her relatives. A third group were also welcomed in. Later she said, 'I love meeting people, you see, all the strangers. If you're left at home with two bairns, you're quite happy to meet people. I liked the company and making conversation.' Living high on the side of a hill, in a sparsely populated area, it is easy to see how weeks or months could have gone by with no or little social interaction. The museum stopped passing motorists and brought people with different life experiences to Elizabeth's door. It was and remains a way of connecting herself to the wider world. There was absolutely nothing bland about it. I had to visit the museum in order to fully grasp the circumstances and the implications of Elizabeth's comments, and the same was true elsewhere.

I also conducted additional interviews at new locations. I spent two weeks visiting museums in Northern Ireland, work that had been delayed by the pandemic, and I visited a series of museums relating to antecedent (or defunct) regiments. The previous interviews had all been conducted in museums of extant regiments, a distinction that escaped us until I started working on the 'War and conflict museums' chapter. Due to the restrictions introduced during the pandemic, a few of the additional interviews were conducted online. These were quite different in tenor and reinforced the necessity of visiting in person. The very fact that we had made an effort to travel long distances and had organised overnight accommodation was taken as testament to our interest in the museum. Many of our narrators acknowledged that effort with offers of tea or lunch, which we always accepted, and took us on tours around the museum or introduced us to other volunteers, members of the family, and friends who had dropped by. They often gave us a lot of their time, and while we did not record those encounters, the casual conversations helped us build up a richer picture of the circumstances in which the founders lived and the museum operated. It also helped build a level of mutual trust. That was all missing from the online conversations.

In total, Toby and I met staff and volunteers at around sixty different museums, and covered over 10,000 miles, although admittedly my mileage included several unplanned visits to garage workshops. We met people who had opened museums as early as 1964 and 1969 and through the decades into the 2020s. RAF Ingham Heritage Centre in Lincolnshire, which I discuss in Chapter 2, was still in the process of being established, and the Black British Museum, which appears in Chapter 4, remains in the planning. Along the way we also interviewed some experts in the field, and while their contributions do not explicitly figure in the text that follows, they helped direct our investigations and provided valuable context. Descriptions of the museums, photographs, and the transcripts are publicly available on the project website, and the audio recordings are available at the Mapping Museums Oral History Archive at the Bishopsgate Institute in London.

The narrative arc

When we met the founders they almost invariably talked about hard work and long nights, about roofs leaking, and about problems with accommodation, but these narratives tended to follow an arc that went from adversity to resolution. Their emphasis was on friendship, becoming part of a community, and creating something of civic value. Above all, they stressed their pleasure and pride in the museum, a response that was perhaps typified at an online seminar to mark the launch of the Mapping Museums oral history archive in 2021.[48] We had invited three of our narrators to speak: Steve Allsop, who had co-founded the Dinting Railway Centre in 1968 and Ingrow Loco in 1990, Anne Read, who had co-founded the Museum of North Craven Life in 1977, and Geoff Burton, who had led on the launch of RAF Ingham Heritage Centre in 2014. When we asked if they had ever regretted their decision to open a museum, they all delivered an emphatic 'no, not for a minute'.

These kinds of response make it easy to interpret the micromuseums boom in a highly positive light, and indeed it was beneficial for very many people and in many different ways, something that we will discuss in the forthcoming chapters. Even so, it is wise to exercise a note of caution. In this section I want to think about the way that the selection process and other aspects of the research had an impact on the stories that we heard, and thus on this analysis.[49]

Although it is rarely mentioned in academic analyses, a large number of museums have closed.[50] According to the Mapping Museums database, 859 museums closed between 1960 and 2022, of which just under 600 were small. We had originally intended to conduct interviews with the founders of museums that had closed as well as those that remained open, but in practice it proved extremely difficult to track down the associated staff. Toby had to search through archived museum websites, online annual reports, the Charity Commission register, newsletters, local press coverage, and even obituaries to piece together a picture of the museums' inception and eventual demise. He tried to find a name, personal email address, or direct phone number of someone involved that would provide a starting point for further investigation. It was time-consuming work.

There were also problems with using the material we gathered. In the first interview that we conducted at a closed museum the ex-members of staff talked about failures of management and how the process of cost-cutting, redundancy, and eventually closure had been immensely stressful for them. The museum was located in a small town and the subject still remained sensitive, so the narrators understandably asked us to embargo the transcript. Given the work involved and the lack of usable outcome, we decided to focus our efforts on museums that remained open. In consequence, most of the staff we interviewed had not only managed to launch museums but, more crucially, to maintain them over the following decades. They had attracted new volunteers and, in many cases, had handed management responsibilities on to the next generation. Their ventures were a success.

Arranging interviews with the founders of museums that had remained open was generally easier. Toby began by telephoning or emailing the museums in question, and in some cases the original founders were still running the museum or remained closely involved as volunteers. In other instances the current members of staff had contact details and made the introduction. As will become clear, the micromuseums boom was largely a voluntary effort. If people were unhappy with how a museum was evolving or were bored or frustrated by the endeavour, they were under no compulsion to stay. Most of the founders we met had continued to volunteer, indeed they had often spent decades establishing and running the museum. They were highly invested in the organisation and were unlikely to question its value. Doing so was tantamount to questioning how they had spent much of their lives.[51]

The optimistic narrative was also reinforced by a degree of judicious self-selection on the part of the museum and the founders themselves. When we contacted museums asking to be put in touch with the founders, the existing staff or volunteers directed us to the person they thought appropriate, who often passed us on once more. In many cases it was clear that members of the original founding team had spoken to one another and had decided who should be interviewed. The oral historian Paul Thompson has noted that researchers obviously need narrators who are happy to speak to them, but that willing people tend to be better educated, more confident, more articulate, and to present particular views of the subject to hand. Less educated, more reticent, inarticulate narrators are not so likely to come forward, yet their viewpoints and experiences are equally important and valid.[52] While we have no way of knowing the characteristics of the people whom we did not meet, we think Thompson's observation probably applied. We certainly met a lot of teachers.

Two other factors are worth bearing in mind. The first is that the narrators wanted to tell a story about the value and success of their museum, even those from the museums that later closed, and they were reluctant to discuss any conflict or failure. For them these were often private matters, and there was a sense that one should 'not put dirty washing out in public'. In regimental museums the discussion of difficult issues was seen as disloyalty to one's peers, and others were reluctant to speak ill of the dead. Some feared that such conversations would reopen old wounds with neighbours or people who were part of a specialist community, if not actively involved in the museum. Even when events lay forty or fifty years in the past, our narrators were quite clear that they would not elucidate or provide any specific details. And, finally, because our focus was on museums of the late twentieth century, most of our narrators were elderly and were remembering events from thirty, forty, or fifty years previously, when they had been relatively or even very young and full of energy and enthusiasm for their new project.

Occasionally, the narrators' accounts were tempered with hints about the difficulty of balancing the demands of establishing a museum against those of work and family life. And despite our selection process and the founders' disinclination to speak about less palatable topics, we did hear some stories of discord and dissension. Some volunteers left owing to a rift concerning the focus of the museum and the degree to which it was public facing; another committee fell out about process. Some of those narratives feature in the chapters that follow, although our focus on the early stages of founding museums means they do not feature as strongly as they might. We also conducted interviews with staff at four closed museums. The sadness and regret of the group who had to close Dinting Railway Centre in Derbyshire when a former supporter hiked the rent is a subject for the next chapter, and the circumstances under which the Asian Music Circuit Museum closed are discussed in Chapter 4.

There are other books to be written about small museums. Not the stories of foundation and of success, when the labour and long nights result in an opening with friends and family, when audiences arrive, grants are won, and the museum wins accolades and even prizes, but of the long slog of keeping a place open, of watching objects slowly decay, and of days when not a single visitor arrives. There are also books to be written about closure, about why it happens, what happens to the collections, and what is lost, as well as the human cost to the founders and staff. It is worth bearing those images in mind as the narratives of community and pleasure unfold.

Micromuseums, gender, and ethnicity

As the research progressed we began to notice some clear patterns in the micro-museums we had visited. The founders of the transport and war and conflict museums were mainly White men, with some women having a backstage role, whereas the groups at local history museums were much more mixed with respect

Figure 0.8 Prince Frederick Duleep Singh, 1921

to gender, and numerous women had led on their foundation. With only one exception, that of Jenny Hurkett at the Criterion Heritage Centre on the Isle of Sheppey in Kent, the founders of the local history museums were also White.[53]

We responded in several different ways. We interviewed the founders of the Glasgow Women's Library and Museum, which at the time of writing was the only museum in the UK specifically dedicated to women's history, and we started talking to women who had founded local history museums about why they were interested in that subject. We also started looking for museums of transport, war and conflict, and local history that were founded by people of colour. We discovered that Prince Frederick Duleep Singh had established the Ancient House Museum in Thetford, Norfolk in 1921, although it fell outside the period covered in our study.[54] Otherwise we drew a blank.

At this point we decided to expand our remit. We knew that the Chinese artist, curator, and poet Li Yuan-chia had founded the LYC Museum and Art Gallery in Cumbria in 1971, and it was possible that there were many more Asian, Black, or

Figure 0.9 Li Yuan-chia outside the LYC Museum and Art Gallery, Banks, Cumbria, circa 1971

other minority ethnic museum founders, just not in the museums dedicated to transport, war and conflict, or local history.[55] We investigated accordingly and put out numerous calls on social media. We found very few such founders. The first Jewish Museum in the UK was founded by the Jewish Historical Society and opened in 1932 at the Jewish Communal Centre in central London, later moving to Camden. In 1947 Polish exiles opened the Sikorski Museum and a museum at the Josef Pilsudski Institute, both in London.

Within the period covered by our research, the Jain Museum and the Sikh Museum in Leicester and the Neasden Temple Museum in London had South Asian founders.[56] Viram Jasani, who opened the Asian Music Circuit Museum, was born in Kenya to an Indian family. There have been four further Jewish museums, three in London and one in Manchester, founded by different groups from within that wider community.[57] Jawad Mella opened the Kurdish Museum alongside the Kurdish community in Hammersmith, London in 2008, and two museums were founded by Romanys. Gordon Boswell opened the Gordon Boswell Romany Museum in Lincolnshire in 1995 as a tribute to his father, who shared the same name and was one of the last British Romanys to be born in a bender (a tent traditionally made from hazel rods pushed into the ground and covered in tarpaulin or sailcloth) on Blackpool Sands, while the brothers Frank, Olby, and Garry Brazil launched the South East Romany Museum in Kent in 2008.[58]

Despite its name, the Black Cultural Archives, which opened in London in 1982, can also be considered a museum. Founded in 1982 by a Brixton-based group led by Len Garrison, it aimed at celebrating African and African-Caribbean history, and especially at educating local Black children about their history. They collected objects as well as oral histories, documents, and books; their first building included a museum repository, and in 2014 they opened a permanent exhibition space. While the archival collections are undoubtedly stronger than the object-based collections, the organisation now self-describes as an archive-museum.[59] To the best of our knowledge it is the only museum with Black founders in the UK.

Tracing information about the identity of founders was difficult and time-consuming. The Black, Asian, and minority ethnic founders whom we identified had established museums that directly related to their belief or ethnicity.[60] In these cases, the focus of the museum meant that their ethnicity was often made evident on websites or printed material, in a way that was not the case in other contexts. It is therefore possible that we missed many other such founders, but we think it unlikely. Rather, it seems that the number of Black, Asian, and minority ethnic museum founders is low in relation to those populations within the UK as a whole.

In the UK, as elsewhere, museum collections often derive from the networks of empire, and for many years promoted a narrative of White superiority.[61] Museums have made active efforts to change the way that ethnicity is represented and mobilised, and to recognise that progress and culture in the West was bought at the cost of immense human suffering and degradation in Africa, the Americas, and the Indian subcontinent, among other locations.[62] Nonetheless, museums continue to be understood as, and arguably still are, a White, Eurocentric cultural form. Given this context, it might seem logical that Black and Asian people in the UK have not flocked to form their own museums.

Yet it is important to recognise that a different situation obtains in the USA. Writing in 2018, Fath Davis Ruffins, curator of Black History at the Smithsonian's National Museum of American History, pointed to the 'flood' of Black museums that opened in North America during the 1970s and 1980s.[63] Unfortunately, it is beyond the scope of this research to compare the foundation of 'minority museums' as they are called in the USA with those in the UK, although that would be a fruitful enquiry. However, in Chapter 4 I account for why there are relatively few museum founders of Black and Asian heritage in the UK.

Writing micromuseums

The interviews ran to over half a million words. The transcripts and recordings include numerous voices: Toby's and mine, and those of the people whom we interviewed. Many of the people we spoke to were talking on behalf of groups or in the stead of friends and colleagues with whom they had worked. They recounted stories about other people and repeated stories that they had been told. Metaphorically speaking, a larger crowd of people stand behind our narrators. We also found and used oral history material in two of the museums we visited, so this account includes their voices.

It is important to emphasise the degree to which an oral history is shaped. The historian Daniel James has commented that 'the apparently self-evident status of the communication and knowledge produced in oral history texts' has a powerfully naturalising effect that compounds 'traditional claims of orality to provide unmediated access to self-knowledge and knowledge of another'.[64] It can seem as if the author is merely describing what took place or is simply recounting someone else's story, whereas in actuality the narrative has been edited, pieced together, and constructed. It has been my job to select from the hundreds of thousands of words, weave the interviews together with the social history research that Jake had undertaken, compose coherent stories, and develop a meta-narrative of the micromuseums boom. The material was plentiful and I could have written many other versions, but I chose material that spoke to the growing number of museums and to the interconnections between local concerns and social or organisational change.

In the chapters that follow I draw on interviews that both Toby and I conducted. I signal our presence within the text as a way to remind readers that the narratives developed as staged conversations. The founders were not just spontaneously remembering: they had been asked to do so; and while some were clearly rehearsing well-worn narratives, they may have told different stories to someone else, or given their narrative a different emphasis. Some sections of this text merge conversations that happened months apart and combine additional information from numerous telephone calls, letters, and emails. Producing a readable narrative involves smoothing over those time lags and differences, and one of the devices for managing disjunctions is to use the term 'we', rather than to switch backwards and forwards between interlocutors.

Throughout the book I have tried to respect the particularity of the individual museums and people. There is a form of academic writing where interview material or other sources are boiled down to make a point. This approach keeps an argument moving swiftly along, but it loses in richness of description. While I have edited the narrators' words to remove pauses, false starts, and repetition, I wanted to keep something of the texture of what people say and to give their narratives space to breathe. One of my aims is to convey a sense of who the founders were and what was at stake for them in setting up a museum. A full list of all our narrators, who interviewed them, when and where is available in the Appendix.

Once I had finished the book and given it to Manchester University Press for review, I also sent relevant sections to the people whose words and museums appear in the text so they could correct or otherwise respond to what I had written. Some of our narrators were delighted and thought that I had captured the intent of their museum. They had a real sense of having been recognised. Others simply said it was fine, and some did not respond. A good number of narrators amended names or details that had been misheard or misunderstood in spoken exchanges, and the volunteers at railway and war and conflict museums corrected my misapprehensions about particular engines or regiments. In an echo of the interview process, the narrators often circulated a text within the group and I received several responses from the same museum, each correspondent correcting or adding to slightly different pieces of information. Some narrators went above and beyond the call of duty. At one point we were grappling with the complex and opaque beginnings of the Heritage Collections at British Leyland Motors. The collections and their management had been split over multiple sites across the UK, the company was long since defunct, and it was proving difficult to establish how they had begun. John Gilchrist, who was Manufacturing Director of the Truck and Bus Division in the 1980s, came to our aid by consulting his ex-colleagues when they all attended their annual reunion dinner, and then sending us an annotated timeline containing the information we needed.

A few of the narrators and volunteers thought that the narrative was strewn with errors, although a closer inspection of the transcripts often suggested that members of the same organisations had remembered events differently. Many of our narrators were recalling events that had happened several decades before, and they brought their own experiences and perspectives to bear on the narrative. Wherever possible we cross-checked the information but, ultimately, our account is a compilation and a construction from many people's memories. In total, I corresponded with around fifty narrators and other informants, often with dozens of emails going back and forth as we discussed details of what they did or did not want in the public sphere. I duly made the changes, and in all cases their input was an essential part of refining the text.

There are also voices that are missing from this account, perhaps most notably those of the audience. In *Voluntary detours: Small town and rural museums in Alberta*, Lianne McTavish focuses on visitors to museums, many of which could be described as micromuseums. She writes about museums situated on major intersections and about long car journeys to out-of-the-way places, teasing out connections between where a museum is situated, who visits, and for what reasons. The differences between visitors and types of visit are beautifully articulated and analysed.[65] In contrast, I have concentrated on the founders and how the museums were established, not on their reception and later use, although occasionally that enters into the discussion.

Nor have I discussed the community archive movement, although there are overlaps with micromuseums. Community archives often collect all manner of artefacts, not just documents, and museums often have archives. Transport museums keep plans relating to the design and production of the vehicles they collect, regimental museums have indexes of service people, and local history museums may have records pertaining to their areas.[66] Smethwick Heritage Centre combines a museum and an archive, and when we visited there was a steady flow of visitors conducting genealogical research. There are also some overlaps in intent. The founders of community archives have generally set out to preserve and present their own histories, whether of an area, a community, or a specific group, and, as we will consider, many founders of micromuseums have similar aims; but other than discussing their role in the restoration of vehicles, few narrators made reference to the archives in their museums, and no-one made reference to neighbouring archives.[67] Exploring the links, overlaps, and differences between the different types of heritage project, be they civic or local history societies, vehicle preservation groups, or community archives, would be a fascinating subject for future research but is beyond the scope of this book.

The first three chapters are self-contained and can be read in any order. Each focuses on museums devoted to a particular subject and explores the connections between their foundation and the wider cultural, social, and economic environment. Chapter 1 examines transport museums, and more specifically how the foundation of railway, bus, and commercial vehicle museums was variously linked to technological development, nationalisation, and de-nationalisation. These founder narratives touch on policy change and mass redundancy as well as songs of steam locomotives, fish and chips on Saturday night, and driving vintage buses in convoy across the UK. Chapter 2 focuses on war and conflict museums, moving from a discussion of military aviation museums to corps and regimental museums, and then on to museums that actively oppose the Armed Forces. In this case the founders' stories connect to the welfare of veterans, how the Armed Forces were downscaled in the aftermath of the Second World War, the Cold War, the Troubles in Northern Ireland and numerous defence reviews. Chapter 3 examines museums of local history and covers local government reform, the modernisation of agriculture, and de-industrialisation, as well as the end of the mining industry, tourism, and second-home ownership. More local concerns about stuffed turtles, a smock, moorhens, and a cobbler's shop also make an appearance.

The three chapters also deal with the emotional weight and affect of opening a museum. In recent years a number of academics have written about audiences' emotional responses to museum objects and to a much lesser extent those of curators and enthusiasts.[68] Here we add an assessment of what the founders and volunteers cared for – the objects of their emotion differ according to the type of museum and its context – and of how they are variously motivated by pleasure, pride, love, affection, duty, loyalty, and a will to help, as well as by dissatisfaction, anger, loss, or a sense of injustice. Chapter 1 concentrates on male friendship and camaraderie among the transport enthusiasts, and Chapter 2 on notions of family, both regimental and biological. Perhaps surprisingly, because the founders of transport and war and conflict museums are mainly men, and those of local history museums predominantly women, the founders of local history museums were less explicit about their emotional attachments. Nonetheless, their interviews did evince a strong attachment to place, which is a point of discussion in that chapter.

Chapters 1 and 2 are both structured in relation to subject sub-categories. The Mapping Museums classification system splits transport into sub-categories of buses and trams, railways, cars and motorbikes, and so forth, while war and conflict museums are similarly divided into regimental, Royal Air Force (RAF), and (non-regimental) military museums, as well as those pertaining to specific events or sites such as the Churchill War Rooms or the D-Day Centre. We planned our interviews and began our analysis of transport and of war and conflict museums in relation to these sub-categories, focusing on the subjects that were most plentiful. I tease out the differences between them, comparing railway with bus museums, or look at the similarities, such as between regimental museums. Chapter 3 is differently structured. When we were devising the Mapping Museums subject taxonomy we could not find a logical way to split the category of local history into sub-categories, and so it remains large and undifferentiated. With no obvious point of departure, I decided to focus on four museums that have contrasting histories and to draw out their commonalities and points of divergence.

Chapter 4 signals a return to Raphael Samuel's arguments. Here, I look across micromuseums irrespective of their subject-matter to examine how they were founded, the buildings they occupied, the flow of objects, who funded them, and who did the work. I also look closely at who opened micromuseums in relation to professional training, class, age, gender, and ethnicity, arguing that there are close links between who set up micromuseums and the circumstances in which they were founded. To close, I think about the implications of that discussion for notions of unofficial history and popular engagement.

Chapter 4 raises questions of institutional sexism and racism within the museum sector. I deliberately separated this material from the subject-based chapters. The people whom we met were not museum professionals and had worked, often for years, in an entirely voluntary capacity. They were generous enough to spend time with us, to offer hospitality, and to tell their stories about their museums. I did not want to judge their museums, much less to suggest that they had personally been exclusive. For me, separating discussions about structural inequality from the detailed histories of individual museums was a means of balancing between the competing ethical demands of respect for the narrators and accounting for the uneven and unequal development of the sector.

The last and concluding chapter provides answers to the question of why people founded their own museums and in what circumstances. I close by briefly considering posterity, the pandemic, and the future of micromuseums.

Stories from small museums

Stories from small museums is the first history of the museums boom. Overall, my aim is to account for why and how it happened and to investigate the motivations and experiences of the museum founders. As such, it challenges and entirely revises the heritage debates, and it puts ordinary people's experience at the heart of cultural production. They are not just visitors to museums, but the museum makers, producing and shaping their own accounts of history.

Chapter 1

Transport museums: loving objects and each other

Transport museums were one of the success stories of the micromuseums boom. All over the UK people started collecting bicycles, motorbikes, cars, vans, buses, trams, locomotives, aeroplanes, and canal boats. Rust was scraped down, metalwork repaired, bodywork resprayed, lettering and decorations reapplied, engines overhauled and oiled, woodwork made sound and watertight, and seats and fittings researched and recreated in exact facsimiles of original styles. Of all the subject areas we consider in this book, transport grew at by far the fastest rate, rising from a mere fourteen museums in 1960 to 240 by the end of the millennium. And of those, railway museums were by far the most common, as individuals and groups bought and salvaged engines, carriages, wagons, track, signage, and station fittings and furniture, among other objects. There are now almost as many train and railway museums in the UK as there are all other types of transport museum combined.[1] The question for this chapter, then, is why did so many groups decide to open transport museums, and given the huge size of many of the objects on display, how did they do so?

The development of transport museums intersects with some of the broad social and economic changes in the UK over the last sixty years. Nationalisation is a major factor, as are changes to policy and the modernisation of public transport. How these factors impacted on the foundation of museums varied depending on the type of vehicle concerned, and in this chapter I begin by looking at museums of trains and railways, and then of buses. While the circumstances in which transport museums are established may vary, railway and bus museums often share similar challenges, namely the pragmatic issues of storing and maintaining large vehicles. It is reasonably common to find a single person or couple who buy cars and motorbikes at auction, develop their own collection, and then put it on display. It is less feasible for private individuals to buy and house a collection of buses, much less railway carriages, steam locomotives, or trucks. It is not a coincidence that one of the few private railways museums in the UK was owned by Sir William and Lady McAlpine, whose family made their fortune in the construction industry, and who had the means to reconstruct a railway on their extensive estate.

In most cases, the costs and labour involved in setting up and maintaining museums of large vehicles are a prompt for the founders to collaborate and work as a group. As I discuss in the second part of this chapter, working collectively has its own effects: camaraderie and friendship, and specifically male friendship, play an important part in the story of how transport museums were developed and sustained. I close with the counter-example of the British Commercial Vehicle Museum, whose origins coincided with the sale of national industries and de-industrialisation, and where the preservation of the collection has a very different emotional weight.

Modernising the railways

The foundation of the Dinting Railway Centre in Derbyshire in 1968 was prompted by the acquisition of a single vehicle: engine No. 45596 Bahamas, a Jubilee class steam locomotive made in 1934 for the London, Midland and Scottish Railway Company. That purchase took place in the context of nationalisation and technological modernisation, as did the formation of the Vintage Carriages Trust and its later incarnation as the Museum of Rail Travel in Keighley, West Yorkshire.

In the early twentieth century, numerous different companies each operated their own railways. After the Second World War the Labour government brought together the track, stations, and rolling stock under the banner of British Railways (later British Rail), which was run as a national company.[2] (Northern Ireland had a separate network to Britain that was operated by the Ulster Transport Authority and subsequently by Northern Ireland Railways.) However, the post-war period also saw the beginning of a shift away from rail and towards road transport. Numerous trunk roads were built across the UK, freight was increasingly moved by road rather than rail, and car ownership became more common. Railways started to go into decline, and in 1955 the network began to run at a loss. Something needed to change and so the government drew up the Modernisation Plan, which aimed at improving speed and safety and making the railways more cost-efficient, thereby winning back custom from the roads.[3] Two of the recommended reforms were to replace steam trains with diesel and electric trains, and to build new rolling stock. Although the process took time, not least because the new diesel trains were unreliable, British Railways duly began to phase out their steam locomotives and to scrap the wooden wagons that had carried passengers or freight.[4]

The transition to diesel required a different kind of infrastructure. There was no need for coaling towers or turntables (diesel locomotives run better in either direction), thereby reducing the need for railway depots, some of which were accordingly scheduled to close. The goods yards were also closing, as containerisation became mainstream and there was less need for short-term storage or warehouses; instead, containers of a standardised size were simply stacked up or moved quickly on to their destinations. And more changes were to come. The Modernisation Plan failed to restore the ailing fortunes of British Railways, and in order to cut costs the Railways Board began closing lesser-used sections of track. That process escalated in 1963 when Richard Beeching, the chairman of British Railways, recommended that over 2,000 railway stations and 6,000 miles of track, a third of the total network, be shut down.[5] The industrial railway network was also closing. Collieries, quarries, and other heavy industries often had their own railway networks to move materials and goods, but the mining industry was declining in size, as were other industries, and these railways were no longer required.[6]

In the 1960s Terry Smith was shedmaster at Edgeley Sheds in Stockport, which was one of the depots on the list for closure, and Bahamas was his favourite locomotive. It was the last named engine left at the Sheds (most are recognised only by their serial or engine number) and it was significant because it had been modified in 1961 to enable it to run on lower-quality coal. This was the last engine on which British Railway

Figure 1.1 45596 Bahamas at Edgeley Sheds, Greater Manchester, 1967

engineers undertook any experiment to improve the performance of their steam loco-motives, and as one volunteer commented, 'the history of steam in this country ran from the Rocket to Bahamas'. So, instead of leaving Bahamas on the sidings ready to be sent for scrap, Terry brought it under cover and continued to maintain it as best he could. He was helped in his endeavours by a group of railway enthusiasts. Steve Allsop, who was twenty-two years old and an engineer, was among them.

In 1967 Bahamas was scheduled for scrap and the group started to negotiate its purchase. The sum required was £3,000. Locomotives were sold at the price of scrap metal, which was calculated by the ton, and Bahamas was a large and heavy vehicle. Steve said, 'You could buy a mansion for that money. An average semi was about £1,000 then.' One of the group members wrote to the *Manchester Evening News* asking for interested parties to help them buy the engine, and the letter proved effective, with Geoffrey Potter, a local businessman, coming forward and offering an interest-free loan. To manage the financial transaction and ownership of the engine the group formed the Stockport (Bahamas) Locomotive Society.[7] Once the purchase was complete, Bahamas was sent to the Hunslet Engine Company in Leeds to be restored.

The next problem to present itself was accommodation. Two members of the group, George Davies, who was a local bank manager and later the Society's chair, and Jack Warburton, who worked in a solicitors' office and had acted on the Society's behalf when they bought Bahamas, started discussing the possibility of buying a redundant railway depot in Dinting, near Glossop in Derbyshire, which was on sale for £1,500. Warburton duly purchased the site and leased it to the group. The place was almost derelict. There was an engine shed, but it had no doors, and the other buildings were in similarly poor condition. Fortunately, they were a practical group. They laid track and road, refurbished existing buildings, opened a café, and bought an old RAF hangar and re-erected it on-site to use as the main exhibition hall. George Davies provided the bricks that formed the cladding. Around a hundred volunteers worked on the site, which opened in 1969, two years after the acquisition of the locomotive.

Over the next ten years or so, the group acquired other engines through a variety of means. Some were bought and some were given. The group paid £500 for the locomotive Nunlow, which came from G. T. Earle's cement works in Derbyshire. In 1970 the North Western Gas Board donated Tiny, which had been used at the Bradford Gas Works and, as the name suggests, was of diminutive size.[8] The National Trust gave an 1888 locomotive known as Coal Tank, which was the last of its type, and had been bought by public subscription. Others were given on long-term loan. Beamish: Museum of the North had bought Jacob, the world's oldest

Figure 1.2 Dinting Railway Centre, Derbyshire; founding group with wives, girlfriends, and children, at the opening on Easter Weekend 1969

Figure 1.3 A view of 45596 Bahamas working during the first Easter Steam Weekend at Dinting Railway Centre, April 1969

petrol-driven locomotive, so called because it had previously been used at the Jacob's factory in Liverpool, famous for producing cream crackers. They were not ready to take possession, so passed it on to Dinting.

Privately owned engines were also added to the collection. One such locomotive was Leander, bought by a Stockport businessman and railway enthusiast who had baulked at the prospect of it being stripped down. Having organised its purchase, it was stationed at the Dinting Railway Centre, where it was restored and maintained by volunteers, as were the Scots Guardsman, Blue Peter, and Bittern. In total Dinting provided a home to some twelve locomotives as well as two diesel engines, two brake vans, a couple of wagons, and a fifty-ton steam crane, while other famous engines, including the Flying Scotsman, were regular visitors.

Like Dinting Railway Centre, the development of the Museum of Rail Travel is closely connected to the modernisation of the railways. Its story begins with the closure of the Keighley and Worth Valley Railway in 1962. This nineteenth-century branch line crosses the steep Pennine terrain between Keighley and the nearby town of Oxenhope in West Yorkshire, and was originally built to service the numerous woollen mills in the area, transporting workers and supplying the coal that powered the looms. Its closure as part of the modernisation programme prompted a huge amount of opposition, and local residents got together to form the Keighley and Worth Valley Railway Preservation Society. They negotiated to buy the line outright and lease access to Keighley station, and British Railways agreed that they could repay the costs incurred over twenty-five years. In 1967 they became the first privatised railway of the post-war period.[9] The Society set out to run a regular train service, and so they bought recently retired railway carriages that they could continue to use. Nonetheless, one member, Tony Cox, was also keen to ensure that the older, less usable wooden railway carriages, which had been phased out during the process of modernisation, be preserved.

Wooden carriages were far more rapidly scrapped than locomotives, and preservationists had to be quick to salvage these vehicles from railways sidings or the scrapyards. The first carriage that Tony Cox bought was a four-wheeled coach built in 1876 that had been used on the Manchester, Sheffield and Lincolnshire Railways. Originally, it had been divided into lavishly appointed first-class, comfortable second-, and basic third-class compartments, but it had since been used as a tool van, and it was thoroughly dilapidated when he acquired it in 1965. In order to help preserve the carriage in the long term Tony worked with a friend, Robin Higgins, to form the Vintage Carriages Trust, which took ownership of the coach. Over the next two decades, the Vintage Carriages Trust acquired other vehicles, including the coaches that had outlived their useful service on the Keighley and

Worth Valley Railway. Their problem was storage, and the carriages suffered in the wild weather of the Yorkshire moors, so in 1990 they happily accepted an offer of space made by Keighley and Worth Valley Railway Preservation Society. They gave the group a site in the goods yard at Ingrow station, where they were able to construct a new building and bring their collection permanently under cover.

The Vintage Carriages Trust had a good track record of raising money. They collected railway ephemera and magazines to be sold in a dedicated shop in Haworth, which generally raised around £8,000 per year; they rented out some of the carriages for use on film sets or on heritage railways; and they applied to PRISM, a purchase and restoration fund that was generally used for the conservation of artworks. The fund covered half of the £1 purchase cost for the Sir Barclay locomotive (Tiny) and £20,000 for its restoration. Members of the Vintage Carriages Trust were also generous, and during the 1980s and 1990s they handed over £34,000 in unsecured interest-free loans. Sometimes the lenders were so pleased by the ensuing work that the loans were converted into gifts, although Trevor England, who joined the Vintage Carriages Trust as a young man and co-founded the Museum of Rail Travel, said that when he told the new secretary about the unsecured financial arrangements, she, 'shall we say, went a little bit white'.

Some of these loans paid for the move to the yard at Ingrow and for them to buy and erect a light industrial unit big enough to house the complete collection of carriages and to provide space for workshops, a reception, offices, and other

Figure 1.4 Trevor English, Museum of Rail Travel, Keighley, West Yorkshire

facilities. It took another few years before they opened their space as the Museum of Rail Travel. Trevor explained that they had originally planned on having a storage shed for the carriages, 'simply somewhere to put them safe. And then we, sort of, gradually talked and said well, actually, we could arrange this so that we could let people in. And if you're doing that, then perhaps it becomes a museum.' Chris Smyth, another founder member of the Museum of Rail Travel and a close friend of Trevor, added that there 'was a dawning realisation that if you were going to put all this work into making these beautiful exhibits then you'd better make arrangements for people to see them'.

The shift from storage space and workshop to museum was ultimately facilitated by a gift from the National Railway Museum in York. They were refurbishing their galleries and passed on a large quantity of raised metal walkways. Railway carriages sit high above the ground, with the bottom of their doors at or above adult head height. It was impossible to see inside the carriages and the carefully restored interiors remained more or less invisible to visitors. The new walkways enabled people to walk alongside the carriages as if on a station platform and to look or step inside. They effectively opened the collection to the public.

The modernisation of the railways and the Beeching cuts both motivated and enabled the foundation of the railway museums we have discussed. The founders were concerned that historic locomotives and carriages not be simply junked in the process of modernisation, while the shift from steam to diesel, and the process of closing branch lines, goods yards, and their related infrastructure, produced a surplus of objects for railway preservationists to buy. These extended beyond locomotives and carriages to the furniture from station waiting rooms, locomotive nameplates, tools, numerous tinplated signs bearing the names of stations, and other ephemera. Some objects were bought directly from British Railways, others from scrapyards, and in some cases they were salvaged from abandoned sites.

Just as the objects became available, so too did the spaces in which they could be stored or presented to the public. Dinting Railway Museum was located at a steam depot that became redundant in the age of diesel. Likewise, the Museum of Rail Travel was located in a goods yard that was closed when branch lines were cut in the 1960s. The combined processes of modernisation and cost-cutting produced both artefacts for exhibition and the sites at which that exhibition could take place.

Nationalising the buses

The Museum of Transport, Greater Manchester has a vast collection of buses as well as a few historic trams and a single fire engine, and is locally known as the Bus

Museum. Like the Dinting Railway Centre and the Vintage Carriages Trust, it started at a moment of change. Its foundation was closely related to the reorganisation of the bus service and to an ongoing process of modernisation.

During the early part of the twentieth century there was a mass of bus companies. Some had municipal operators and others were privately owned with single bus operators running alongside large companies that owned over 300 vehicles.[10] After the Second World War, the Labour government moved to consolidate the bus and tram services. The Tilling Group, one of the two large conglomerates that operated bus transport, sold its stock to the government in 1947, and the following year London Transport was nationalised, with British Electric Traction Company, the second major group, continuing to operate on an independent basis until 1967. Unlike the railway, which was centrally organised, responsibility for the newly acquired bus and tram services was passed to individual local authorities. At the time, the structure of local government in the UK was even more complex than it is now, and the conurbation surrounding Manchester was no exception. Not only did it cross the two counties of Lancashire and Cheshire, it also straddled eleven municipal boroughs, with Bolton, Bury, Leigh, Oldham, Ramsbottom, and Rochdale to the north, Manchester and Salford in the centre, Ashton-under-Lyne and Stalybridge to the east, and Stockport to the south. Each of these boroughs ran their own bus services. They all ordered different types of bus and they all had different liveries. The double-decker buses used in Rochdale were made by Daimler and were blue and cream; Bolton had cherry-red buses that were at the forefront of 1960s bus design; and Ramsbottom, which was the smallest operator, bought one bus a year, making sure that the model could easily be maintained by a small crew.

In 1968, the Transport Act created a new structure for public transport to ensure that it was co-ordinated across and within large areas. One of those newly created authorities was the South East Lancashire and North East Cheshire Passenger Transport Executive (SELNEC), which took over responsibility for public transport within the expanded area. At this point, all the vehicles that had belonged to the former municipal undertakings were passed to SELNEC. They designed a new corporate livery, and any bus that had four or more years of working life was painted orange and white. However, there was a nascent interest in bus preservation, and various employees banded together to buy some of the buses as they were being phased out. They were supported by two of the senior managers, Harry Taylor and Jeff Harding, and in 1970 they arranged to keep an Atkinson double decker, the only one of its kind. The Preston company had made it as a prototype, but the gearbox malfunctioned and there was stiff competition in the commercial vehicles market, most notably from British Leyland, only a few miles to the south.

Initially, the preserved buses were scattered among the various company depots and maintained by small groups of enthusiasts, who usually worked at or from those same garages; but, encouraged by senior management, who were keen to deal with a single group rather than scattered individuals, some came together to form the SELNEC Transport Society. One of the aims of this loosely convened group was to open a museum, and the catalyst for this came in 1972 when SELNEC decided to hold an open day. The Society ran the event, it was well attended, and everything went smoothly. Their credibility established, SELNEC gave the Society space to house their buses in a Salford garage, and then in 1977, when a huge 1901 tram depot on the edge of Manchester city centre became vacant, gave them permission to move in to the larger building.

The tram shed had been used by the Post Office to maintain their vehicles, and it needed considerable work to be made ready to house the buses and be opened to the public. Paul Williams, who was fifteen at the time and still at school, was one of the group who undertook that work. He told us that the place was filthy, with oil ingrained in every surface, a room that was ten foot deep in sand, and piles of bricks stacked over floors. There was asbestos, and tanks with contaminated fuel set into the ground. The group cleaned and repaired the site, and built a makeshift shop, a café, and women's toilets, as the tram shed had been entirely occupied by men.

Figure 1.5 Upper Exhibition Hall prior to opening, Museum of Transport, Greater Manchester, circa 1978

The museum opened to the public in 1979, but its direction and aim were already a matter of some contention. Paul said that the 'founding fathers were often hobbyists, people who like to restore buses and drive them out to events'. However, once the group acquired a building they started to attract new volunteers who were interested in setting up the museum. They did not generally own vintage vehicles. The two factions were divided over the question of whether the place was 'a shed full of buses that was open to the public or a museum where we also restored buses'. Paul explained that the dilemma they faced was 'the trade-off between professionalising the museum to attract more visitors, grant funding, etcetera, and accepting the loss of freedoms that go with it. If you're in a high-standard museum, you can't have lots of buses absent each weekend because the owners have taken them out – the display must be robust. And the public likes to see some work in progress; by and large, though, they want a museum that is full of restored exhibits.'

The disagreement came to a head at the Annual General Meeting of 1980, and over forty years later Paul could vividly remember the vote. The museum-minded group had lobbied hard for support and they understood how to make use of the proxy voting system. Against expectations, they won the day. Paul observed that small independent museums often had a moment of conflict, 'a fork in the road at which you decide what kind of place you're going to be. And that was ours.' With the museum in place, SELNEC (by then known as Greater Manchester Passenger Transport Executive) agreed to keep one bus from each corporation and pass it on to the museum for safekeeping. They have since built up an extensive collection.

Other bus museums had quite different trajectories, and their foundation was not directly connected to legislative change. Jasper Pettie set up the Scottish Vintage Bus Museum in Fife, which slowly evolved out of his and his colleagues' interest in bus restoration. As a young man he took a job in Vancouver, where he worked with a group of enthusiasts to restore an old bus. That fired his own enthusiasm, and in 1970, when he returned to Scotland to take up a position as accountant to the Scottish Bus Group, he decided he would buy his own vehicle.

Jasper wanted a Guy bus, because those were the vehicles he'd travelled in as a small child. Bus companies usually retire vehicles when they have reached around twenty years of service or occasionally earlier, when there are major design changes. For instance, the introduction of buses on which passengers paid the driver on entry meant that buses that required a conductor and were thus more expensive to staff were retired more speedily than would have otherwise been the case. Guy buses were manufactured in the 1940s and were long past their sell-by date, but through his contacts at work Jasper found one that was still in operation. The company agreed to sell it for £100 scrap value, and over the next few years he worked with a group to restore the vehicle. When that was finished, he bought another bus, more decrepit than the first, from a showground family, who had used it to move fairground equipment and to tow caravans. And so it continued, until he had restored eight vintage buses.

A double decker is generally around ten metres long and four and a half metres high. Obviously, they do not fit into an ordinary domestic garage, and parking them outside leaves them prey to vandalism and to damage from the weather. It is possible to lease industrial units to use as a garage, but secure tenure tends to be expensive, and so enthusiasts often opt for short-term measures. After losing accommodation at short notice, Jasper decided to buy his own space. He approached his second cousin Hilda Noble for a loan, and with her help he purchased a British Rail shed (that had become available after the Beeching reforms) and a secure yard that was capable of housing up to fifteen buses. This gave him enough room to offer storage to other bus owners, who paid a monthly rent, and he was able to defray costs and gradually pay off the loan. The arrangement was successful, and when the debt was covered Noble was happy to lend a further sum of money, which in 1985 enabled the group to move to a larger space that could accommodate up to forty buses.

At this point Jasper registered the company as a charity, mainly because it meant that they qualified for remission on the rates. They also started to run an annual open day. Bus companies and other owners would come and bring their vehicles, and the events became so popular that they organised off-site car parking at a local school and ran a shuttle bus between the two sites. The shuttle bus was a vintage vehicle, and it was then that Jasper realised that 'people – particularly kids – love to travel on buses', and that this was one of the reasons why they are so popular compared with, say, vintage cars or tractors or lorries. He said, 'You can look at them, but you can travel on a bus.' The open days gave the group a sense of the potential public interest in their vehicles.

Ten years later, in 1995, they moved again, this time to a Royal Navy stores depot. At 45 acres, the new site was considerably larger than their previous premises, and it provided more possibilities for income generation. They used some of the hangars as garage space, and within five years there were around 175 vintage buses on-site, generating a rental income of some £72,000 per annum. They also let the space to other groups for events and training, including courses for riot police, and they developed a members' group for people who did not have their own buses. For £20 a year, members could use the facilities, get involved in vehicle

Figure 1.6 Jasper Pettie, annual open day at Scottish Vintage Bus Museum, West Lothian, circa 1988

restoration, and come along to the various activities and events organised by the group. The funds from these various activities were reinvested in the site, and over the following years the group embarked on an ambitious programme of redevelopment and expansion. They paid for the roof on a major building to be replaced, completely rewired other spaces, and installed a workshop for the use of the members, a weighbridge, a function hall with a bar and dance floor, and a bunkhouse for members should they want to stay overnight. On one occasion, Stagecoach hired the site to host the Scottish Business awards and re-landscaped the grounds for the event. The group subsequently extended the lawns and planted flowerbeds.

Once the buildings were watertight and usable, the group set up an archive containing records and photographs from coach-building companies that bus owners could consult when restoring their vehicles, and they opened a museum.[11] Jasper commented that it was a 'eureka' moment. They had 'wonderful buildings, cash in the bank' and, so far as they knew, no-one had an exhibition devoted to buses. They earmarked one of the large hangars as an exhibition hall and constructed glass display cases around the walls, which were then filled with models of buses, ticketing machines, company uniforms, and historic photographs of drivers and conductors, most of which were donated by fellow bus enthusiasts and supporters of the museum. In the centre of the hangar they parked around two dozen fully restored buses. Two or three of the vehicles had been bought by the museum; the rest were in private ownership.[12]

In one instance, then, the foundation of a museum was a direct response to the reorganisation of public transport in the UK. The fleet of buses on display at the Museum of Transport, Greater Manchester first became available through the reorganisation of the public transport system and was initially retained by people working for the newly formed company (although that later changed, with many of the volunteers coming from outside the industry). In contrast, the Scottish Vintage Bus Museum was not directly linked to the reorganisation of public transport, although it did benefit from the modernisation of the railways in that it found accommodation in a redundant British Rail shed.

Second families

Many of the founders we spoke to became involved in vehicle preservation when they were young. Steve Allsop joined the Bahamas Locomotive Society and helped at Dinting Railway Centre in 1968, when he was twenty-two years old. When we first interviewed him, in 2017, he was wearing a pair of overalls covered in grease, having spent a cold winter's day working with a group of apprentices and fellow volunteers on restoring the locomotive Coal Tank. Paul Williams is still closely involved with the transport museum that he helped set up when he was a boy, as a trustee and running their social media channels and press. Jasper bought his first bus in 1970, when he was twenty-five years old. When we met him in 2019 he had recently returned from a run down to the Beer and Buses Festival on the Isle of Wight. It had taken the group four days to drive from the north east of Scotland. These three men have spent decades, indeed their entire adult lives, working to preserve and display locomotives and buses. The same is true of Trevor England, who volunteered on the Keighley and Worth Valley Railway and joined the nascent Vintage Carriages Trust in the 1960s, becoming the first treasurer of the Museum of Rail Travel in the 1990s. He was later appointed and remains chair. Why would they dedicate so much of their lives to these projects? What have the projects given them and why have they stayed?

In the late 1980s Dinting Railway Centre was forced to close, and the volunteers' response to that transition provides a useful indication of its importance within their lives. The Centre had proved popular. When the Flying Scotsman came in 1973, the queue to stand on the footplate was an hour and a half long, and the line of cars waiting to enter stretched out through Dinting and backed up on to the main trunk road. However, they faced a problem. Jack Warburton, who had been a supporter and had bought the site and leased it to the group, kept trying to increase the rent. The group repeatedly used the Landlords and Tenant Act to contest the rise, but in the mid-1980s their solicitor missed a deadline to appeal, which meant they were no longer protected by legislation. The rents were raised and the costs became unsustainable. In 1989, following a dispute, the group gave notice to quit.

Once again they had to look for accommodation. Steve said, 'I don't think we had any other option. Well, there was one other option: we could have just sold up and packed it in, but we didn't want to. You just couldn't pull out and sell it to somebody else after twenty odd years.' There were several possibilities for new accommodation, one of which involved a clandestine meeting at a motorway service station, but they decided to accept an offer from the Keighley and Worth Valley Railway Preservation Society and to resettle at their site at Ingrow, where the Museum of Rail Travel was also opening its new premises.

Ingrow was forty miles from Dinting and on the other side of the Pennines, the range of mountains that divides north-west and north-east England, and the group had a limited amount of time to make the move. Steve said that 'there was just so much to do that year; we had to shift absolutely everything. We were on the phone

Figure 1.7 Nunlow leaving Dinting Railway Centre, 1990

day after day with people like Goodman, the transport man, people with cranes, people at Keighley for reception of things. Every week we had to decide what to move, sort things out from store, get them on a lorry, get them across the Pennines, get them unloaded again. You know, it was continuous effort all the time; you kept going. Sometimes when you look back on it now, it was fantastic really, what we did.'

The move was partly financed by a lawsuit. The group sued the solicitor's firm for negligence and the compensation helped fund the costs of moving the collection, although not all of the locomotives made the journey across the border. The new space was far smaller and there was no room for the privately owned engines that the group had restored. Jacob was moved to the Beamish Museum, the Scots Guardsman went to the Birmingham Railway Museum at Tyseley, and the Bittern and Blue Peter went to a collection in the North East. The Avonside tank engine, which was owned by the museum, was sold to help finance the relocation, and in the end the group were only able to retain Tiny, Nunlow, Coal Tank, and the foundational locomotive, Bahamas.

For Steve there was little time to mourn the end of the museum. 'You obviously saw that you were pulling down what you'd built over the previous twenty years, but I don't think we were feeling sad about it as such, because it was just so hectic – there was just too much going on. There wasn't time to sit back and think whether it was right or wrong.' For others, though, the loss was more keenly felt. Mike Bentley, an ex-British Rail driver and one of the original volunteers at Dinting, said, 'The departure of Leander was the first. I couldn't even bring myself to accept that. That was a low ebb that was for me. My wife Pat used to say, "Don't you think you ought to go and give a hand?" and I said, "I can't face it. Can't face that, not pulling it all apart". It hurt.'[13] Like some of the locomotives, a number of the older members of the group never made the transition across the Pennines.[14]

The reconstituted museum opened as Ingrow Loco in 2003 and featured a small display about the Dinting site. Before the exhibition was completed Pete Skellon, who had been involved with the group since 1968 and became the volunteer collections manager at Ingrow, embarked on a project called Steam in Our Soul. He worked with Graham Allen, another volunteer, and George West, a sound engineer with the BBC, to interview the people who had been involved in setting up Dinting Railway Centre. They used their stories as the basis for a cycle of songs that moves through the purchase and preservation of Bahamas to working at Dinting and the eventual loss of that site.[15] Members of Pete's local folk club recorded the songs, and the completed audio documentary was released as a CD in 2002.

The project is testament to how much they cared about the locomotive, about each other's experience, and about the change of site. Pete kindly shared that interview material with the authors, and we draw on those transcripts and the CD in our discussion here. One of the songs on the CD is called 'Dinting Engineman':

I first went up to Dinting when I was just thirteen
I covered myself in dirt and oil to get the engines clean
I quickly made some friends amongst the lads who were there
And I learned my fireman's duties and locomotive care

Chorus: *For I'm a Dinting Engineman I'm proud of all we do*
And what I've learnt from older hands I'll gladly teach to you

I p'rhaps had twenty brothers maybe twenty uncles too
You felt secure in knowing that they'd all look after you
The more we laughed and joked we found the more we could achieve
And the quality of the work we did some found hard to believe

Well Dinting men go everywhere was something I was told
So I went with all the lads to Crewe, Hereford, and Bold
And there were lots of other places where the engines would appear
And when we'd cleaned and serviced them we tried the local beer

So if you wish to know some more about the age of steam
Why not come and join us and be part of the team
Get into your overalls, and fill your can with tea
Let's climb aboard the engine it's the only place to be.

As the song suggests, the older men taught the younger men how to repair and drive the engines. Some of the volunteers were ex-railwaymen and they retained the original training structure from their days at British Rail. The young volunteers started off by cleaning the locomotives, then progressing to being a passed cleaner (which meant that they could work as a fireman when required), to being a full-time fireman, and only finally to being a driver, a process that could take many years: as the song goes – 'I learned my fireman's duties and locomotive care'. Steve commented that 'they were great to us really; they wanted to show us how it was done, and we were just like sponges – give us more, you know; the more they could tell us the more we would want'. In turn the younger men passed their skills on: 'And what I've learnt from older hands I'll gladly teach to you.' Steve, now in his seventies, is still training new volunteers how to repair and maintain a steam locomotive.

Structured training and the acquisition of skills gave the volunteers a level of self-respect. One of the men Pete spoke to was Steve Peach, otherwise known as Peachy, who said that 'I was treated as an older, more responsible person than I was at school. At school I was thirteen, when I was at Dinting, you know, I was one of the cleaners, one of the oinks, like, but you just got the feeling that you were that bit more special.' Working at Dinting also set them up for future careers in engineering. Peachy reports that 'I went into mechanical engineering because of Dinting. I saw all these welding, fitting skills. Found I could do them. Found that I was interested in them enough to want to make a career out of it.' Having worked at Dinting 'I could weld, I could scrape, I could use a lathe, I could use a milling machine, I was familiar with the process and I think it made me stand out a little bit.' At seventeen he won an Apprentice of the Year award.

The song also gives a sense of the volunteers' pride in the finished object – 'the quality of the work we did some found hard to believe'. There was a delight in restoring the locomotives to their former glories and seeing them in full steam. Fred Barnes, one of the founder members and a former toolmaker, who in the early days was in charge of engineering, was also interviewed in the making of the CD. He remarked that 'after Bahamas was done up and was standing there highly polished up, lovely engine, the rest of the shed looked like the black hole of Calcutta. And this just stood out, it was above everything else. And at that stage you thought, well, that was worth it, well worth it. I thought so anyway – still do.'

Above all, though, 'Dinting Engineman' conveys the camaraderie of the group. During the week, the volunteers would go to Dinting after they finished work and then leave for last orders at the local pub, although as Steve recalled, 'we had lots of energy as young guys, nothing's too hard, so you do things like night turns and not think about it. Something special: we've had to stay up all night to look after the engine – we were real railwaymen now.' At weekends somebody was usually designated to go into the nearby town of Glossop and bring back around twenty portions of fish and chips. Working, eating, and drinking together served to build bonds. Peachy said that 'I'd never had any brothers. I only had two sisters, and there I was at sort of thirteen or fourteen with this group of lads. I'd just got that feeling that they really would look after you right to the hilt.' And they did look after him. One night he was catching the last train home when some older boys accosted him. He recalls the incident: 'I remember running back along the foot-bridge and shouting to Andy Jones or Big Smith, I think it was, "There's some lads here trying to get us," and everybody just dropped everything and these lads they went berserk. There was about fifteen blokes come haring round the side of the New Shed and the boys just screamed and ran, you know.' For Peachy, the group

Figure 1.8 Steve Peach on the footplate of Coal Tank during a visit to Severn Valley Railway in 2015

provided him with something akin to family and a level of automatic support, hence the lines 'I p'rhaps had twenty brothers maybe twenty uncles too / You felt secure in knowing that they'd all look after you'.

Simon Bryant, who served for 36 years as the Society's chair, made the point even more forcibly when he said, 'We've survived because of our love of the steam locos we look after and, dare I say it, our love of each other.' For some of the volunteers, working at Dinting was so important that they asked for their ashes to be spread at the site.[16]

These experiences all find overlaps and parallels with the experiences of the founders and volunteers in the other transport museums that we visited.

For Jasper, the pleasure of restoring buses was in the process, not in the finished object. When we visited in 2019, he had recently sold several of the buses that he had bought and so carefully restored as a younger man. When we asked what he had felt, he said, 'There was a slight sort of welling up in my throat. I was surprised in a way that I wasn't more emotionally attached.' He then went on to explain that he liked the restoration process because 'at the end of each day you've got something to show for it', and because 'I learned a lot of skills which I hadn't had before'. He also enjoyed the hunt for replacement parts. For instance, he reported that: 'I've got a bus; we don't have any seats for it. Well, we do – we've got a huge seat store and my next job is to ferret through and find a set of matching seats, and I love doing that sort of thing. You think: "Right, now where can I get a set of interior lights of the correct pattern?" So you make a few phone calls, you send a few emails to a few contacts, or as has happened quite recently, an old bus has been discovered on a farm which is totally derelict but it's got a load of bits on it, so off you go to have a look.' In contrast, 'When a bus is finished, I think, well, what can you do with it? You can drive around, have a bit of fun and admire it and everything else but, you know, that's it.'

Restoring the buses required the acquisition of new skills and incremental work, both of which were satisfying. It also involved detective work. The restorers had to identify exactly what was missing and track down the correct replacement, which often took them on something of a treasure hunt. For Jasper, the finished bus was testament to those endeavours, but it was not particularly interesting in and of itself. It was the process that captured his interest and, despite his slightly disparaging remark on the subject, the pleasure of driving it around. He said that that in the 1970s there were no meets for bus owners, so a group of enthusiasts usurped an annual car rally, arriving in a convoy of forty or more buses. As more rallies were established, they travelled further afield, taking the vintage buses on road runs through towns and villages. Later, after he was married, his family would accompany him on rallies. They would pack a picnic on to one of the restored buses and set off to drive from town to town. There was no shortage of space on board so his wife and two boys would invite their friends along, and sometimes their friends' families. It was, Jasper says, tremendous fun.

As with the group at Dinting, the work of restoring buses and taking them on outings builds camaraderie and trust. This can be particularly valuable for volunteers facing personal difficulties. Jasper said that the Vintage Bus Museum is 'a huge man shed' that provides 'a breath of fresh air in what are possibly strenuous lives. They may be looking after aged relatives, they may have domestic problems,

Figure 1.9 Vintage bus rally, Leven, Fife, 1971

Figure 1.10 Edinburgh running day, undated

they may be divorced, there may be all kinds of things, and I know that people look forward to coming up here. Coming up to work on the buses is actually what keeps them together, keeps them going.' Explaining further, he said: 'I suppose it's an unspoken rule that you just don't say, "Oh what happened to your divorce?" or something. You don't have to talk too much. You can have a banter. You can retreat into whatever you're doing or you can go and chat to other people, but that's the great thing about this place, you're valued as a member of a team and a lot of people are very lonely. They live on their own and coming to a place like this reinforces their self-worth, you know.'

Trevor England and Chris Smyth also had first-hand experience of this kind of unspoken care. In the early 1980s, when they were both members of the Vintage Carriages Trust, Trevor met and married Jean and they introduced Chris to her close friend Sue, and they also got married. Sadly, the two women both died at a young age, and Trevor and Chris were widowed within eighteen months of each other. When we met in 2020, Trevor said, 'We still miss them.' He went on to explain that when he was married, he had worked a five-day week at the steelworks and on Saturdays the couple would do the shopping together. Then he would spend one Sunday 'playing on the railway, where she would do other things, and on the following Sunday I'd take her for a run out in the countryside and enjoy trips about'. After she died, he went to the museum most weekends. 'I found when I lost Jean that the extended family was too close and too possessive, and I needed freedom but still needed support. So, coming to the railway and having friends helped me through the bereavement process. The railway then became our saviour, to a certain extent… we've actually had a second family to support us for years'. Trevor paused and said, 'I don't know how Chris felt on his side of it, but that's how it worked for me,' and Chris nodded: 'Yes, that right.' For them, volunteering at the Vintage Carriages Trust and setting up the Museum of Rail Travel meant that they could get out of their houses and be with other people. Their companions knew of their bereavement and were kindly towards them, but they were not cosseted or expected to talk about their loss.

In this instance, caring for the locomotives, carriages, and buses provided a point of connection for the men involved. The vehicle was the lynchpin around which the groups came together and provided a reason for the men to meet. There was no suggestion that anyone joined the groups purposefully seeking friendship, much less out of emotional need, and yet in the process of repairing the vehicles, and of teaching and learning the skills required to do so, they all built a community. As Paul Williams said, 'It's a niche interest and it's a pleasure to sit in the tea room with like-minded people boring each other silly talking about buses.' The point is that they do not bore each other silly. Friendship, support, and even love for one another were developed and articulated in relation to the locomotives, buses, and carriages. Indeed, while the objects were the locus of that companionship, and formed the basis on which those friendships were built, the men often stayed involved because of the ensuing friendships. Their connections with one another superseded those with the vehicles.

A sense of duty

The Dinting Railway Centre and the Vintage Carriages Trust and their successor bodies, Ingrow Loco and the Museum of Rail Travel, all have their origins in the nationalisation and modernisation of the railways. Likewise, the foundation of the Museum of Transport, Greater Manchester is closely linked to the nationalisation and modernisation of the UK bus service. Along with the Scottish Vintage Bus Museum, these museums provided a space where men came together, repaired vehicles, taught and learned new skills, went to the pub and enjoyed day trips, had fun, and supported one another through difficult times. Other transport museums have emerged through quite different routes and have generated other kinds of emotional attachment. Here I turn to the British Commercial Vehicle Museum, which opened in Leyland, Lancashire in 1986. Its origins lie in the process of de-industrialisation and ultimately in the sale, not the creation, of nationalised industries.

In the post-war period the UK was the world's biggest vehicle exporter. Even so, by the late 1960s a lack of investment and, increasingly, competition from Germany, France, and Japan was beginning to bite.[17] The then Labour government had a hands-on approach to industrial management and they approached British Leyland with a proposed merger. British Leyland, which owned Triumph and Rover, would join forces with British Motor Holdings, which owned Austin, Morris, MG, and Jaguar, to form a mighty conglomerate that could compete in the international market. The two firms agreed, but the reality was somewhat different. Factories were overstaffed, in urgent need of modernisation, and there was a series of strikes over pay and conditions. In the early 1970s the merged British Leyland Motors was on the verge of collapse. It employed around 250,000 people in the West Midlands alone and so its closure would have been calamitous for the local and national economy. Harold Wilson's government stepped in with a huge £2.4 billion bailout, which made the government one of the company's major shareholders.[18] Thus, when the Conservative party came to power in 1979, they had a say in the management and future of the company. The new Conservative administration took a very different approach to UK industry, preferring to trust in the free market, and the ensuing battle over the fate of British Leyland Motors became symbolic of competing political and economic policies. After years of fraught negotiations, its constituent parts were gradually sold off. The Truck and Bus Division was one of the first to go and in 1987 Leyland Trucks and Freight Rover vans were merged with the Dutch company DAF Trucks, with DAF being the majority owner.[19]

Over the years British Leyland had accumulated examples of vehicles it had manufactured in eighty years of production, although it was by no means a complete set. In 1975, the company established the Heritage Collections to recognise these vehicles, with the vintage commercial vehicles falling under the purview of the Truck and Bus Division, which was based in Leyland. At this point the vehicles were parked in a large display space that was mainly used for corporate events and hospitality. Then in 1983 the company formed four independent charitable trusts to take over the management of the different collections: the British Motor Industry Heritage Trust, Austin Rover Heritage Trust, Jaguar Daimler Heritage Trust, and the British Commercial Vehicle Trust. Under these new arrangements the Leyland collection was opened to the public.[20]

Unusually, responsibility for the museum was given to John Gilchrist, the manufacturing director of the Truck and Bus Division. It had previously been with Gavin Barlas, the head of sales and marketing, which made sense as the museum was used for corporate hospitality, but the role was shifted in a minor dispute over noise. Les Wharton, the chief executive officer, always ate a sandwich lunch in his office. Two doors down, Gavin used the time for private trumpet lessons with the leader of the British Leyland brass band, so Les was forced to listen to a beginner going through his scales. Tensions built. Then one day Gavin burst into a meeting and insisted that Les deal with some problem relating to the museum. Already irritated by the trumpet playing, Les pointed at John who happened to be in the room and said, 'You're not sorted out – he's getting the museum.' There was no possibility of discussion and from then on John took up the reins.

This meant that when Leyland DAF went into receivership in 1993, John had responsibility for the museum. He recalls that he was in Eindhoven in the Netherlands, at the parent company, when he heard the news about the imminent bankruptcy. 'I think we all suspected that there was something wrong,' he said. 'DAF kept telling us they had plenty of money to draw down. Suppliers kept telling us they weren't getting paid. The chief executive got the management team together and said they had gone into administration. After the meeting, which was only about half an hour, I said to him, "What are we going to do about the UK?" He said, "I don't know. Don't know." He said, "This is terrible. I don't know." So I got the plane back. When I arrived back, the receiver was waiting at ten o'clock at night. The receiver was in my office.'

The Dutch and Belgian governments bailed DAF out but the UK government declined to help Leyland. Meanwhile, Murdoch Lang McKillop of Arthur Andersen, who had been appointed as receiver, stepped in and tried to maintain production. 'That was a bad time,' John said, 'and it went on for about eighteen weeks. There was all sorts of interest from other companies, but we just had to keep going. The receiver had to try to get the suppliers to keep supplying, because the only way he could make any money was to keep trading. There was lots of jobs shedding. The receiver was handing out notices of severance and everyone was frightened to death that they were going to get a brown envelope. The guys on the shop floor were more pragmatic, to be honest, but the middle management found it more difficult. One of the perks of the job was that you got a very low-cost rental car. They had to put the keys back in that day. Managers that had good jobs had to get the bus home, but they didn't know where the bus stop was. It was as bad as that, you know – trauma. So that side of it was quite a shock for everybody.'

Leyland DAF employed some 5,300 people in UK and another 12,650 in the supply chains.[21] All of them stood to lose their jobs or their investments, and in an odd coincidence Jasper Pettie, who established the Scottish Vintage Bus Museum, was one of them. He had bought into a company that manufactured exhaust systems for commercial vehicles, and Leyland DAF was one of their main customers. Its demise pushed his company into receivership.

John proposed a management buy-out of the Truck and Bus Division. He started working with Stuart Pierce, the head of human relations, and a small group of colleagues who were convinced that the factory was still viable, and so it proved to be.[22] (They also restarted trading with Jasper's resurrected company, after they managed to buy themselves out of debt.) At the same time, John and his colleagues worked with the receiver to secure the future of the museum. They arranged to have a space in one of the redundant factory buildings and were given enough money to cover the running costs for the first few years, although from that point on the museum had to rely on ticket sales, donations, and grant funding for its survival. Along with the ownership of Leyland Trucks, John and Stuart and their colleagues took on responsibility for the museum, becoming its trustees. They held quarterly management meetings and largely ran the museum as a small division of the company. Andrew Buchan, the newly appointed public relations officer, was made museum manager. In fact, John did precisely what his CEO had done earlier: he delegated the museum to another member of staff.

The trustees of Leyland Trucks did not agree to launch the British Commercial Vehicle Museum because they loved, or even liked, commercial vehicles. At one point in our conversation John said, 'I would have preferred cars.' When we asked why the group had worked to keep the collection and to open it as a museum, he replied, 'Obviously, a lot of people mourned the passing of "the motors", as they fondly called it. They even shut the sports and social club, which was just about the end, you know – it was gone.' The collection 'was part of Leyland history and, you know, people in the factories live in the town and they work in the town, so it's kind of good relations to not be sour and just shut it down, you know. That would have been wrong, I think. It was something that was left intact. It was there, so I think we should be thankful for that and just carry on with it, you know.' Here, there is a complex mix of care, strategy, and pragmatism at play. The residents of Leyland and the people who worked in the town all felt some affection for British Leyland Motors; it was part of the local history and community. Its closure also led to amenities being lost, including the sports and social clubs being closed, which had an impact on the town that reached far beyond the Leyland employees. Given that the collection had been retained, John and his colleagues felt that it was incumbent on them to preserve it in the long term. The new museum embodied something of the defunct company and gave it a continuing and visible presence within the town; it provided an amenity, and it was strategically useful because it demonstrated that the new company cared for the history of Leyland.

Opening the museum also provided a place to house the company archive. As John said, 'I mean, nobody likes throwing away history, to be honest. You know, there's all these photographs and all that stuff. What else were we going to do with it if we didn't keep it? You know, we'd have had to destroy it. Nobody wanted it.' Again, the decision to keep the archive had an ethical and emotional dimension in so far as it would have felt wrong to dispose of the historical records of the company. And, finally, when we asked him why he had stayed with the museum for so many years, he wondered, 'A sense of duty? It's not that onerous but I've been determined to find a way of sustaining it, making it sustainable, and I think we are probably well on the road to that now.' After many years of making do, in 2016 they won a £1.8m Heritage Lottery grant, which enabled them to make the building watertight, install adequate heating, and redevelop their interpretation.

The British Commercial Vehicle Museum started life as a private collection that functioned as an archive of the company's output and added colour to their events. The slow collapse of British Leyland Motors – nationalisation, asset-stripping, and eventual bankruptcy – meant that the collection no longer had a home, but it also made it available for a different audience and use. Working with

Figure 1.11 British Commercial Vehicle Museum, Lancashire

an ethical purpose and out of a sense of duty and responsibility, the receivers and ex-managerial staff at British Leyland relaunched it independently of the factory. Unlike the other transport museums we have discussed, the British Commercial Vehicle Museum did not start as a passion project. Even so, John observed that 'exactly the same camaraderie and teamship between participants is generated'.[23] In terms of emotional attachment, the company museum had an identical dynamic to those opened by enthusiasts.

Museums by default

The conditions that enabled and motivated these new transport museums are complex and their foundation is overdetermined. The creation of the British Commercial Vehicle Museum was directly tied to the decline of vehicle manufacturing within the UK, which was in turn connected to problems with nationalised industries, a lack of investment in technology, competition from overseas, and to the sale of nationalised companies. The emergence of railway museums is intimately linked to the introduction of the new diesel technologies and the drastic overhaul of British Railways, which were in turn related to the rise of road transport, private car ownership, and the decline of industries that had relied on rail transport to move their goods. The drastic reconfiguration was itself only possible because

British Railways was a nationalised service and changes to policy could be implemented wholesale and from above. Thus, foreign competition, nationalisation, the rise of road transport, public policy, and technological change all contributed to the circumstances in which it became possible to launch transport museums.

Other organisations and events were important in the emergence of new transport museums. Heritage railways had an indirect role in how railway museums were established and continued to function because they supplied retired carriages for restoration, hired restored carriages for special events, and provided track for locomotives. They provided space for museums of railways and of other subjects, including buses. Dai Woodham, who ran the Barry scrapyard in Wales, decided not to scrap the engines he had salvaged, providing a source of spare parts for the repair and maintenance of the preserved vehicles, and giving railway enthusiasts time to raise funds to buy locomotives in their entirety. He is widely credited with enabling and supporting the railway preservation movement.[24] Car and bus rallies provided focal points for meeting other enthusiasts and forging networks across the UK, as did steam events that showcased locomotives and carriages. Publishing also played a key role. The Ian Allan ABC guides created a community of trainspotters, as to a lesser extent did magazines devoted to vintage vehicles. The Museum of Rail Transport has a whole room packed with complete runs of the relevant journals, which are collected in their own right.

The foundation of new transport museums also relied on the availability of particular skills and on them being shared. Some of the original volunteers at these

Figure 1.12 Woodham's scrapyard, Barry, Glamorgan, 1968

museums had been bus or train drivers, firemen, mechanics on steam locomotives, or engineers, and they passed on their skills to the younger volunteers, enabling them to restore, maintain, and run the vehicles in question. They oversaw the necessary licences, since vehicles need to comply with current safety legislation if they are to carry passengers or to be run on road or rail. Crucially, however, the technology that they were dealing with is not particularly complicated by today's standards. Whereas diesel trains and contemporary vans and buses have an array of systems relying on computer processing and micro-electronics, and maintaining them lies beyond the skill of most amateur mechanics, it is possible for anyone with competencies in welding, engineering, or carpentry to tackle much of the work involved in restoring older vehicles. This allowed for new volunteers to easily join in.

Restoring vehicles requires multiple skills and considerable financial investment, and so it is more likely to be the focus of collective endeavour. Although some of the founders and volunteers reported petty disputes, or instances when egos had clashed, working with others had huge emotional rewards for those involved. They variously described their pride in acquiring new skills and in restoring vehicles to pristine condition, the self-respect and self-worth derived from being a valued part of a team, the sense of being looked after and cared for by others, the pleasures of banter, sociability, and friendship, fun, the alleviation of loneliness, and the sense of doing the right thing. Some men had emotional attachments to the objects; in other cases, care for the objects provided a means by which they could care for one another or demonstrate their care for a community and its history. The objects enabled participants to build camaraderie and helped keep groups together over time, sometimes over a series of geographical moves.[25]

It is notable that the founders' and volunteers' motivations do not always relate to the museum itself. Most of the founders and the volunteers that we interviewed had been initially motivated by the desire to preserve a collection of vehicles, or individual buses, locomotives, and carriages, and to engage in the work of restoration, and then by the prospect of spending time with like-minded people in a shared enterprise. The group at British Leyland Motors had a slightly different focus in that they were concerned to preserve the archive and the vehicles but were not specifically interested in restoration. They were also keen to create a museum as a public amenity in the wake of the factory closing along with some of the services it provided. None of the founders were primarily moved by a dream or desire to open a museum per se.

The museum was not the most important component in the configuration of the organisations' interests. Even when they had a collection or opened a centre of some kind, it took some time for the museum to emerge as such. The Bahamas Locomotive Society predates the foundation of the Dinting Railway Centre, and when they moved to Dinting the group was far more concerned with restoring locomotives than with curating exhibitions. They only set out to create coherent displays after the move to Ingrow. The Scottish Vintage Bus Museum, the Vintage Carriages Trust, and the British Commercial Vehicle Museum were in existence for decades before it occurred to anyone to open the sites and collections to the public. For the Vintage Bus Museum, the decision to open to the public on a regular basis was precipitated by the move to a new site that had numerous huge hangars and plenty of space to spare. The foundation of the British Commercial Vehicle Museum as it now exists was formed at the behest of the receivers who dealt with the collapse of British Leyland Motors, while the inauguration of the Museum of Rail Travel occurred almost inadvertently when it acquired raised walkways that enabled visitors to see the carriages properly. The exception here is the Museum of Transport, Greater Manchester. Like the other groups, the founders were primarily interested in preserving vintage vehicles, and opening a museum was a means of achieving that end; but unlike the other groups, there was a shift in power and the balance of the organisation, resulting in the museum being given a higher priority.

The founders are proud of their museums. Steve Allsop went out of his way to show us the new and highly professional education coach at Ingrow Loco and to point out the interpretative panels that he had assisted with. Trevor England and Chris Smyth were clearly proud of the work they had done in turning the Museum of Rail Travel into a properly accessible public space. After decades at opposite ends of the yard these two museums have now joined forces to form a single entity called Rail Story, which will allow them to further professionalise and consolidate their visitor provision. Nonetheless, these groups and societies opened transport museums by default. They were the by-product of other activities and passions and became museums through a process of transition. In some cases that transition was conflictual, as at Manchester; in others it was the result of difficult external circumstances, as at Leyland and to a lesser degree Dinting. At the Scottish Vintage Bus Museum and for the Museum of Rail Travel it was more akin to a slow realisation that something was possible.

Chapter 2

War and conflict museums: muttering in the corridors of power

During the late twentieth century the number of war and conflict museums rapidly increased, making it one of the most popular subjects for a museum in the UK. The new war and conflict museums addressed a wide range of periods in history – from the 1066 Battle of Hastings Museum to Kelvedon Hatch Secret Nuclear Bunker – and covered a plethora of topics – from the Jersey War Tunnels to the Museum of Cipher Equipment – but some topics were more common than others. In 1960 the RAF was a relatively new service and there were no military aviation museums, whereas there were sixty by 2020, and the number of corps and regimental museums grew from fifty to 132, becoming the single largest group within the category.[1] Although some of these museums were national, and others belonged to local authorities, the majority were small and independent and established by groups and individuals. The question, then, is why did so many people choose to open museums of war and conflict?

The war and conflict museums that opened in the late twentieth century often took decades to develop as such. They emerged slowly within a long history of conflict and their foundation was closely interlinked with changes to the character of warfare, government policy, and the structure of the Armed Forces. How exactly that took place depended on whether the museums in question focused on aviation or on Army corps and regiments, or on other areas of war and conflict, each type of museum having a markedly different trajectory. In this chapter I take them in turn, beginning with military aviation museums, moving on to corps and regimental museums, and then discussing two museums that are unaligned with the Armed Forces, even oppositional to them: the Museum of Free Derry in Northern Ireland and the Peace Museum in Bradford. In each case I examine who established the museum, why, where it was accommodated, the source of the collections, and who did the work. My analysis covers topics including audience, institutional and governmental support, and social privilege.

Irrespective of their precise subject, museums of war and conflict are sites of emotional management. As our research developed it became increasingly clear that the museum founders were aiming to support members of their communities in processing difficult or traumatic experiences and histories, and they were also deeply concerned with family. I thread the discussion of emotional experience, memory, and family throughout the chapter, asking whose feelings are being managed, what or who constitutes family, and how such matters have a bearing on the numbers of museums founded.

Time walking in empty airfields

When Peter Scoley was a small child he lived on a farm just outside the village of Metheringham in Lincolnshire. Then in 1942 some of the family's land was requisitioned to build an airfield and they were given three days to quit. The Scoleys moved out of the farmhouse and a huge crew of Irish labourers arrived to build a standard Class A bomber airfield that consisted of three concrete runways, set at different angles to cope with the strong winds that sweep across the fens. One of them is still there, an unusually wide and empty road cutting between fields of potatoes. The workmen also built a control tower, hangars, and lines of Nissen huts, which provided mess halls, offices, dormitories, and other facilities for the crew.

The 106 Squadron was posted to Metheringham in October 1943 to find that the site was still under construction. Writing in the log book, Group Capt. Ronnie Baxter commented unfavourably on the unfinished, muddy accommodation, and it was widely rumoured that he was considering returning the squadron to their previous, more comfortable quarters. Conditions grew worse and that winter was one of the coldest on record. The site was snowbound and there was a flu epidemic. As Andy Marson, who was chair of Metheringham Airfield Visitor Centre remarked, 'Of course, this part of Lincolnshire, the next bit over there is Siberia,' neatly conveying a sense of the freezing conditions. They stayed until VE Day in May 1945, during which time they flew Lancaster bombers on over 200 missions.

Bombers were largely flown by young civilian volunteers from the UK and the Commonwealth and were commanded by a relatively small group of older officers. The death rates for bomber aircrews were extraordinarily high, and in the course of the war 51% of aircrews were killed in operations and another 12% killed or wounded in non-operational accidents – for instance, during training. A further 13% were taken prisoner of war, and it is estimated that only 24% escaped physically, if not psychologically, unscathed.[2] Like other crews, the 106 Squadron suffered horrendous loss. Sixty-five of their planes were lost, crash-landed, or shot down. Each plane had a crew of seven, and almost 300 men from the squadron died in the space of nineteen months.

As well as providing a base for the bomber aircrews, Metheringham was also used as a transit point for US troops. After the Normandy landings, the largest seaborne invasion in history, the Americans flew their wounded into Metheringham, moving them on to the 162nd US General Hospital, which was close to the base. Those men who recovered were also flown out of Metheringham on the first leg of their journey home, with around 1,600 US personnel passing through the base.

Meanwhile, the Scoley family continued to farm the surrounding fields. When the war ended the Metheringham base was closed, as were some 700 airfields in the UK, and the land reverted to its original owners.[3] The family returned from their temporary accommodation, moved back into the farmhouse, and put the airfield buildings to use: the large gymnasium became a cowshed and the ration store was used for rearing heifers. Then, in the 1970s and 1980s, airmen started coming back to Metheringham. They remembered the Scoley family and would often stop at their house to say hello. By now, Peter Scoley was running the farm, and he would spend time with the veterans, asking them inside for tea, listening to their stories, and showing them around the derelict site. He eventually decided that the family 'should do something more', and his wife Zena agreed. At the time, she was the deputy lord lieutenant of Lincolnshire and chair of the county council, and she secured a small grant from North Kesteven District Council to convert the old ration store cum cowshed into a museum.

The Scoleys formed a group to help in the work of establishing a museum, which opened in 1994. Andy explained that to begin with the Heritage Centre only had a few small artefacts on display. Over time, the group bought a Merlin engine of the kind used in the heavy Lancaster bombers, and they were also given the wreckage of a Lancaster bomber. The Dutch Royal Air Force, which excavated planes that were shot down or crash-landed in case they contain unexploded ordnance, found one with a serial number that linked it to Metheringham airfield, and they arranged for the wreckage to be returned. A group of airline pilots also donated a plane, although this one was in perfect condition. They had bought a Dakota, the type of plane used to transport the American soldiers out of Metheringham, but the costs of storage proved too high for them to keep it as a leisure aircraft. It is now housed in a huge light industrial unit at the edge of the site and visitors can climb inside to see where the invalids were strapped into stretchers.

Figure 2.1 Brick-built memorial with a salvaged propeller, Metheringham Airfield Visitor Centre, Lincolnshire

Andy had a long career in the RAF. He flew Vulcans and Tornados in the 1970s and 1980s, later joining the Battle of Britain Memorial Flight, a RAF unit that holds aerial displays at state and commemorative events. Sometimes the planes are landed and the crews meet with the public. Andy flew a Lancaster bomber and would invite any of the RAF veterans who had flown in the planes to climb inside.

In the aftermath of the world wars, the veterans were not always encouraged to remember or talk about their experiences and what they had felt at that time. Even long afterwards, many found it profoundly difficult to talk about their more troubling memories and were unable or unwilling to articulate them. However, getting inside the planes often had a profound effect, and Andy said that they talked in a way that they rarely, if ever, had before. 'A lot of them talked about the raids. A lot of it, again, is the people they knew. They're remembering the people they knew – that was part of it as well.' It brings back 'the bad memories, but in getting them back they also got the good memories as well, of friends and colleagues. And, of course, the social side of it as a crew. You were a crew – it was family.' For Andy, this was a highly positive process: 'I think they bottled up their memories for so long and it's got to them – It's a bit like PTSD in a way. And once they sit down there, it's all just, "Hang on, I've been worrying too long and there's been no problems at all. I've remembered my friends, I've done it, I can now actually talk to my children and my family about it." A lot of them didn't and once they talk about it, of course, half the anxiety that they bottled up goes.'

Andy compared that experience of getting back inside a bomber with visiting the Metheringham site. He said that for the veterans who had been based there, it was a means to 'assuage the ghosts… It's walking – time walking again, where they've been, is what it is.' Wandering along the miles of redundant runway and around the buildings where they lived and worked awakened embodied memories and emotions. They time walked, slipped into the past, and then brought those memories, both good and bad, back into the present. Some of those memories

Figure 2.2 Scale model of RAF Metheringham airfield at Metheringham Airfield Visitor Centre

were construed as a form of haunting. In visiting the airfield and in remembering the people whom they had lived and worked with, they were acknowledging those who had died. It was cathartic and it was akin to paying their respects at a graveside.

Lincolnshire is known as Bomber County. Its flat land and proximity to the coast of western Europe made it an ideal place to station aircrews, and by the end of hostilities it had forty-five airfields. Several of the other decommissioned Lincolnshire airfields have also been made into museums, including the RAF Ingham Heritage Centre, which, like Metheringham, was built on requisitioned farmland, and which I turn to now.

After the invasion of Poland by Germany, thousands of Polish men and women fled their country to fight with the French and the British Armed Forces, and between 1942 and 1944 three Polish bomber squadrons were based at Ingham. After the war the land and buildings reverted to the Rose family, and they moved some parts of their business into the redundant RAF buildings. Perhaps most notably, they used the airmen's mess for the manufacture of machinery that could enclose objects in wrappers, such as razor blades, soap, Lucozade bottles, or chocolates. Cadbury later bought the design, hence the trade name Cadbury Roses.

The site also continued to be used for housing Polish servicemen and women. After the war, Poland became part of the Eastern Bloc. For many Poles, the prospect of living in a Communist regime was not appealing, and as some of the soldiers who returned were suspected of spying, it could be actively dangerous. In order to cope with the displaced Poles and in recognition of their services, the UK government passed the Polish Resettlement Act, which in 1947 gave British citizenship to over 200,000 service personnel. They needed housing, and Polish Resettlement Units were established to provide accommodation for single people, married couples, and families. Ingham was one of them, and Polish families lived on the site for many years.[4]

Geoff Burton first came across the Ingham base in 2003 when he moved with his family to the nearby village and was intrigued by the ruined site. At the time he was working for the RAF and stationed in Kuwait. Geoff told us that he sometimes worked night shifts and 'after about one or two in the morning, there was nothing to do so, through the early hours of the morning, you could find me in front of a screen, researching the Polish Air Force. I was there for four months so, most of the nightshifts, after two in the morning, I just used that opportunity to research. It's the time you would never get in your normal life to do stuff like that.' In the Falklands, Geoff was based at Mount Pleasant, which was nicknamed the Death Star, after the space station in *Star Wars*. The staff had one day off a week, and while some went to the gym and others to the bar, Geoff had brought copies of the operational records from RAF Ingham and he continued his studies, making separate records for every person who was stationed at the base.

In 2010 Geoff decided to make his material public and with help from his wife Deborah arranged a one-day exhibition at the village hall. Over 200 people turned up, and many expressed an interest in forming a local heritage group. The newly formed group met and quickly decided that they wanted to do more than research the airfield. They wanted to open a museum, and they approached the Rose family, who were sympathetic to the plan and leased them part of the site on a peppercorn rent. In this instance, the landowning family did not instigate the foundation of a museum, but they were certainly supportive of it.

At the time the site was derelict and in need of substantial work. The group cleared the dense mass of saplings that had self-seeded around the buildings, built concrete walkways, restored a food preparation building for future use as a café, and rebuilt a Nissen hut, featuring original parts and furniture from the resettlement camp. Geoff and Brendan Pritchard, a project manager who became one of the driving forces of the heritage group, also proved to have considerable powers of persuasion and of fundraising. They arranged for the Royal Engineers to lay an access road and a car park as part of their training programme for new recruits, and they successfully applied to the Armed Forces Community Covenant, which funds projects that integrate serving and ex-serving people with their local communities. That grant covered the costs of installing utilities on the site and the construction of a large light industrial workshop. The members of the group now have a space to restore original machinery and vehicles and to work independently on their own projects.

Geoff and Brendan also built close links with Polish organisations. A local Polish Scout troop spent a weekend clearing the ground for a memorial garden, which was then paid for by the Polish Royal Air Force Association Charitable Trust. The garden has two memorials to the squadrons, one written in English and the other in Polish, and a roll of honour that lists the names of over 160 members of the squadron who lost their lives during the time they were based at RAF Ingham. Next to the garden is an evocative sculpture featuring life-size steel cut-outs of an aircrew. They are positioned with their backs to the fields, as if walking from the fields into the base. The Polish Ambassador came to formally open the garden and the Embassy continues to support the project.

Until now, no museum has documented the history of the four Polish bomber squadrons, and RAF Ingham Heritage Centre aims at telling the 'forgotten story of the Polish men and women who came to fight here for our freedom and theirs'. For

Figure 2.3 Memorial at RAF Ingham, Lincolnshire

Geoff, though, as for other members of the group, that story does not begin and end with the squadron itself, but includes the cooks on the base, the cleaners, and the Polish families who lived on the site after the end of the war. At the time of writing, the exhibition spaces and displays are unfinished, although one of the volunteers, Christine Bojen, who is of Polish descent, has already established a tiny vegetable garden outside the recreated Nissen Hut to show what the Polish families would have grown and cooked. The group have also raised money to record oral histories associated with the site, including that of Wanda Pietras, a WAAF (Women's Auxiliary Air Force member) who lived in the barracks during wartime and then stayed on with her husband. The video of her testimony will be played on a loop alongside the photographs that she donated. Rather than being a purely military history, the volunteers at RAF Ingham Visitor Centre are keen to present 'a human story about the Polish resettlement'.

The memorials and the planned exhibitions at RAF Ingham Heritage Centre are not primarily intended to help veterans remember; indeed, its relatively recent date of foundation means that few veterans will have had the opportunity to see it. Instead, Geoff and the rest of the group hope that the museum will enable the veterans' descendants to better understand their heritage. He said that 'our wish is that future generations will be able to come, even if they don't remember their grandma and grandpa, or great-grandma and great-grandpa; as it is, they will be able to come back, possibly see them talking (on film), certainly see evidence of what they did, old documents, photographs and things like that'. He noted that there has since been economic migration from Poland and said that the museum is also intended for migrants, so that they might find out more about historic links between Poland and the UK.

There are some clear parallels between Metheringham Airfield Visitor Centre and RAF Ingham Heritage Centre. Both airfields were hurriedly built during the Second World War and then decommissioned at the end of the hostilities, making them available for other use. They then provided space for agricultural buildings, businesses, and domestic accommodation, and only later transformed into museums. In one case the landowner instigated the museum; in the other the landlord was sympathetic and made the site available on a low-cost basis. The two museums focus on the site itself, how it was occupied by specific squadrons, and on the residents who followed, and they are also memorial spaces, although who is doing the remembering varies. At Metheringham it was the veterans themselves, and it is only more recently that the museum volunteers have begun to concentrate on supporting their families, while at Ingham the founding group focused more on their descendants – and Poles more generally. Both sites have also had external support. The local council helped Metheringham with start-up costs, and Arts Council England with acquisitions, while a range of groups and institutions supported Geoff and Brendan; and, lastly, the two museums have commonalities in that they were established by people who had close links to the Air Force, either by growing up alongside a base or being in its employ.

Opening museums slowly

Metheringham Airfield Visitor Centre and RAF Ingham Heritage Centre both began with a series of derelict buildings. The objects on display were acquired later. Regimental museums have the opposite trajectory: they begin with a mass of stuff. The circumstance of their opening, and who sets them up and to what ends, is also quite different from the two airfield museums discussed above, and is closely related to regimental structure.

In the Air Force, squadrons are not permanent units but are formed or reformed as and when they are needed. For instance, the 106 Squadron that was based at Metheringham was established for eighteen months during the First World War, re-established between 1938 and 1946, and then deployed as a strategic missile squadron between 1959 and 1963. The same is true of the Navy, whereas regiments are the organisational basis of the Army. This system has its origins in the seventeenth century, when monarchs and Parliament commissioned landowners, aristocrats, and professional soldiers to raise, equip, and lead troops. The regiments had individual identities and retained close connections to their areas of origin.[5] Julian Farrance, regimental liaison officer at the National Army Museum, explained: 'If you join the Navy in Edinburgh or if you join the Navy in Portsmouth, it doesn't make any difference: you're in the same thing and it's pretty much the same with the Royal Air Force. You're in one large structure.[6] But the Army, going way, way back, to the point when it was founded back in the 1640s, is made up of individual tribes.' Over time, some of these individual tribes were renamed and their remits necessarily changed. For instance, the Royal Hussars were light infantry and later became an armoured division, but by and large they continued as such and remained individual entities. That changed in the post-war period.

During the Second World War, the British Armed Forces employed almost 5 million personnel, with 2.9 million on active service.[7] Training, accommodating, and arming so many servicemen and women required depots, barracks, fortifications, airfields, and naval bases. Although the number of servicemen and women was greatly reduced at the end of the war, the Armed Forces remained sizeable. National Service remained in place, and the UK fought in Palestine, Malaya, Korea, Kenya, Cyprus, and Suez. Then in 1957 the government held a major review of UK defence policy.[8] They needed to cut costs and they were increasingly aware that the principal threat came from the possibility of nuclear warfare, not from land invasions, and that a large standing army did not provide sufficient security in the Cold War period. They made a decision to rapidly develop military science and technology, to end compulsory service, and to reduce the size of the standing forces.[9] The last call-up duly took place in 1960, with the number of serving personnel dropping from around 868,000 in 1953 to 400,000 in the early 1960s.[10] Further reviews and cuts followed in stages, and by the end of the millennium the numbers of servicemen and women had halved again, to around 200,000, and numbers now stand at around 144,000.[11]

As the number of service people dropped, the structure of the Army was correspondingly changed. Through the 1960s, some regiments were disbanded and others were combined to form new units; there were localised changes; and in 2006 the government amalgamated several infantry regiments to form new super regiments.[12] The practical and emotional repercussions of these changes often led to the formation or the transformation of regimental museums.

The Suffolk Regiment Museum was first established in 1935, after the First World War. An early photograph shows a sizeable room with a tall glass vitrine

Figure 2.4 Suffolk Regiment Museum, Bury St Edmunds, circa 1955

in the centre and two flat cases to either side. They variously contained the regimental silver used for formal dining, sporting cups, maquettes of soldiers, and
historic dress swords. A stack of side and tenor drums elaborately decorated
with regimental crests sit beneath the tall cases, uniforms hang to the rear of the
room, and a series of flags swing down from the ceiling, including the regimental flag, the Canadian flag, and a flag captured from a 'Bandit Camp' in Malaya
in 1951.[13]

Over time, the museum received many more donations, mainly from
ex-servicemen or their families. Some were substantial, such as a historic collection of rifles, or valuable, such as a Victoria Cross, while other donors gave objects
from the soldiers' day-to-day lives, including pay books, camp-beds, boots, and
kit. Relatives gave the letters that informed the next-of-kin that a husband, brother,
or son had been taken prisoner of war and the certificates that were issued after he
died. These objects have all been added to the displays.

The museum was attached to the officers' mess in the regimental depot in Bury
St Edmunds. Depots were large sites that functioned as the home base for the
regiment and variously included the administrative headquarters, a training
ground and quad, living accommodation for the regiment, weapons stores, and the

officers' and sergeants' messes. Apart from occasional open days they were 'behind the wire' – that is, subject to military security and were thus inaccessible to the public. Hence, the Suffolk Regiment Museum was more of a private collection than a museum as such. That situation began to change in 1959, when the Suffolk Regiment was amalgamated with the Royal Norfolk Regiment to form the 1st East Anglian Regiment, and they moved into new and larger premises. The original depot was subsequently demolished with only the keep being retained. It provided space for the regimental administrative headquarters and for the regimental collection.

Once the regiment had left, the status of the building changed. It was no longer part of a military base and was not subject to the same levels of security. Anyone could visit, and civilians gradually started coming to see the museum. Brigadier Tony Calder, chair of the Suffolk Regiment Museum, remembered the transition and said, 'I don't think it happened all at the same time. I don't think it was a public announcement from the MOD (Ministry of Defence) that you were to open all our museums; it certainly wasn't that. It would have been very difficult to have the room in the depot as a public museum, but when they became more publicly available buildings there was no security issue, so, you could open it up to the public – why not?' The museum opened slowly, without fanfare, and to a large degree by default.

An almost identical set of circumstances obtained at the Black Watch in Scotland. Like the Suffolk Regiment, the Black Watch had trophies of war, regimental silver, uniforms, and other items at their depot, the Queen's Barracks in Perth. Col. David Arbuthnott remembered that 'there was something at the depot before the war, downstairs, left-hand room, with a shiny linoleum floor'. 'A brown floor', he added and explained that 'there was nothing to tell you there was a museum inside. You had to go in through the gate, right across the square, and know where it was in the officer's mess. I can't remember now whether there was a separate door or not. It wasn't a public museum: it was a family museum, a regimental museum.'

Unlike the Suffolk Regiment, the Defence Review of 1959 did not lead to the Black Watch being amalgamated; that happened much later, in 2006, when they became a battalion within the Royal Regiment of Scotland. Even so, its depot was closed, and in 1961 the soldiers moved into a shared space at Stirling Castle, while the administrative headquarters was relocated to Balhousie Castle, also in Perth, as was the museum, which was allocated five rooms. The original museum had been formed under the direction of Col. Rusk, and he organised the new displays by period.[14] After he retired, it came under the purview of the regimental secretary and his assistant, as was common elsewhere, and slowly began to transition into a public museum. Maj. Ronnie Proctor was the Black Watch assistant regimental secretary from 1999 until 2006, and he explained: 'I think it was a gradual creeping evolvement. So, first of all, it was veterans who would go back and have a pilgrimage type thing. And then these veterans would take Mum, Dad, and Aunt Marge who would maybe say to cousin Jimmy down the road, oh, you want to go and visit this. It was just an evolution as to when the public came in. And to be honest when I went there in 1999 it was primarily for the serving and returning members of the regiment.'

In both cases the museum developed over time. They began with extensive regimental collections that were organised into museums in the 1930s, although they were only open to soldiers and visiting personnel. Changes in the structure of the Army resulted in both regiments losing their depot, thereby forcing the museums into other quarters. This move made it possible to open them to other visitors and for them to become public, which for us is one of the criteria for somewhere being considered a museum.

Figure 2.5 The Black Watch Museum, Perthshire

Networks of influence

The histories of the Suffolk Regiment Museum and the Black Watch Museum hint at the rich resources available to regimental museums. They had existing collections and available accommodation, and the running of the museums fell within the purview of the regiment, and later the regimental association. Both regiments had the infrastructure that made it comparatively easy to establish a museum. That support system is nicely elucidated in two accounts of the foundation of Horse-Power: The Museum of the King's Royal Hussars, which were published in the regimental journal in 1981.

The 10th Royal Hussars and the 11th Hussars were originally raised in 1715 and were merged to form the Royal Hussars in 1969. At that time Lt Col. Peter Upton was regimental secretary, an honorary position that is usually given to a retired commanding officer, who is then expected to 'fly the flag', to encourage recruitment, and generally raise the regiment's profile. Upton decided to start a museum. This took some time, and in 'Museum Saga' he provided a chronology of his lengthy and generally abortive attempts to find accommodation. Upton first approached Osborne House (Queen Victoria's vast holiday house in the Isle of Wight) to ask if they would provide space for a museum, before moving on to Berkeley Castle (a twelfth-century fortress house), Wimbourne St Giles (a seventeenth-century house owned by the Earl of Shaftesbury and at that point largely empty), and Salisbury City Museum, all without success. The Earl of Bathurst invited them to establish a museum in the old barracks in Cirencester, but the cost of restoration proved too high, and negotiations with Lord Leigh to place the museum in Stoneleigh Abbey (a Grade 1-listed historic house) came to a similar conclusion. Upton describes how they then drew up detailed plans to house the museum in Dodington (a privately owned eighteenth-century historic house with Capability Brown gardens, which was already open to the public), and when that failed they embarked on a plan to jointly open a museum with the Duke of Edinburgh's royal regiment in a spacious Navy, Army, and Air Force Institutes (NAAFI) building in Salisbury. These too came to nothing, and Upton's frustration is evident when he remarks that 'detailed plans were again made … and submitted to the Ministry of Defence through the normal and tediously slow channels'. Three other potential locations were inspected and found wanting before Upton had a chance meeting with General Sir Patrick Howard Dobson KCB, who was then quartermaster general and responsible for supplies and accommodation for the army as a whole. Dobson agreed to help, and in 1978 the Ministry of Defence offered the regiment a space at the Lower Barracks in Winchester, which had been the depot for the Royal Hampshire Regiment until they moved out in 1959. They were also awarded £15,000 towards its restoration, and the museum finally opened in 1981.

Angela House adds detail and humour to the account in her article 'A Bird's Eye View of the Birth of a Museum', the title being a period-specific pun on her status as 'the only woman in the man's world of an Army Unit'. She wrote that 'we were all united in our Despair when Denis's skilfully drawn up plans fell apart: in our Determination to find yet another site when the last one went the way of all others, and in our Dislike of all Government Departments as they muttered vaguely down the corridors of power that our request would be dealt with in due course'. Denis was Maj. Wheyman Meakins, clerical officer and assistant to the regimental secretary, who oversaw the process of drawing up and costing plans for each possible site on a full-time basis.

Angela also described the process of building the displays and establishing the museum. While Denis 'bayed along the trail of bureaucracy', Angela sorted out the

Figure 2.6 Angela House (left) at the opening of HorsePower: The Museum of the King's Royal Hussars, Hampshire, 1981

exhibits: 'rich cloaks, inlaid workboxes, plumes, gold and silver braid, and a treasury of faded letters and first-hand accounts of the charge of the Light Brigade'. Denis then retired and was replaced as clerical officer by Don Spencer, who usefully enough was 'a first-class carpenter and skilled craftsman'. Along with Maj. Bob Macdonald, 'who was employed as a Museum Orderly', and Mr Potter, a volunteer who had previously served with the 11th Hussars, Spencer worked to create the displays for the museum. The three men built a series of dioramas and made a 'small army of dummies', which Angela attempted to render a little more lifelike with the judicious application of some of her leftover make-up. Pride of place went to Trooper Fowler's cupboard. During the First World War, Fowler was behind German lines when he was separated from his regiment. A French woman and her daughter gave him shelter, and despite German soldiers being billeted upstairs he remained safely hidden in their kitchen cupboard for over three years. Angela noted that in order to 'create the tableau of this famous incident, we produced some wooden sabots and clothing from Belgium, potatoes from Bob's garden, and a candlestick from my kitchen'.

While Angela's account conveys a strong sense of the fun of putting together a museum and its rather ad hoc quality, there are clearly high levels of interest in and support for the project. The places that Peter Upton and Denis Wheyman Meakins looked to for accommodation were mainly privately owned historic houses, castles, and to a lesser degree military and local authority buildings. They were able to get in touch with major landowners and aristocrats, and to negotiate with them, and in several instances those people contacted the museum's founders to offer space, rather than the other way around.

Their ability to network at high levels is also evident in the comments about the founders muttering 'their way down the corridors of power', and how the Treasury 'dumped our file on the DOE with instructions to start work' (DOE is the Defence Operations Executive). Although the group may have been frustrated by the slow pace at the Ministry of Defence, they were nonetheless able to access government, to speak to one of the most senior officers in the Army, and to gain his influence for their project. HorsePower additionally benefited from financial support and support in kind. The Ministry of Defence gave them a building, a grant to refurbish it, and supplied the workmen, and all but one of the people who helped establish the project were on the payroll. Peter Upton's honorary position was paid, Denis Wheyman Meakins was ostensibly employed as a clerical officer, Angela House as a secretary, and the Ministry of Defence covered the salary for Bob McDonald, the only person specifically tasked with working on the museum.

Other kinds of small museum would struggle to leverage equivalent influence or benefit from comparable levels of staffing.

Similar levels of support are evident in other regimental museums. For example, Guy Farage (father of Nigel) explained that when he worked to found the Kent and Yeomanry Sharpshooters Museum in 1966, the mother of one of the other serving officers gave them space at her home at Squerryes Court, a seventeenth-century manor house in Kent. She later needed that space to cater for growing numbers of visitors, so one of the founder members of the museum called in a favour from a colleague whom he had helped place in a job at Hever Castle, the ancestral home of the Boleyn family. The Lord Lieutenant of the county, who had also been governor of the Bank of England and was an Honorary Colonel in the Kent and Yeomanry Sharpshooters, put his weight behind the request and the museum duly moved. Initially they occupied a large room at the top of the castle, which made physical access difficult and was apt to be damp, but with the help of Sir Nicolas Soames MP, the grandson of Winston Churchill, the trustees persuaded the Guthrie family, who owned the castle, to erect a new, purpose-built museum in the grounds. They needed to raise £200,000 to fit out the space, which they did with the help of a professional fundraiser, while the landowners paid for the building and covered the cost of the services.

Regiments have historic links to the landed and aristocratic families that formed them, and some, particularly the cavalry, have links to the royal household. In the post-war period, public schools had a near monopoly on places in the cadet training colleges, and the ranks of captain and above were held almost exclusively by public school men. That dominance increased rather than decreased over time, and by the time that HorsePower and the Kent and Yeomanry Sharpshooters Museum were being established, the officer classes were more homogenous than they had been at any point since 1800.[15] Given these circumstances, it is not surprising that officers had connections to people in positions of authority and had exceptionally strong financial, social, and institutional support networks. In this context, starting a museum was a relatively straightforward business.

The regimental family

It is clear that the regiments had extensive resources and were in a position to open museums, if they wished. It was less clear to us why so many regimental collections had been retained and opened as individual museums. The regiments were being dissolved or amalgamated, so why not the collections? Surely it would make economic and practical sense to merge them? After all, every regiment is part of the British Army. Our questions on this topic drew strong responses. Tony Calder said, 'Put it this way – if you said the Suffolk Regiment Museum is gone tomorrow, there would be a huge outcry mainly from veterans and their families. They would say, we've lost the memory, we have lost the achievements of what those people did all those years ago. They want to keep those memories alive; it's our family. The army is very much a family business.' 'But you wouldn't necessarily be losing the memory,' we suggested, 'just some stuff,' to which Tony replied, 'Yes, but there wouldn't be a focus for the memories of the Suffolk Regiment, the soldiers. To lose that and to have it dissipated or put into store or something would, to them, feel like a betrayal.' All the other officers we met made similar remarks and many reiterated the notion of family. These sentiments require some unpacking.

The notion of the army being a family business works in different ways. In the late Victorian era, the military authorities preferred officers and other ranks to remain unmarried, at least during the first phase of their service. They wanted officers and men to remain free of intimate ties so that they could devote themselves to the army. In return the regiment promised to provide them with a support network akin to that of an extended family: the regiment became the soldiers' family.[16] David Arbuthnott used the term in this sense when he referred to the museum as being a family museum.

When we met David he was in his mid-nineties. For the officers a generation below, the notion of the regimental family had slightly different connotations. In the post-war period the army found it hard to recruit and retain soldiers, who understandably wanted a family life, so restrictions on marriage were reduced and the number of married quarters increased. When Tony Calder was a child he 'lived on a patch of 200 houses where all the families were military'. His use of the word 'patch' is itself a military description, being the nominated location for the married quarters associated with a specific barracks or camp. The battalion was usually relocated every few years and the families would move with it. Tony Slater remembers the 'battalion moves – the quartermaster, who organised it all, would sort out the officers' mess and the sergeants' mess and the soldiers and he would then get down to the real problem – moving all the families. The family officer would be tearing his hair out because he had, whatever it was – 200 married quarters to find, and slot in the right people and the right things. Moving a battalion, the soldiers, was the easy bit.'

In addition to the camp being relocated, the soldiers were routinely posted overseas and would be away for up to six months at a time. The wives and children were therefore trebly isolated. They were living in a barracks, so they were separated from their own extended families; it could be hard for them to form links with the local community; and their husbands were absent for long periods of time. Discussing the difficulties of the situation, Tony Slater said, 'But, of course, that's why you need a family – a regimental family.' Tony Calder agreed: 'the regimental family is enormously important when the chaps go abroad, go off to Afghanistan or Iraq or wherever it happens to be, because you're all in the same area. So, they all have to get together to support each other.' For the two Tonys, the regimental family comprised the soldiers, their wives, and their children. They also pointed out that it had become more expansive in recent years and included partners of soldiers, both male and female, grandparents, and indeed anyone who was affected by the soldiers being away from home.

Tony Calder's comment 'It's our family' also applied in a very literal sense. The officers often followed their fathers and grandfathers into the same or related regiments, and they often married within the regiment. Tony said, 'My father was, my son was, although he is now a Fusilier. My wife's uncle was and her grandfather, all in the same regiment. They were Norfolk and Suffolk, but it filtered down to Royal Anglian.' Six out of his seven grandsons have also joined the army. Ronnie Proctor's wife was also from a military family, and her grandfather and two of his brothers had served in the Black Watch. Ronnie told us that when he first met Sonia's grandfather, the older man had enquired after his regiment and rank. A few days later her cousin Jacqueline's new boyfriend was greeted with the same enquiries. Ronnie recounted the incident. 'She said, "This is Charlie my boyfriend, Grandad," and old Billy said, "Oh, aye? What regiment are you in?" He said, "I'm in the Army Service Corp." And old Billy said, "That's the galloping grocers. Why don't you join a real regiment like Ronnie at Black Watch."' Ronnie added, 'Sonia's grandad, he and I were really great, great friends.' In other words, the regimental link helped him secure family approval. One of Ronnie and Sonia's sons also went on to join the Black Watch; indeed, father and son served together in Northern Ireland. And their daughter, Fiona, spent her gap year working at the Black Watch Museum. Their family history and their family life were interwoven with the regiment.

Thus, there are at least three overlapping ways in which the regiment is understood as family: it supersedes the soldiers' biological family with respect to practical support and emotional bonds, it is comprised of soldiers and of their extended families, and, as family members tend to follow one another, the regiment often includes blood relations. By extension, the museums are also family collections. They tell the story of the regiment, which is imagined as a family, features members of the regimental family, and for many founders and visitors connects to the history of their biological family. In some cases it may do all three. For example, the text at the entrance to the Black Watch Museum reads 'every soldier of the Black Watch is part of the Regimental family and a Son of the Black Watch'. When we visited, Ronnie drew our attention to a Kevlar vest that had belonged to Cpl Tabua, a young Fijian soldier who had fought in Afghanistan. The vest had saved his life. At this point Ronnie paused and then said that Tabua had subsequently survived a blast from an IED in Afghanistan only to be later diagnosed with inoperable lung cancer. When he died, his wife wanted him to be buried with full military honours, and although the Ministry of Defence automatically covered the costs of repatriating his body, they did not pay for other members of the regiment

Figure 2.7 Kevlar vest on display at the Black Watch Museum, 2021

to attend the funeral. Ronnie said that the Black Watch Association 'stumped up the balance for that, so we paid to send a guard down as the firing party'. Looking at the vest he remarked, 'Now for someone who didn't know –' For many visitors, the Kevlar vest is just that, a piece of protective kit once worn by a soldier, whereas for Ronnie and for others who knew him, it is Tabua's vest. It embodies the story of a man who survived real danger only to die tragically young, and it stands for his wife's respect for the Black Watch and the support that the regimental family offered.

Close to the vest is a photograph of Ronnie as a young lance corporal sitting on the back of an AFV 432 armoured personnel carrier in Germany in 1964. At the other end of the gallery is a photograph of Maj. Gen. Robert Arbuthnott. He commanded C Company of the 1st Battalion The Black Watch in the First World War, during which time he was awarded a Military Cross. He was also David Arbuthnott's father. Regimental history, the stories of the soldiers, the founder and their families, are all closely intertwined.

Julian Farrance remarked that the regiments were like individual tribes. The officers we met described them as families. For members of the extended regimental family, the prospect of losing the objects connected to the regiment is inconceivable. Closing the regimental museum would be akin to throwing away the family silver, junking your grandfather's photograph album, or selling your father's medals when he had died in the process of achieving them. These objects have a huge emotional weight, which if anything has increased since the regiments were dissolved. The museums and the regimental associations are now the only places that actively retain and preserve those regimental identities.

In other cases, though, a museum is formed to consolidate a new military identity. For instance, in 1992 the Corps of Royal Military Police, the Royal Army Pay Corps, who were the Army's financial administrators, the Royal Army Educational Corps, who instruct and educate personnel, the Army Legal Corps, who provide specialist legal advice, the Military Provost Staff Corps, who provide custodial advice and support, and the Women's Royal Army Corps were merged to form the Adjutant General's Corps. The amalgamation made them one of the largest corps in the Army. The original corps had their own museums or collections, but after the restructuring there was a feeling that the collections ought to be consolidated into a new museum that would conserve, display, and articulate the history and heritage of the antecedent corps.

Unlike regiments, which work as a unit, corps train specialists, who then go to join other units as required. Their members are far more accustomed to working with others, which can make mergers relatively painless, and the Royal Army Pay

Corps, the Royal Army Education Corps, and the Army Legal Services pooled their collections, while the Royal Military Police agreed to loan and gift objects to the new museum.[17] Lt Col. Tony Figg explained that representatives of the four corps all worked together, he chaired the process, and everything proceeded in a relatively straightforward fashion. Here, the ability of the founders to amalgamate collections and create a new museum was closely linked to how corps had historically operated. Like the regiments that wanted to preserve their family collections at all costs, the founders of the Adjutant General's Corps Museum followed their training to co-operate across units and to become part of a new entity.

Conflict, close at hand

So far, the museums that we have discussed in this chapter are located in England or Scotland. It is now almost eighty years since UK residents experienced war or sustained conflict on their home ground. Unless they are employed by the Armed Forces or have arrived as refugees, few people living in England, Scotland, or Wales have direct experience of war or of prolonged civil unrest. That is not true of Northern Ireland, where residents lived with the Troubles for three decades and are still negotiating its ongoing legacy. This history of conflict has inevitably had an impact on where and when museums are founded, why they are founded, and the emotional management required.

Ireland's relationship with Britain is complex and highly contested, as is its own history.[18] Even place names and the terms used to describe events are a matter of dispute. Very briefly, for those readers entirely unfamiliar with the situation, during the sixteenth and seventeenth centuries English and Scots Protestant settlers colonised Ireland. Decades of resistance to British rule culminated in the Irish War of Independence of 1919 and in 1921 with Partition. Six of the nine Ulster counties, which were largely Protestant, remained part of the UK and became known as Northern Ireland, with the rest of Ireland, which was mainly Catholic, gaining independence.

The new Unionist administration in Northern Ireland was highly discriminatory towards the Catholic minority. Gerrymandering ensured that they held control of the local authorities, while voting was only extended to homeowners and primary tenants, and since Catholics were discriminated against with respect to education, employment, and housing, many were effectively disenfranchised. Tensions grew between the two communities and in 1969 a group marched in Derry/ Londonderry in protest against discrimination. They were targeted by Loyalists, who saw the civil rights movement as a front for Republicanism and the reunification of Ireland, and the largely Protestant Royal Ulster Constabulary did little to help. Rioting ensued and the British Army was deployed to keep the peace. Initially welcomed by the Catholics, who saw them as relatively neutral, they rapidly became an occupying force. Armed conflict escalated and continued over the next three decades until a ceasefire was negotiated in 1994. The Troubles officially came to an end with the Good Friday Agreement in 1998, although the British Army did not leave the province until 2007. It was the longest continuous operation in British military history.[19]

In many ways, the history of the Royal Irish Fusiliers Museum in Armagh resembles that of other regimental museums. The regiment established the collection for its own members, it was displayed in the barracks, and it became a public museum by degrees, slowly opening to a wider audience. It differed in exactly how the collection was established and how that increased accessibility finally came about.

When the Royal Irish Fusiliers Museum first opened in the field officers' mess in the Gough Barracks in 1932, its displays were definitely skimpy. The regiment did not have a pre-existing collection, and while members and supporters had been asked to donate objects, the response had been disappointing. The regimental journal implored its readers to 'ferret around' in pursuit of relevant artefacts, a request that was reiterated later in the year, and this time the authors listed the gifts received so far.[20] They included old grenades, fuses, and cartridges, a twisted stick from the Peshawar valley, a wooden bowl from the Hazara expedition, a Kaffir pillow, and a carved wooden spoon with no apparent link to the regiment or to their campaigns. The accompanying photographs of the time show a single room with an exhibition that mainly comprised framed prints. Two rifles lean against a window ledge and a Union Jack hangs rather limply from the ceiling. It does not look particularly inspiring.

The museum had decidedly improved by September 1941, when it was rehoused in a former dining hall and cookhouse. The *Journal of the Society for Army Historical Research* reviewed the new museum, praising the ample space, interesting exhibits, and the 'extremely attractive' displays.[21] Unfortunately, its occupancy was relatively short-lived because the reorganisation of the Army in 1959 led to Gough Barracks being closed and the regiment moving into new, shared accommodation. The regimental headquarters was to stay in Armagh, and the General Committee of the Regimental Association decided that the museum should likewise remain in the city. They set about finding accommodation and, according to the regimental journal, faced no real difficulties in that Sovereign's House, previously the mayor's house, was up for sale. The War Office covered the purchase costs while money from the regiment, local authority, and an anonymous donor paid for its refurbishment.[22] The museum reopened in spring 1963, sharing space with the regimental headquarters.

Sovereign's House is an impressive townhouse on the corner of the Mall, a Georgian terrace that runs down the side of a city-centre park. For the first time, the museum was in a public rather than a military space, and at the opening ceremony Sir Norman Stronge, the Colonel of the Regiment, hoped that many more people would be able to visit. Capt Armstrong reiterated this view, reporting that Armagh County Council were proud to have assisted in the venture and that 'it had been arranged that the museum should be open to the public'.[23] The convoluted phrasing – 'should be', rather than 'would be' open – gives an indication of the situation. The current curator, Caroline Covan, the first Catholic to hold the post, went to the museum as a child in the late 1970s. Her father was knowledgeable about military history and would sometimes visit, taking his children along with him, and she remembered that you needed an appointment – that they would always ring in advance. The curator, Maj. Alistair Boyne, was reputed to have said that 'if you open the doors, the public will just come in', and Caroline remarked, 'I don't think he particularly liked the public. I don't think he minded people that he knew in military guise. So, yes, if you were in the know you got in, if you were just Joe Bloggs off the street, you didn't get over the door.'

Unlike the Black Watch and the Suffolk Regiment museums, the Royal Irish Fusiliers Museum did not drift towards greater public access. Rather, the doors were literally blown off when the IRA exploded a 1,000lb bomb outside the courthouse on the Mall in 1993. Sovereign House was caught in the blast, and although no-one was hurt, the building needed extensive repairs, which were largely funded by English Heritage. A new curator, Amanda Moreno, was appointed, and the museum reopened in 1997 with additional rooms and extensive public-facing displays. A series of large, visually impressive vitrines showed how military uniform and weaponry had changed, and professionally produced wall texts gave information on the social history of the Army. As with other regimental museums, the gradual shift towards public access was accelerated by external events, except in this instance it was an indirect consequence of the Troubles, of conflict rather than regimental restructuring.

Regimental museums were intended to 'wave the flag' for the regiment, to remember and honour the dead, and to provide a focus for the regimental family.[24] For the founders whom we met, it was unthinkable that their displays would acknowledge the difficult episodes in their histories. Indeed, when we visited David Arbuthnott, who served with the Black Watch and helped establish the regimental museum, his wife Sonja commented that to do so would be disloyal, like airing your family's dirty linen in public.

If airfield and regimental museums in Britain have celebrated the British Armed Forces and largely ignored their demerits, the Museum of Free Derry pointed directly at one of its shameful episodes.[25] In 1972 British soldiers shot at demonstrators at a protest march in Derry. Thirteen marchers and bystanders were killed, with a fourteenth later dying in hospital. The Army claimed that the marchers had been armed and fired the first shots, a version of events that was upheld in the original tribunal. Twenty-five years later the Bloody Sunday Trust was formed to assist the bereaved families and to continue the campaign for justice. Then in 1998 prime minister Tony Blair announced that Lord Saville would lead a new investigation into the events of the day, an inquiry that lasted a decade and ultimately found that the victims had been unarmed and the shootings unlawful. The Trust also supported the group through this process.

Alongside support work and campaigning, the group decided to preserve the history of Bloody Sunday. At first, there were just a few objects laid out on tables in the Gas Works community centre in the Bogside, the area where Bloody Sunday had taken place, but they quickly began to think about opening a museum. Adrian Kerr, who was one of the founders of the museum and is now its curator, explained their thinking: 'We had a history that was very famous: there had been a lot written about it, a lot of discussion, but always from the outside. You know, we had British government views on it, we had official reports, we had politicians, journalists, authors – nobody was giving the point of view of people who had actually lived through it, or very few; there were some voices trying but they were basically struggling in the wilderness. So we wanted a place that told this very, very important history from the point of view of people who were affected by it, for want of a better phrase, who owned that history.'[26]

The group started looking for a site and settled on a block of post-war flats in the Bogside that had been at the heart of the day's events. Two marchers – Jim Wray and William McKinney – had been killed directly in front of the block, which had been preserved pending investigation. The group were able to buy the site with money from the Saville Inquiry, who paid rent for using the city Guildhall. The council disbursed the rental income to various community groups, including the Bloody Sunday Trust, and the £200,000 it received was enough to cover the purchase cost. The group gutted the space and in 2007 opened with a basic display while they set about raising enough money for a new building and a more ambitious exhibition.

Figure 2.8 The Museum of Free Derry

The new museum opened on the same site in 2017. The ground floor is covered with rusted metal that closer inspection reveals to be an artwork, the patterns on the surface replicating the sound waveform of the Bloody Sunday marchers singing the civil rights anthem 'We Shall Overcome'. The first storey is white and angular, housing an education room that leads out on to a small, grassed terrace looking out over surrounding housing. Two murals are painted on the gable-end walls, one showing people on the march holding placards reading 'One man one vote', and the other depicting a child standing in front of an armoured car. Inside the museum, visitors walk through a gallery with a chronological display that moves from the civil rights protests of the 1950s through Bloody Sunday to the end of the Saville Inquiry in 2010. Video footage shows the then prime minister, David Cameron, apologising for the earlier injustice and footage of family members speaking out on the report. There are numerous wall texts explaining the events and issues and two large vitrines containing associated objects, most notably clothing worn by some of the people who died that day.

One of the central displays comprises a near life-size version of a photograph taken on Bloody Sunday. Now famous, it shows Fr Edward Daly waving a white handkerchief above his head while behind him four men are carrying Jackie Duddy out of the line of fire. He was shot in the back while trying to run away. The handkerchief that Daly held has been mounted above the image. Adrian explained that Daly later pushed the handkerchief inside the boy's jacket to staunch the wound. When Duddy died, the handkerchief was returned to his family with the

Figure 2.9 Display including Fr Edward Daly's handkerchief, Museum of Free Derry

rest of his clothes and his father kept it until he too passed away. It was then given to his sister Kay, who carried it in her handbag until an attempted mugging made her anxious that the handkerchief might be lost and she decided to give it to the museum for safekeeping. Adrian said that she borrowed it back when the Saville report was being released. 'She wanted to be carrying it on that day. She's described it at various times as being like a comfort blanket.'[27]

When we met, Adrian commented that the Trust could not have been established and the museum opened at any earlier date. Up until the ceasefire in 1994 the staff and volunteer team 'would have been just constant targets for harassment and abuse. They'd never have got anywhere with it – British soldiers through the door constantly, and it literally wasn't safe to do work like that during the conflict.' The ceasefire also meant that 'there started to be a bit of breathing space'. As he pointed out, 'It is hard to deal with one issue of justice when there's a new one happening almost every day. That was really the first time where it really could happen.'

Other factors were important in the foundation of the museum. By the year 2000 the city council had started to promote tourism in Derry, and they supported both the first and second incarnation of the museum. Then, Adrian said, when the Saville Inquiry announced its conclusions in 2010 there was 'an acceptance within the city, within local government that, yes, the story had to be told, but they couldn't really take it on, so it was better if somebody else was doing it'. Whereas civic and national museums have an obligation to cater to the community at large, an independent museum was 'free to tell their community story the way they want to'. The local authorities provided around £175,000 towards the new building and other funding was also available; most notably, the European Regional Development Fund was offering grants to improve Northern Ireland's economic competitiveness, specifically targeting small and medium enterprises, such as the museum. They gave £1.2 million towards the total cost, with the National Lottery Heritage Fund and Stormont departments both awarding around £800,000. It is unlikely that such funding would have been forthcoming before the conclusion of the Saville Inquiry, at which point the Museum of Free Derry changed in status. Whereas it had been an activist museum, campaigning on an issue that was extremely contentious within the wider establishment, the Saville Inquiry validated their cause and endorsed that history.

Taken from a political standpoint, the Museum of Free Derry and various Armed Forces museums that we have discussed are diametrically opposed, but there are links between them. Bloody Sunday is part of the history of the British Army, not just of the Bogside or of the population of Northern Ireland. As Adrian recognised, funding the Museum of Free Derry was a means for public bodies to acknowledge some of the wrongdoings of the past, while simultaneously maintaining some distance and hence apparent neutrality with respect to the British Army and the Catholic and Protestant populations of Northern Ireland.

There are other parallels between the regimental museums and the Museum of Free Derry. In both cases the museums were set up by and for a specific community but they became used for wider purposes. Once they opened to the public, regimental museums were seen as a means of having a foothold in areas where there was no military base, and of being a form of soft recruiting. Regimental museums effectively publicised the merits of the Army and commonly provided information on how to join up. The Museum of Free Derry also operated as a mouthpiece for a group, albeit of a very different sort. It was a means of making their version of events public. Above all, though, there are similarities in the status of the objects on display. A protective vest stands in for a dead comrade, a wife's love, and a sense of duty, while a handkerchief is an emblem of a murdered son but also of strangers' bravery and care.

The Peace Museum

There have been around 400 museums of war and conflict open in the UK over the past six decades. To our knowledge there have only been four museums that actively contest the received history of the British Army, all Irish Nationalist, and only one museum that actively opposes warfare in all its forms. The Peace Museum in Bradford grew out of the Peace Tax Campaign, which was formed in 1977. It was one of many activist groups that objected to the arms race, military expenditure, and the escalation of the Cold War. Comprising mainly Quakers, they observed that the Armed Forces were supported by public money and argued that taxpayers' money should be used for creating security in a non-violent manner if they so requested. Some members of the group withheld that percentage of their tax bills in protest.

Gerald Drewett was one of the founders of the group. He was also a tax inspector. We asked him whether his colleagues had looked askance at his position. 'No,' he said, 'I had no problems whatsoever. They even took some of my papers to supply the collectors of taxes with an understanding of why people refuse to pay. It is a matter of conscience.' To these ends the group decided to register themselves as a charity, as it would exempt them from paying the taxes to which they objected. They were called the Give Peace a Chance Trust and one of their aims was the creation of a national peace museum. To this end, they invited Peter van Dungen, a lecturer in the Peace Studies department at Bradford University, to join the working party, and he suggested holding an international conference. The Trust agreed, and funded the event, which Peter organised. Founders and curators came from peace museums in Australia, Austria, Switzerland, Japan, Norway, the USA, and Germany, and on the last day there was a planning workshop where the group drew up detailed plans for a UK Peace Museum, making recommendations for its historic and geographic scope.[28]

One outcome of the conference group was the creation of an International Network of Museums for Peace (INMP). Another was that the city of Bradford gave their support for a peace museum in the city. One of the conference delegates, David Kennedy, had responsibility for tourism in the area, and he offered the group an empty warehouse. Then when the conversion proved too expensive he allocated them free office space in the city centre. The group was also funded by the Quaker Rowntree Charitable Trust, which paid for an administrator, Carol Rank, to organise temporary exhibitions, including one at Leeds Armouries. Then in 1997 Gerald secured a space above a NatWest Bank in the city centre, which the owners were prepared to let for a nominal sum.

In the years after the conference, members of the peace movement had donated hundreds of campaign posters; these went on display, as did material relating to conscientious objection, the Campaign for Nuclear Disarmament, and the Children's Peace Monument in Hiroshima. The Ferguson Trust, run initially by

Figure 2.10 Peace Museum, Bradford, West Yorkshire

John and Elnora Ferguson, who had belonged to the original Peace Tax Campaign, initially paid for staff, and the museum continues to have many Quaker supporters, who give an annual donation. As Gerald noted, several thousand small donations accrue to a reasonable sum, which greatly contributes towards the costs of utilities and paid staff.

When we asked Peter van Dungen why he thought a peace museum was important, he replied, 'Peace has a history. Textbooks all focus on wars and revolutions, and it cannot be denied they are important turning-points in social history and so on, but if you are lucky you get a footnote about the anti-war movement.' For him, though, the museum did not go quite far enough.

Peter was one of the few people to express any disappointment or disagreement with the museum they had helped found, which given the subject of the museum can be considered ironic or as entirely fitting within an important tradition of dissent. He had been opposed to accepting the free office space that was offered by Bradford council, saying that 'my idea always was only London will do; when you really want to make an impact only London will do'.[29] He also felt that the museum lacked ambition. As well as documenting campaigns and celebrating peace movements Peter wanted it to be more explicitly anti-war, and imagined Tolstoy's quote – 'Soldiers are murderers in uniform' – being painted across the walls and windows, or that of Frederick the Great, who said, 'If my soldiers were to begin to think I would have no army left.' 'Oh my goodness,' he said, 'people would throw bricks through the windows if we put that statement up.'

Downsizing the Armed Forces

It is clear that the rise in numbers of war and conflict museums was closely connected to the downscaling of the British Army. The end of the Second World War resulted in many sites being abandoned and buildings being made redundant. Metheringham Heritage Centre and RAF Ingham Visitor Centre were located on decommissioned airfields and took the history of those sites as their subject-matter. The Black Watch Museum and the Suffolk Regiment Museum were both housed in buildings that had been occupied by their regiment and which became accessible to the public after they were decommissioned. HorsePower: The Museum of the King's Royal Hussars and the Adjutant General's Corps Museum both moved into an empty barracks in Winchester. The situation in Armagh was slightly different, where the regiment bought a new building to house their association and museum after the barracks closed.

The Armed Forces also provided the objects and infrastructure for many of these museums. At the airfield sites that we visited, the space and buildings were the focus of the museum, while most of the corps and regimental museums had pre-existing collections that formed the starting point for the displays, with additional items later acquired and given. The huge institutional infrastructure of the Army made it especially easy to open regimental museums. Costs were covered and the workforce was often deputed or seconded to set up a museum.[30] Where there were hiccups, the founders of regimental museums could walk the corridors of power, call in favours, and leverage influence. Setting up the military aviation museums was more demanding, in that support had to be more actively established, collections developed, and volunteers recruited. Nonetheless, they also received support from the Armed Forces, from allied organisations, landlords, and on one occasion the Scouts.

Museums operating outside of the Armed Forces relied much more heavily on public money, charitable foundations, or individual donors, and they did not have the same levels of access to power, or at least not initially. At different points in its inception, the Museum of Free Derry received indirect funding from the Saville Inquiry and direct funding from the Northern Irish government and the European Union. The Peace Museum had a more modest income but nonetheless was enabled by grants from charitable organisations and is maintained through the generosity of its supporters. In both cases, the objects on display were given or loaned by supporters. Without exception, the foundation of war and conflict museums relied on institutional support, whether in kind or through funding, although, unlike the other museums we have discussed in this chapter, the Museum of Free Derry is now principally reliant on ticket sales.

With the exception of the Peace Museum, which had a strong educational mission, all the museums we visited grew out of a concern for their immediate community, however that was construed. Metheringham Airfield Visitor Centre was set up for returning veterans and was intended to help them in their process of remembering and recovering, and the founders at RAF Ingham wanted to develop and maintain links between families across the generations. The regimental museums functioned as the family albums for the regimental families, in both the narrow and the expanded sense, while the Museum of Free Derry was the work of a group expressly established to support the families affected by Bloody Sunday. In their various ways these museums all helped their constituencies to manage change, to commemorate their dead, to acknowledge bravery and injustice, and to help those involved or affected by conflict.

Establishing the museums was also a way for the founders and some of the later volunteers to manage their own relationship to past and present conflict. Andy Marson, who became chair of Metheringham Airfield Visitor Centre, served in the Falklands War and was a lead navigator during the first Gulf War. He was responsible for putting the system for laser-guided bombs into service, and was briefly deployed to Tobuk. David Arbuthnott served with the Black Watch in Korea, Kenya, Cyprus, and Northern Ireland, while Ronnie Proctor saw active duty in British Malaya, Korea, Libya, Northern Ireland, and Belize. Tony Calder, trustee of the Suffolk Regiment Museum, was deployed to Aden and Northern Ireland, and Tony Slater also served in Northern Ireland, while Adrian Kerr, curator of the Museum of Free Derry, was born in Northern Ireland as the Troubles began. He said that he 'was 25 before I knew what it was like without a war going on all around'. In different ways they had all been in involved in conflict. Setting up museums and honouring other people who had died in conflict was also, arguably, a means of assuaging their own ghosts, of maintaining their own communities, and of recognising and validating their own experiences. Like so many of the other founders discussed in this book, they were part of the history that they told and commemorated.

Counter-intuitively, the foundation of the Peace Museum can also be linked to the process of downsizing. Reducing the standing forces and infrastructure was conducted in tandem with an increased emphasis on technological development, and the Peace Museum grew out of the protests against the ensuing nuclear escalation. Its remit also points to one of the main requirements for starting a museum. Adrian Kerr commented that the Museum of Free Derry could only open when it was safe to do so and when the community was not caught up in the day-to-day struggle of negotiating the Troubles. It is perhaps an obvious point but nonetheless worth underlining – people do not generally launch museums in wartime. The proliferation of war and conflict museums, and indeed the micromuseums boom more generally, is part of the history of peace. Even museums of war and conflict require basic stability and security. Remembering and preservation happen after the fact.

Chapter 3

Local history museums: at the centre of the universe

Of all the museums in the UK, local history museums are the most common. They account for almost one quarter of the total number of museums in the UK and it can sometimes seem as if almost every hamlet, village, town, or city has one of their own.[1] Despite their number, there is little obvious variation: local history museums can be rather homogeneous.[2] They usually have displays on local industry, famous people, significant events, and the archaeology, natural history, and geology of the area. Photographs of school groups abound, as do sports cups, sportswear, and children's toys. There are often images of young men in uniforms on display alongside relics of the two world wars, huge amounts of outdated domestic equipment, crocheted blankets, and lacework. Likewise, the exhibitions routinely include agricultural implements, rakes and spades, anvils and hammers, and maybe a plough or seed drill with the saddlery for a heavy horse. Many of the objects tend to be of a similar vintage and so the overall content and timeframe is fairly similar, stretching from the late Victorian period through to around 1950.

Considering this plethora of undistinguished objects gave us little insight into the circumstances in which museums were founded. It was all generically 'past'. On closer inspection, however, local history museums turned out to be far more heterogeneous than they first appeared. While the types of object on display are broadly comparable, the circumstances in which they were opened and the founders' aims for the museums were notably varied: they used similar material for quite different ends.

In this chapter we focus on four local history museums to examine why and how each was opened. The founders of the first pair of museums, Nidderdale Museum in the Yorkshire Dales and the Brynmawr and District Museum in South Wales, were both concerned with salvaging something of the past, although the circumstances that prompted them to do so were markedly different. The founders of the second pair of museums, Perranzabuloe Museum in Cornwall and the

Aldbourne Heritage Centre in Wiltshire, both talked at length about newcomers arriving in their villages, but they did so in distinct contexts and from quite different perspectives. Here we pay attention to both the commonalities and the variations between them.

By definition, local history museums have a particular relationship to place. Where they are matters, not just with respect to the circumstances of their foundation and the stories they tell, but in relation to why the museums were opened and indeed why they are so plentiful. Place turns out to be important in explaining the spread of local history museums, and I close the chapter by considering that point in more detail. As in the rest of this book, the museums I discuss are small and independent, and in this case were all opened by community groups, privately owned local history museums being comparatively rare.

Disappearing histories

Eileen Burgess and Muriel Swires both lived in Nidderdale in the Yorkshire Dales. In the north of England, 'dale' is the term for valley, or, more precisely, for a wide, open valley as opposed to a narrow ravine, or 'gill'. The Yorkshire Dales cover hundreds of square miles of moors and hills, dotted with stone-built villages and small towns. The area is now protected as an area of outstanding natural beauty and forms part of a National Park.

Figure 3.1 Upper Nidderdale and Great Whernside, North Yorkshire

In the 1960s Eileen and Muriel attended a Workers' Educational Association class on local history, and under the guidance of their tutor the group embarked upon a huge archival research project that culminated in them publishing a history of Nidderdale.[3] A few years later the group were considering their next project, and over a cup of tea at an annual general meeting, Eileen and Muriel came up with the idea of starting a museum. Other members of the group agreed, and they duly formed a museums committee, inviting other local residents to join. Almost fifty years later we asked Eileen what had prompted that decision. She said, 'Farms were being sold up; there was a farm sale nearly every week, and stuff was going out of the dale. And the final straw was that just down the road here, we had had a cobbler's shop. When he died, it just went. And we felt that the whole of the history of the dale, belonging to ordinary people, was disappearing, and would soon be gone.' They were concerned that the material culture of the valley was being lost and that they needed to preserve it before it vanished completely. Nidderdale Museum was a salvage operation.

There had been major changes in the area, mainly relating to farming. During the Second World War, the combination of labour and food shortages led to the rapid modernisation of the UK agricultural sector, and tractors, combine harvesters, and other machinery increasingly replaced horses and labourers.[4] Post-war, the Agricultural Act of 1947 introduced financial incentives that further encouraged the mechanisation of farming, and this made it possible for farmers to work at a larger scale. Hedgerows were removed, larger fields created, and properties amalgamated. Between 1949 and 1999 there was a 65% decline in the number of farms, a 77% decline in farm labour, and an almost fourfold increase in yield.[5] Productivity soared, but the number of people actually living and working on farms plummeted. As a result, many small holdings and farmhouses became redundant and were sold off, people had to look elsewhere for work, often leaving the area, and the associated infrastructure of services also began to change. Nidderdale was no exception in these respects.

Other changes were also evident in the dale, and one had a direct impact on the foundation of the museum. Until 1974, the UK had a complex and uneven administrative structure. Individual counties were variously divided into municipal boroughs, rural districts, urban districts, and county boroughs, each having their own councils and each operating with a degree of autonomy. That changed when the Local Government Act (1972) introduced a two-tier system and reduced the number of administrative units from 1,500 to 500.[6] Numerous parishes and smaller areas lost their councils to the larger towns and cities, and Nidderdale was among them. Their rural district council was dissolved, the premises vacated, and the administrative functions transferred to Harrogate, some fourteen miles away. For hundreds of communities the reorganisation of local administrative boundaries involved a dramatic loss of local power, and it was deeply unpopular in Nidderdale, as it was elsewhere. Eileen explained that 'it took away our status; and you felt instead of being a large fish in a small pond, we were a minnow in a big pond'.

One of the upshots of the reorganisation was that numerous civic buildings were left empty, including those in Pateley Bridge, the main town in Nidderdale. Partly as a means of mitigating ill feeling, the new borough council in Harrogate offered the old offices to the museum group, generously proposing a donation of £14,000 to cover the initial start-up costs, and an annual grant of £7,000 a year for running costs. The group were appalled because they thought that if they accepted the money it would become Harrogate's museum.[7] 'We were going to have the hard work of getting the museum together,' Eileen said, 'and we knew that Pateley people, Nidderdale people would give things to Pateley people. They wouldn't give it to Harrogate because there was a terrific animosity about going into Harrogate.' The group decided to reject financial assistance but accept the building and the offer of help with redecoration.

The group took possession on 3 January 1975 and instantly put out a call for local residents to donate objects, stipulating that they had to be relevant to life within the dale. Eileen had been right when she said that Nidderdale people would give things to a group from Pateley, and local residents quickly started arriving with potential exhibits. She listed some of the donors. One of the first was Jack Hollingsworth, who brought his grandmother Frances Mudd's dairying equipment. Frances and her daughters were prizewinning dairymaids, winning numerous competitions for their elaborate butter sculptures. Heather Swires' family gave their collection of traditional agricultural equipment, Joanna Dawson gave a collection of china made for and used in the Methodist churches that are dotted around the dale, and the chemist Frank Pepper gave bottles made for perfume and perry (which is like cider but made with pears rather than apples) that his predecessor had stocked in the 1880s. Many brought single items – 'family treasures', as Eileen described them – and two members of the group bought the contents of a cobbler's shop that they first loaned and then later donated to the museum. It was the only thing to come from outside the dale.[8]

A few of these artefacts were displayed in cases, perhaps most notably the Methodist china, while the remainder were combined to recreate a schoolroom, pub lounge, and kitchen. Over the years the series was extended into a long and impressive series of rooms, including a tackroom, general store, saw pit, dairy, joiner's shop, Victorian parlour, workhouse, chemist shop, mine, and wash house.

Figure 3.2 Eileen Burgess in Nidderdale Museum, North Yorkshire, 1991

Later the group acquired the fixtures and fittings of a local solicitor's office and a courthouse, which were installed to create additional rooms. Some of these spaces were reconstructions or were directly connected to named individuals. A small tableau about dairying includes photographs of the Mudd family with their dairy sculptures, and the certificates they won, while the recreated cobbler's shop has a photograph and information about Christopher Binks, who was a travelling cobbler. In the 1920s new reservoirs were built in Nidderdale, and a large semi-permanent encampment grew to house the workers and their families. These were high in the hills and some distance from nearby villages, so Binks would cycle to take orders and collect the workers' boots for repair, later returning to the camps to drop off his finished work. The tableaux provided a way of documenting and remembering the lives of the Mudd family and Binks among others. They were also a way of depicting ways of life in the dale more generally, of showing where the permanent and temporary inhabitants lived, worked, shopped, worshipped, and learned.

The group had researched and documented the history of the dale for their book. They had written about the various residents, industries, and ways of life, but for Eileen, 'What we had done in the group wasn't concrete enough.' For her,

Miss. P. L. Mudd.
First Prize. London Dairy Show. 1926.
Butter Flowers.

Figure 3.3 Miss P. L. Mudd, First Prize Winner for butter flowers, London Dairy Show, 1926

the history of the dale was embodied in its artefacts, and when the cobbler's shop was sold, the history disappeared. So long as the objects were kept within the dale then something of that history would also be preserved. Notably, though, Eileen's perspective changed: she said that by the time she stood down as secretary in 2003 it had 'dawned on me that it was becoming a museum of objects, rather than story', and so she encouraged the group to refocus. Following that lead, Joanna Moody, the incoming museum secretary, published *Nidderdale in 40 Years and 40 Objects*, which consists of a series of object biographies, one being about Binks' bicycle. The shift in approach is consonant with thinking within the museum sector – that objects are not self-explanatory – but it also points to the original founders' tacit knowledge. They knew the people who gave the objects that went on display. Many of them remembered the farms when they were working, the horse-drawn ploughs, and the cobbler cycling over the hills. For them, the objects were rich with

Figure 3.4 Cobbler's shop display, Nidderdale Museum

meaning and history, and so salvaging them, simply having them to hand, was enough to conjure the memory of those people and that way of life. It took the group a while to recognise that not everyone knew the same stories.

In collecting the objects that had belonged to ordinary people and later in telling the stories, the museum founders consciously distanced themselves from more established forms of history that privileged great events or the experiences and artefacts of the aristocracy. Eileen said that this was history from below, and anyone who wanted to find out about the aristocrats could go to visit Ripley Castle, a grand fourteenth-century house some miles away. From today's perspective, displays of milk churns and boots may seem conventional, even dull, but at the time it was a clear assertion that working people also mattered and that their stories were important, and as such it marked a real shift away from top-down notions of history. Nidderdale was an example of people documenting and exhibiting histories about people whom they had lived among, been related to, or identified with.[9]

Nidderdale has a history of industry as well as farming but nothing on the scale of the Valleys in South Wales, which was one of the earliest areas in the UK to be industrialised. Brynmawr is a small town at the head of the South Wales Valleys and originally developed in the late eighteenth and early nineteenth centuries to serve the huge Nantyglo and Beaufort ironworks. It later functioned as a dormitory town, with residents travelling two or three miles to work at the Ebbw Vale steelworks or in the nearby coal mines, which were opened in the late nineteenth century, while residents in the post-war period found employment in the Brynmawr rubber factory (later Dunlop Semtex), the Tuf Shoe factory, and the Danimac factory, all of which opened in the immediate area.

The area has been through several serious economic upheavals. During the late nineteenth century and up until the First World War there was a 'coal boom', with miners earning good wages, but the Great Depression of the 1930s led to unprecedented levels of unemployment. Brynmawr was particularly hard hit because the ironworks had closed and the coalfields and other industries tended to prioritise work for local men. Although Brynmawr was only a few miles away, the workers travelled in and so were not deemed to be local. At one point 90% of the Brynmawr men who paid National Insurance were out of work. The economy then partially recovered only for it to slump again. The rubber factory closed in 1982, and the mining industry, which had been in slow decline, more or less ended after the miners' strike of 1984.[10] The Conservative government had sought to weaken the power of the unions and to privatise national utilities, a strategy that brought them into sharp conflict with the National Union of Miners. After almost a year on strike, the miners lost, returned to work, and a decade-long programme of pit closures ensued. In South Wales 25,000 miners lost their jobs.[11] Then in 1986 the Danimac factory shut down, in 2000 the Tuf factory closed, and in 2002 the Ebbw Vale Steelworks closed, with the loss of another 780 jobs.[12]

The collapse of mining and the other industries had a profound effect on the area. Families fractured as people moved away to find work, the town centres emptied out, and there was – and still is – high unemployment. Most of the work that is now on offer is low-skilled. There are very high rates of ill health and disability. Social deprivation in South Wales was and remains acute even in comparison to other ex-coalfield areas in the UK.[13] Frank Olding, who is the heritage officer for the Blaenau Gwent Museums Service and helped set up the Brynmawr Museum, said that there was a long period when no-one wanted to remember what had happened: 'Feelings were very raw, and people, the guts had been pulled out of these communities, there's no way of getting round that and, yes, raw is the right word, raw and beaten up and embittered and despondent, and it took a while to get over that.'[14]

Early in the millennium the Town Centre Partnership, a group of shopkeepers who work together to try to improve the town, mooted the idea of a museum. They approached the Local History Society, who then held a series of public meetings to gauge local interest in the project. People were keen. In 2003 a local shopkeeper offered a temporary space above his shop, and a few months later the local authority gave them a more permanent space in an empty nineteenth-century library building. As in Nidderdale, the council refurbished the space, stripping out old bookcases, painting the space white and laying carpet in preparation for the museum moving in. The group agreed to pay £10 per annum rent and to cover the costs of utilities and insurance, which they manage via subscriptions to the History Society and weekly, well-attended coffee mornings.

The museum group was also approached about a donation of furniture that had been produced as part of the Brynmawr Experiment. During the 1920s recession the Quaker Society of Friends launched a scheme to improve the area and to provide support for the unemployed. Volunteers came from across the UK and Europe and collectively built a swimming pool, a nursery school, and a park. The Quakers also launched a number of new businesses that were intended to provide training and employment for local people. These included a furniture factory that was run by Paul Matt, a young Quaker designer. The factory produced simple, well-made arts and crafts items that could be made by people who were still learning their craft. Within a decade the factory was employing around fifty people, and the furniture was sold in a dedicated London showroom as well as in several major department stores across the UK. Unfortunately, the impact of the Second World

Figure 3.5 Workers at the Brynmawr Factory, Blaenau Gwent, 1939

War on furniture manufacturing and the withdrawal of government funding led to the workshop's untimely closure in 1940.[15]

When he was based in Brynmawr, Paul Matt had lodged with the Morgan family, later marrying Sally, one of the daughters. Her sister Cissie Morgan stayed in the family home, which she furnished with items made during the Brynmawr Experiment. By the time she died, early in the millennium, the furniture had become collectable but, nonetheless, her nephew offered it to the newly founded museum. They were delighted to accept and decided to make the furniture the centrepiece of the museum. Several members of the group had family connections to the Brynmawr Experiment, including Vivienne Williams, whose mother's cousin had been employed in the workshop, later becoming the woodwork teacher in the local high school. Interested in that history, Vivienne had previously bought several items of the Brynmawr furniture at auction, which she now loaned to the museum, adding to their collection. Once the furniture was on display, word spread, and people arrived at the museum with more tables, chairs, desks, and other items in the boots of their cars. Vivienne said that the donations often came from Quakers whose family members had been part of the Brynmawr Experiment and who wanted the furniture to 'come home'.

When we asked the museum founders why exactly they had wanted to start a museum we got a variety of different answers. Sandra Plaister made a link with the changes to local authority boundaries, saying that 'since we've become part of Blaenau Gwent – I know I'm being quite controversial – everything seems to be centralised in Ebbw Vale and we've lost our identity as a town. I think in that respect, it's a good thing to have the museum here for people to know that we did have an identity. We weren't always Brynmawr in Ebbw Vale, Blaenau Gwent; we were Brynmawr.' Alan Williams said, 'I don't think Sandra is by herself on that; I think a lot of Brynmawr people object to the change.'

In contrast, Vivienne Williams' motivation for opening a museum was connected to her memories of the town. She was born in 1939, and said, 'It's hard to admit, really, but this is not the town that we grew up in; it's dead now compared with what it was. It was a very vibrant community at one time. There were independent shops but now they're all closed – it's so sad – and the market died. When I was a child, Saturday morning, everybody came from everywhere to Brynmawr Market.' She also had a huge extended family living in the area. She explained that: 'my mother was one of nine and of course they had aunties and uncles everywhere and cousins, but now I've got cousins that are living in Gloucester and Birmingham and I think we just about exchange Christmas cards, you know? Then we were in and out of each other's houses and it was a community, but now it's not so much that at all. I think the museum is so people know what the town was like in the past.' She added: 'I think it is important to try and keep the town alive.'

Frank had a similar viewpoint. He said that 'people wanted their kids and grandkids to know what it had been like', that it hasn't always been like this. 'There were times when these communities were thriving places, even within living memory. People felt pride in what had gone before and then, despite the fact they had taken a kicking, there is still a pride in where we come from, and what our background is and what we've done and why we're all here in these valleys.' For him, Brynmawr and the other new museum in the area 'are part of the healing process because they help people to look back, and a sign of having been healed, in that

Figure 3.6 Vivienne Williams at Brynmawr and District Museum, Blaenau Gwent

they can look back: they're an indication that people are ready to go on to the next stage'.

The people involved in establishing Brynmawr Museum had a variety of reasons for wanting to do so. The Town Centre Partnership was keen to make the town centre more attractive to residents and to visitors and thought that a museum might help. It also meant that a handsome building was kept in use, and from the local authority's perspective, it meant that the bills were covered. For the people who put the work into collecting objects and arranging exhibitions and later running the museums, it was a means of reasserting their identity as a distinct town, as somewhere the residents could be proud of, and as a means of keeping the community alive. To some extent it has worked, and the museum does function as a means of creating and maintaining community. Vivienne told us that most of the group who volunteered at the museum had all gone to the same school, and almost everyone had grown up and spent their adult lives in the town. Every Thursday morning the museum is open for coffee and they meet to plan and talk, with other local residents also dropping by. Around fifty people attend every week.

There are some clear parallels and some obvious differences between the Nidderdale and Brynmawr museums. They were both set up on a voluntary basis by local history societies, they both wanted to reassert their identity after changes to local authority borders resulted in a loss of their autonomy, and they both received help from the local authority. Both relied on donations to establish their collections, and both displayed items relating to named individuals who lived in the town. Lastly, in setting up a museum the founders in the two locations were responding to seismic changes in the nature and availability of work, and in the associated social changes. Here, though, the stories diverge, because the changes in Nidderdale were prompted by the mechanisation and increasing industrialisation of farming, whereas those in Brynmawr were the result of de-industrialisation.

There is also a difference in exactly what was being accomplished in setting up a museum and why. At Nidderdale, Eileen wanted to document a way of life and to render the past concrete before it disappeared. The implication is that this past way of life had not entirely gone. It was still possible to reach out and salvage the associated artefacts and document the associated stories. In turn, grasping that history and creating exhibitions was a means of showing respect to previous inhabitants, of recognising the ordinary people who had shaped that town and landscape. Among other things, Nidderdale is an exercise in acknowledging what had been. The situation was much more stark in Brynmawr. As in Nidderdale, the Brynmawr group wanted local residents and visitors to know what the town was like for earlier generations, but there was also a strong sense that the past could be and needed to be used to recuperate the present. They variously spoke about the town having died, or the need to keep the town alive. That way of life had already gone. They also raised the possibility of the museum mobilising a sense of pride for people who may have lost that regard for their community, and by implication for themselves. Perhaps the key difference is that although Pateley Bridge was economically depressed in the 1960s and 1970s, in recent decades it has become both a tourist hotspot and a very desirable place to live, whereas the people of Brynmawr still face unemployment and real social deprivation. It is no coincidence that the centrepiece of their museum is furniture made as part of a utopian project that offered a struggling community the chance to reinvent itself and to thrive.[16] It is precisely what the town needs now and what, in its own practical, educational, and symbolic way, the museum is attempting to offer.

Newcomers, incomers, dabchicks

The parish of Perranzabuloe takes its name from a newcomer. In the seventh century Saint Pirran sailed from Ireland to north Cornwall and built an oratory on the shoreline where he landed. In medieval Latin 'Pirran in the sands' is written as *Perranus in Sabulo*, hence the name of the place. Perranporth is the main village in the parish and is now a popular tourist destination. Holidaymakers come to enjoy the wide, white-sand beach and to surf the breakers rolling in across the vast Atlantic Ocean. There are numerous campsites and hotels, and the high street is

Figure 3.7 Perranporth, Cornwall, from the air

packed with shops selling plastic inflatables, bodyboards, postcards, ice-cream, and fish and chips. In summer, crowds fill the streets and the beaches.

Betty Pitman was also a newcomer to the area, and in 1986 she proposed that the Oddfellows Hall, an empty but impressive building in the centre of the village, be converted into a museum. Many of the county's towns and villages have an Old Cornwall Society, which focuses on the history and traditions of the county, and some of the members of the Perranzabuloe branch were keen to pursue Betty's suggestion. As in Nidderdale and Brynmawr, the group was concerned that changes to the area meant that older ways of life would be forgotten and lost. They duly arranged to rent the hall at a peppercorn rate, and with the help of trainees from the Manpower Services Commission programme, which provided training for school and university leavers, volunteers refurbished the building.[17] Initially they let the ground floor to small arts businesses to cover their costs and then, when that proved unsuccessful, to the public library, which has been a reliable tenant.

In this instance, the changes to the area were largely due to the influx of tourists, second-home owners and in-migration – that is, people who move from within the UK. Chris Easton and Linda Higgins, two of the founder members of the Perranzabuloe Museum, explained that the area had become a popular tourist destination. As a result, some of the older buildings were knocked down to make way for things that were 'new and shiny and for tourism'. The popularity of the location had also pushed up house prices, making them unaffordable for most of the people who lived in the area. 'People who need to live here can't,' said Linda. Substantial numbers of extra houses had been built but many were rented out to tourists or bought as second homes, as were older properties. 'I live in a row of nine cottages and three of them are holiday lets,' Chris said. 'I've got no problem with people having a second home or a holiday let, but you know that those houses, there's nobody going to run the football club, there's nobody going to train the surf club, they're not going to join the surf club, they aren't going to be in the local choir, they'll never be in the WI, they're never going to be part of the community.'

Cornwall has experienced both a population rise and an increase in tourism. From the 1960s onwards there were high levels of in-migration. Some of the returnees were Cornish people who had spent much of their adult lives working elsewhere, while others moved from urban centres, most notably London, to settle in Cornwall, and between 1960 and 2001 this influx led to the population increasing from around 340,000 to over 500,000. Many of the in-migrants were looking for a more leisurely way of life and to spend time exploring Cornwall's spectacular landscape and coastline.[18] The same qualities also attracted tourists, and the numbers of holidaymakers increased from around 1.4 million in 1954 to 2.1 million in 1964, 3 million in 1991, and 5 million a year in 2019.[19] The number of in-migrants and the significant rise in second-home ownership and holiday lets inflated property prices, which are high by any standards. At the same time, the growth in population and tourism has coincided with economic decline and with Cornwall becoming one of poorest areas in the UK.[20] There is relatively high unemployment and wages are far below the national average, so housing is often beyond the financial reach of the existing residents, although not beyond that of the newcomers, who tend to be wealthier, more able to buy their own home, and more able to afford homes on the coast and in the more attractive areas, such as Perranporth.[21]

Chris and Linda were both keen to stress that they were not opposed to new residents per se and cited Betty Pitman as an example. Linda said that while she was 'a newcomer, she was one of those that threw themselves into everything. She was tied up with the surf club, wasn't she, very much.' 'And the rugby club,' said Chris. 'I mean Betty was one of those people that moved in who had that interest, but there were lots of people who moved in who were just interested in running a café and making as much money as they could.' Chris and Linda were understandably concerned that their village and the surrounding areas were being emptied out. Newcomers were welcome but only insofar as they lived in and contributed to the village and did not further the inequalities within the existing community.

For them, it was a problem that Perranzabuloe 'was very much viewed as a holiday place, bucket and spades, there's not much else here. Even other areas of the parish really were looking at Perranporth as being sort of just a holiday destination.' They explained that Cornwall had ancient trading links with Brittany and Spain, and a long history of tin and copper mining that connected the county with the rest of the globe. Then when local mining industry went into decline in the late nineteenth century thousands of Cornish miners migrated and found work in Argentina, Brazil, Cuba, Mexico, and Australia, among other destinations. Their skills meant that they were desirable workers elsewhere. These histories are embedded in the place names and landscape of the area but are often unregarded. Linda said that the museum ran a project about the mine workings at the end of the headland and that 'the vast majority of people thought they were natural caves. One chap said, "I've been coming here on holiday for seventy years – I never knew that." They've got no idea about what's behind it all.' Chris reinforced the point, saying that 'people were ignoring the history of the parish and I suppose, growing up here, I was very aware of that and thought there's a danger of it being lost'. 'Being on the beach is lovely,' said Chris, 'but the thing is it's not just buckets and spades.'

In Perranzabuloe, the process of documenting and communicating the history of the village prior to the influx of holidaymakers and second-home owners was a means of pushing back against change, and of emphasising the area as a place of work and industry, not just of leisure.[22] That position is complicated and to some degree compromised because the group needs to appeal to tourists who will potentially visit the museum, and they see the museum as having a role in sustaining the tourist industry on which the local economy largely depends. Linda said that 'heritage has got to be a pulling-point for people, and we've got to keep that going', and Chris added: 'At the moment, I guess the obvious one is the Poldark thing, because we get quite a bit of interest in that.' Here, he was referring to a series of twelve novels set in the late eighteenth and early nineteenth centuries. They begin with the protagonist Ross Poldark returning from the American War of Independence to his home in Cornwall only to find the woman he loved about to marry his cousin, and the family's copper mines in a state of collapse. When we visited, the most recent television adaptation of the Poldark novels had reached its fourth series, and Cornwall's gift shops were full of cushions, mugs, kitchen coasters, and other consumables emblazoned with the face of the actor who played the lead character. Chris said, 'Winston Graham lived in Perranporth for 32 years and wrote all of his Poldark stories here. So, that's the story that's worth getting across at the moment,' illustrating how the museum catered for, as well as resisted, tourism.

Opening a museum helped some of the founders negotiate the demographic changes in the area and the consequent social disjunction. For Linda, that process was highly personal. She said that her family had moved to the area when she was in her early teens, and then laughed and commented that, 'I'm almost naturalised now because I married a Cornishman.' Linda learned Cornish, too. She said, 'I wanted to know what all these place names and things meant, so I took an evening class in Cornish language and learned it, and they said, oh yes, you can do three years of it.' She then carried on with her studies and became a bard, participating in annual language festivals. Like marrying a Cornishman and studying the Cornish language, founding a museum was a means for her to become local.

The same pattern of studying local history or setting up local history museums as a way of accommodating to being in a new town or village is evident elsewhere. When we met the three main founders of Aldbourne Heritage Centre in Wiltshire we asked them how they had become involved in opening a museum. Terry Gilligan had started to tell us about his interest in the history of an eighteenth-century bell foundry in the village when his friend and colleague John Dymond interrupted and said, 'I think Terry's missed out something, which is the fact that of the three of us Terry is the native of the village; he's a dabchick, which is the name for natives of the village. Alan and I are both incomers.' Alan Heasman concurred. 'Exactly. Terry has been born and bred here and has a good knowledge of the village. I came fifteen years ago.'

We asked why Alan and John had moved to the village. Alan explained that he was a meteorologist and he and his wife had mainly lived in a busy area of Reading. When he retired they wanted to be somewhere a bit quieter and just stumbled across Aldbourne. Something similar happened to John and his family. They had lived in Switzerland for eleven years and were relocating to England. He needed to be in commuting distance of Slough and so he and his wife started visiting nearby estate agents. One of them asked the couple to describe their ideal location and they replied, 'We want to live somewhere that is a real old English village with a really good English community, lots of activities, and a good school.' The estate agent replied, 'You need to go to Aldbourne.' It is an exquisitely pretty place. A twelfth-century church sits on a rise above a large village green surrounded by cottages with deep thatched roofs. Ducks paddle across a small pond and, somewhat incongruously, a large Dalek is parked

Figure 3.8 Aldbourne, Hampshire

outside one of the pubs, while the other has a second sign reading 'the Cloven Hoof', both objects being a reference to 'The Daemons', a *Doctor Who* series that was filmed in the village in 1971.

Having arrived in the village, both Alan and John started to research its history. Alan said, 'Well, I was a newcomer, wanting to learn about the village I was living in – well, the parish strictly,' and then John picked up the conversation, saying that he 'came to the village 32 years ago. At that time, I was a computer geek and a computer consultant, but I was also interested in family history as a genealogist. And for the last twenty-five years I've been studying the families of the village. I've transcribed the registers, censuses, and the marriage licences of the village and reconstructed a number of family trees, including Terry's, back for a good number of generations, and published them on my website.'

For the three men, researching the history of the village puts them in contact with the deep past. Terry said that it 'brings us closer to the people that lived in that time, or even beyond, and I feel quite an affinity with them, and particularly with the bell-ringers who are buried in the churchyard'. Terry is also a bell-ringer, as were earlier members of his family, who are among those interred in the village churchyard. 'There is one grave in particular outside the back of the church, where an old bell-ringer named Broom is buried,' he added. 'There is a hole in the grave and when we're showing tourists around, we always say, "What did you think of the ringing today then, Broom?", and we answer in ghostly tones, "'Rubbish!'" The statement is playful but in his imagination he is talking to the people who rang the same bells as he now rings. For John, too, there is a sense of continuity. 'We are also lucky I suppose in that the village hasn't changed much in 200-plus years. The actual buildings, cottages where these people lived are still here and still being used. We haven't suffered, if that's the right word, too much degradation. There is a little bit of modern building on the outskirts but not in the centre.' The village is perceived as quintessentially English and as unchanging.

The idea of opening a village museum had been in circulation for some time. At the turn of the millennium a group of local residents staged an exhibition as part of the annual village festival. They showed agricultural implements and gathered together a collection of bells that were all made in the local foundry, which operated between 1720 and 1825. Terry said that it helped them realise 'just what the history of this village is. Because for a village of only, what, fifteen or seventeen hundred people maybe, we have a history that goes from the Bronze Age right through to such things as *Doctor Who*.' It also takes in the history of the 101st Squadron, the American airmen who were stationed in the village during the Second World War and whose role in the conflict was documented in the television series *Band of Brothers*. The villagers decided that there was 'enough history here in the village and we're proud enough of it that we could and should have a museum'.

Setting up the museum took some time. The main problem was that there was no building available for use. The temporary exhibition had been held in an old fustian mill, which was scheduled for renovation, and Terry said, 'We would be hard pushed to find any other buildings of that type in the village. All are occupied for one reason or another; it's not like a town, where you might find the odd industrial unit that becomes available. The parish council didn't own any property as such, unlike town councils that often have older disused buildings.' Some years later, however, the district council announced that they would no longer fund the public toilets in the village and that the building would revert to the parish council. Terry gathered other enthusiasts together and they proposed that the building be converted to provide space for a museum. He lost out to the youth club and an internet café, an enterprise that proved popular, so much so that in 2014 they relocated to bigger premises, leaving the refurbished toilet building empty and available for use as a museum. In the meantime, the local Civic Society had organised an archaeological dig in the football field, unearthing a bell, medieval brooch, and sardine tins from the American camp, all of which went to form the core of the first displays.

Aldbourne Heritage Centre is supported by the 120 members of the Heritage Society, a remarkable achievement in a small village with many other societies and activities competing for their time. That support was made particularly tangible when the group wanted to buy one of the bells made in Aldbourne that was coming up for auction with an estimated price of £500. The donations totalled £2,000, giving the group one of the only acquisition funds that we have encountered in a local history museum. For John, the success of the heritage centre is due to the combination of newcomers and more settled families. He said: 'I think it's the case that the people who grew up in the village knew the history innately, it was in their blood, but they were never really able to pull a museum together, whereas the newcomers, when you move into a village you're more curious to know why the church was there and what's that over there.' It was precisely because the newcomers were unfamiliar with the village and its history that they were prompted to investigate further and to join in the enterprise of opening a museum. It has also proved a means for them to repay kindness. Alan said, 'It's such a welcoming village. Not all villages are. People like Terry have been very open so you want to give something back. My interest in history and the heritage group is my little contribution.'

Figure 3.9 Aldbourne Heritage Centre, Hampshire

Having arrived in the village, the incomers had to find ways to make themselves at home. Unlike holidaymakers and to some degree second-home owners, they needed to settle in and make friends. For Alan and John, local history was one means of becoming familiar with the terminology of the village, its stories, local inhabitants, and past ways of life, and setting up a museum enabled them to publicly demonstrate that interest. Local history and the museum also provided a meeting point. Although two of the three men were neighbours and all three had known each other previously, local history gave them a collective aim and helped them to further develop a friendship. The museum and heritage group put them in contact with 120 members: it created a space where they could spend time with like-minded people.

Both Perranzabuloe Museum and Aldbourne Heritage Centre opened in repurposed buildings. The founders of the museum in Perranporth had been keen to save the Oddfellows Hall from demolition, while in Aldbourne empty buildings were in short supply and the group had taken what was available. Both museums had been established by groups that included newcomers and people whose families had lived in the area for generations, and in both cases establishing a museum had provided a means for newcomers to demonstrate their commitment to the village and their engagement with its history. In doing so they were able to better integrate with and be absorbed into the existing community.

The differences lie in how the histories of the villages were conceived and thus in the motivations for establishing a museum. The founders of Perranzabuloe Museum felt disenfranchised by the large numbers of holidaymakers, second-home owners, and in-migrants, and in telling the story of the village before the influx of newcomers they were able to symbolically assert their prior rights to that locale. They were not necessarily resisting wholesale change but trying to modify and negotiate that change and its worst effects. In contrast, the founders of Aldbourne Heritage Centre were heavily invested in the notion of historical continuity. While they acknowledged that things have changed in the village, including the presence of the American soldiers in the Second World War, the arrival of commuters, and the demise of many local shops, there is a feeling that any alteration has been and can be encompassed without too much undue interruption. Unlike the other museum founders whom we met in the course of researching this chapter, there is not even a hint of a rift, of a before and after. Instead of the museum providing a means of catching hold of the past or trying to counter recent changes, it is a celebration of a 'real old English village' that is perceived to have endured throughout the ages and continues to prosper.

A sense of place

The founders all emphasised the specificity of their village or town and their groundedness within it.[23] Their sense of place was generated partly in relation to the past and present industry in the area: to the industrialisation of farming in Nidderdale, to the loss of heavy manufacture and coalmining in South Wales, to tin mining in Cornwall, and to the bell foundry in Aldbourne. It related to migration into and out of the area, and how that impacted on their community, to notable individuals, including Christopher Binks the cobbler, the Mudd family, Paul Matt and the Morgan family, St Piran, and Broom the bell-ringer, and to notable events such as the short-lived Brynmawr Experiment and the filming of *Doctor Who*.

A sense of place was also generated in relation to local differences and hence identities. In Nidderdale and Brynmawr the residents fiercely resisted the reconfiguration of local authority boundaries and their amalgamation into the larger conglomerates of Harrogate and Blaenau Gwent. The two other groups were equally adamant about their borders, but on a smaller scale. When we met the founders of Perranzabuloe Museum we asked them about their relationship with other museums in the area, and Linda said, 'We do talk to St Agnes occasionally.' Chris replied, 'But not if we can help it.' They both laughed, and Chris said, 'it's village rivalry'. Linda clarified, saying, 'We do get on, we talk to each other, but we haven't done any joint projects or such, because we're a local museum.' Continuing the theme, Linda and Chris started to compare the two neighbouring museums. Chris explained that while their museum had a better building, they didn't have many objects, whereas the opposite was true of St Agnes Museum. 'They had a turtle,' said Linda. 'We were jealous of their turtle.' It had been washed up on the St Agnes side of the parish boundary and was now on display in the St Agnes village museum. The two museums also had 'a bit of a dispute' over a farmer's smock. The farmer it had belonged to lived in St Agnes, but his relatives had given it to Perranzabuloe Museum. 'Anyway,' Linda said, 'it was donated to us and we decided we were going to hang on to it because it was a lovely item and we didn't have much. He only lived just over the border,' she added. 'I'm sure he wore it when

Figure 3.10 Stuffed turtle, St Agnes Museum, Cornwall

121

Figure 3.11 Postcard depicting 'the Legend of the Dabchick re-enacted'

he came into our parish.' Here, Perranzabuloe's identity is affirmed in distinction to St Agnes, which is a mere three miles away. St Agnes is the place with a turtle and Perranzabuloe is the place with the smock, and on no account should the two villages be confused.

Likewise, the word 'dabchick' originated in a small-scale local rivalry. Terry told us that at some point in the far-distant past a strange bird was seen on Aldbourne village pond. No-one could identify it and so the oldest inhabitant of the village was put in a barrow and wheeled down to the pond to have a look. He pronounced it a dabchick, the dialect name for the little grebe, a bird that is common on the nearby River Kennet, if not in Aldbourne itself. On hearing the story, the villagers in nearby Ramsbury ridiculed their neighbours as being too dimwitted to identify the bird, and started using 'dabchick' as an insult, especially at inter-village sporting events. Since then, villagers have adopted the name. In 1901 they re-enacted the event, a picture from the time is on display in the museum, and the village magazine is called the *Dabchick*.

While insisting on their boundaries, the groups at both Perranzabuloe and Aldbourne understood the identity of their villages as deriving in part from their local, national, and international connections. Linda and Chris mentioned Cornwall's links with Brittany and Spain, and Chris said, 'The thing with Cornwall was, it's a peninsular, so sea trade was very easy. Now, we're stuck on the end of somewhere but at one stage –', and Linda finished his sentence '– we were the centre of the universe.' In a tone of slight self-parody she added, 'We are still the centre of the universe as far as we're concerned. They just don't understand it. Can't even get the trains down here sometimes for goodness' sake.' 'They' in this instance is everyone who is not Cornish, and more specifically the non-Cornish people in charge. For the founders, then, Perranzabuloe is both distinct from and in rivalry with their immediate neighbours St Agnes, is part of Cornwall (which clearly St Agnes is too), is unreliably linked to and simultaneously distinct from England, and is connected to Europe.

The Aldbourne group saw the village as connected to towns within commutable distance. Alan pointed out that 'people go to work in Swindon, which is reasonably important financially, and at the Honda Motor Works. People also go to Newbury and even perhaps up to Reading from here on a daily basis.' The airport in Southampton links the village to Europe, and John said that he goes to the airport almost as often as he commuted to Slough. The village also had global connections in terms of the diaspora of original residents. During the nineteenth century many of the villagers emigrated, including the Liddiards, who moved to Australia. In 2016 the family organised a worldwide reunion, and over 150 Liddiards gathered in Aldbourne. They met again in 2019. Likewise, descendants of the American airmen who were stationed in Aldbourne during the Second World War come to visit, as do tourists who are following the *Band of Brothers* tour around Europe. Here, the founders' conception of place derived from a sense of the village being part of much wider geographic, economic, and social networks.

Lastly, landscape plays a role in the founders' notions of place. Eileen Burgess explained that the group that set up Nidderdale Museum had decided to confine themselves to the structure of the dale. When we asked why, she said that 'Nidderdale is a small dale. It is the smallest of the major dales; and the watersheds are pretty well defined.' She explained that 'to the south of the watershed it's a Midlands dialect; from here northwards it's a Northern Yorkshire dialect', and that 'in some instances there are completely different words for the same things'. Different parts of the dale are culturally distinct. Nonetheless, the group decided to make some exceptions and included artefacts from Washburndale, a very small dale to the south, because they shared the same textiles industry. Nidderdale is understood in relation to the contours of the land and the watersheds, which in turn relate to dialects and working practices.

Likewise, Frank Olding made a link between the landscape, the industrial, social, and cultural development of the towns and villages, and the sense of place.

In addition to helping set up the Brynmawr and District Museum, he was involved in the development of several other local history museums in the immediate area. When we asked why there were so many museums in a comparatively small space – by our reckoning, nine in a few square miles – he said, 'People are very definitely from a valley. I was born and brought up in this valley. I didn't see the next valley until I was about ten.' One of the issues is that the valleys are steep and high and there is no direct route between them; rather, the road system follows the ridge along the heads of the valleys, with smaller roads running down into each individual valley. In order to cross into the next valley travellers must walk or drive to the highest point, before dropping back down, and a journey that is a mile or two as the crow flies becomes a much longer and more demanding trip. Visiting the different museums certainly tested my elderly campervan.

Frank then went on to explain how and why each of the valleys 'had their own character'. Tredegar had a library, a radical debating club, and high levels of welfare provision, most famously in the form of the Medical Aid Society. The mining companies and the individual workers made a contribution to the fund, which covered the costs of Harley Street surgeons who visited for two days per week, and later paid for a dedicated surgery. Frank said, 'That's the kind of money they had, and that was socialism in action. It was very bottom-up.' Aneurin Bevan was a member of both the Tredegar debating club and the Medical Aid Society, and when he became an MP he took the Medical Aid Society as his model for the National Health Service, which was rolled out across the UK. For Frank, the 'very fiery, very vocal tradition of Aneurin Bevan is very strong in Tredegar and you can see how he came out of that background, and the people are still the same. People in Abertillery, virtually the same, pretty vocal, independent-spirited.' Both Tredegar and Abertillery opened local history museums in 1972. 'Ebbw Vale is a different matter,' Frank continued, 'because everything was done by the company there.' In Ebbw Vale the steelworks organised all the services and there was no town council, so, in contrast to Tredegar, the organisation was very top down. Notably, it was the works manager who first mooted the idea for a museum in Ebbw Vale, and Mel Warrender, the technical manager, was asked to carry the proposal forward. Indeed, the Ebbw Vale Works Museum, which opened in 1998, was initially established as a means of preserving a record of the company, only later expanding to address the community of the valley more generally. Brynmawr is different again: Frank said, 'it's part of another county; historically, it's in Breconshire, which makes a difference, and there weren't pits in the town, whereas in other places, where I grew up, the pit was right in the middle of the village. Brynmawr grew up as a dormitory town for two ironworks and that's been its personality ever since, really.'

Thus, as Frank explained, the neighbouring valleys and towns had distinct identities. These were a product of political organisation and whether services were run by representative committee or the company, and indeed if there were services at all. It was related to the formation of societies and political debate, and to the place of industry in relation to domestic life. Living in Brynmawr, a market town, and commuting to work was quite different from living in one of the houses next to the pit, as was the case in other nearby villages. And established boundaries had an impact. Brynmawr was historically part of Breconshire, which is rural, whereas Tredegar and Ebbw Vale were in Monmouthshire, which is largely industrial, and had links with the Marches, the land along the border of England and Wales. The valleys, towns, villages, and surrounding areas had developed their own history and culture.

The museum founders' sense of place was established in relation to where the village or town was not (Harrogate, Blaenau Gwent, St Agnes, England, Ramsbury, Stroud) and where it was connected to (Brittany, South America, Australia, England, Washbourne). It also derived from a concatenation of material qualities, cultural factors, and social relations, including the industry, tourism, the price of property, local authority boundaries, nicknames and dialect, genealogical research and family reunions, war-time residents, the height of the mountains, the direction of the rivers, road systems and commutable journeys, early socialism and company hierarchy, and the possession of a turtle or a smock. That sense of place is not static but changes and morphs as the cultural, social, and physical environment alters. Nonetheless, it remains specific.

Distinct histories

There are real differences between the local history museums we have examined. The four museums were established in divergent circumstances and had differing aims. Nidderdale Museum was established as farming in the dale was in the process of changing and was a salvage operation, retrieving historic objects before they were thrown away or destroyed. Brynmawr Museum was established a number of years after the collapse of local industry and was a means of remembering a past that had already gone. They tried to mobilise that past in order to provide a point of pride and to give hope for the future. Perranzabuloe Museum was founded after a wave of in-migration to Cornwall and as the number of tourists was rising, and it strategically presented an alternative image of the area. In all three of these cases the museum seeks to retain some aspect of local identity that they value but is under threat, and to some extent to pose more ethical alternatives. Aldbourne

Heritage Centre was opened in a settled, affluent area and celebrates the deep history of the village. Its founders do not need to resuscitate pride in the area, and while it similarly functions as an expression of local identity, it is not intended as a mode of resistance or protest.

There are also some clear parallels between the four museums we have discussed and the circumstances in which they were founded. All four museums were founded by or grew out of an existing group: Nidderdale Museum from the adult education classes in local history and the Local History Society, Brynmawr also from the Local History Society, and Perranzabuloe Museum from the Old Cornwall Society. The formation of Aldbourne Heritage Centre was prompted in part by the archaeological dig organised by the Civic Society. These groups provided a space for residents to learn about the history of their area, so they already had a knowledge base when they decided to start a museum. The groups also brought the participants into contact with other people who lived in the area and had similar interests, thereby creating networks and friendship groups that formed a platform for further projects, such as opening museums. The museums strengthened and built community.

The four museums acquired their collections free of charge. All of them relied on donations and, in addition, Aldbourne benefited from the objects unearthed in an excavation. Almost nothing was bought. This process of object acquisition helps account for why local history museums often bear a superficial resemblance to one another. There are exceptions, such as the Methodist ceramics at Nidderdale Museum and the furniture at Brynmawr Museum, but donors rarely give items of real economic value, as these are more likely to be sold or kept within the family. Instead, they give redundant objects that they were nonetheless reluctant to throw away.

The resemblance between local history museums is often amplified by their accommodation. Three of the museums we discussed are located in disused civic buildings – council offices, a library, and a public toilet – with the fourth being in Oddfellows Hall. Local history museums are understood to be appropriate tenants for civic and society buildings and in all these instances were only charged a nominal rent. Local authorities have also been generous to local history museums. Three of the museums were offered financial support, Aldbourne being the exception, with Nidderdale turning it down. The local authorities in Blaenau Gwent also supported heritage officers who advised and supported the foundation of small museums in the area, although, unfortunately, Frank's post was cut after he took voluntary redundancy, despite the volunteers saying how important he had been in setting up new museums.

Above all, the founders all had a strong sense of place, and it is this that under-pins the proliferation of so many local history museums. Residents of Brynmawr felt that the town should have its own museum, as did those in the neighbouring valleys of Abertillery and Tredegar. Despite their proximity, each area was understood to be distinct and the local history was understood to be sufficiently different to warrant a separate narrative. Likewise, the residents of Perranporth felt they needed to address their precise history, as did those in St Agnes. Nidderdale's story was not the same as Harrogate's, and Aldbourne's differed from Ramsbury's. Each place is quite rightly recognised as not being the same as any other place and thus as requiring its own museum.

Chapter 4

The museum founders: getting on the footplate

The historian Raphael Samuel argued that history is the work 'of a thousand pairs of hands'.[1] In this chapter I ask: whose hands exactly? Who founded the micromuseums of the late twentieth and twenty-first centuries? Conversely, who did not? And if not, why not?

I start by assessing the founders' prior experience and whether small independent museums were established by or with the help of museum professionals. I consider the founders' skills and the types of expertise they brought to their museums, social class within founding groups, and the age and the gender of the participants. A survey of 2016 suggested that there are more women than men in the museum workforce.[2] The opposite is true so far as the micromuseums we visited are concerned, and here I consider the reasons why women founders tend to congregate in particular subject areas. I then investigate inclusivity with respect to ethnicity, and it transpires that the founding groups were almost invariably White. In response, I concentrate on the Criterion Heritage Centre, the Asian Music Circuit Museum, and the Black British Museum, which have Asian or Black founders, to find out more about their motivations for opening a museum.

There is no reason why anyone should necessarily want to establish a museum; after all, there are plenty of ways to develop histories, tell stories, create community, or otherwise engage in cultural activities. The question is whether structural factors contributed to the uneven authorship of museums.[3] The last part of the chapter attends to that issue. At the most fundamental level, setting up a museum requires accommodation or a site, something to put on display, and someone to undertake the work involved. I examine how these requirements were met. While micromuseums may often appear to be DIY enterprises, put together on a wing and a prayer, the reality is often more complex than it first appears, and I close by arguing that there is a connection between how the museums were founded and who opened them.

The museum founders

In the previous three chapters of this book I concentrated on museums of transport, war and conflict, and local history, explaining how each of those museum types had a specific history and trajectory of development. In this chapter I draw on and develop that analysis, presenting material on a wider range of museums where appropriate.

Professional training

Who, then, opened the new small independent museums?

Occasionally, the individuals and groups who founded micromuseums included museum professionals. Peter Marsden was an archaeologist at the National Maritime Museum. Concerned that wrecks were not being preserved and that they were prey to 'treasure hunters', he founded the Shipwreck Museum in Hastings, which opened in 1986. Likewise, Edward Paget Tomlinson, who was keeper of maritime collections at Merseyside Museums, was one of the founder members of the National Waterways Museum at Ellesmere Port in Cheshire in 1976, as was David Owen, a senior curator at Manchester Museum. Peter Ingham was trained as a carpenter and employed as the technician at Worcestershire County Museum in Hartlebury Castle, later founding the Romany Gypsy Museum in Hampshire.

There are also instances where the museums received help from one of the various museum services. Anne Read, who co-founded the Museum of North Craven Life in the Yorkshire Dales in 1977, said that 'right from the very beginning we got excellent advice from the Area Museum Service. The director visited us in Settle and said that whatever you do don't just become another collection of bygones – have a proper theme.' In consequence the founders decided to use the museum as an orientation point for visitors, enabling them to 'automatically and easily be able to learn about the area and not just about the town itself. Then, when they went out and started exploring they would understand the landscape, why the fields were the shapes they were, and know about the local industries.' Having a coherent approach 'more or less from day one' enabled the group to successfully apply for funding that paid for a professionally designed exhibition. Likewise, the volunteers at the Brynmawr and District Museum were fulsome in their praise for Frank Olding, the heritage officer at Blaenau Gwent Council and how he had helped them get started; and the founders at Aldbourne in Wiltshire similarly praised their local museums development officer, who had tutored them through the process of opening.

More usually, the founding groups had no previous experience of working in a museum and no or little input from museum professionals. Instead, they visited numerous museums that addressed similar subjects, took notes of how their displays were organised, and often emulated the things that they had enjoyed or admired. Eileen Burgess, one of the co-founders of Nidderdale Museum told us that she had requested numerous books on museum practice from her local library, and followed their recommendation that all objects be catalogued. After a few years they decided to apply for Museum Accreditation, and Eileen told us that 'the person inspecting us came. It was Tuesday morning at ten o' clock. I remember this very clearly. She asked, "And what is your backlog of cataloguing?" and I said, "If you'd asked me at four o' clock yesterday afternoon, I should have said, no, nothing, we're up-to-date, but unfortunately three things were brought in yesterday evening." I felt quite triumphant.' The founders were museum autodidacts.

Figure 4.1 Tony Brooks with radon detector in the Great Condurrow Mine, Cornwall, 1978

While the founding groups did not usually include museum professionals, they almost always had subject specialists as part of the team. Tony Brooks was head of mining at the Cambourne School of Mining in Cornwall when he led on the foundation of the King Edward Mine Museum. The school, which is now part of Exeter University, had an international reputation for teaching and research in mining, tunnelling, mineralogy, geology, and geophysics, among other subjects. When Tony took up his position he inherited responsibility for King Edward Mine, which was the oldest complete mine in Cornwall, having been preserved as a training site for students. Tony and his work colleagues were keen to open the mine as a museum and so they formed a group that included lecturers, mining technicians, and members of the Carn Brea Mining Society. Likewise, Richard Larn, who co-founded the Charlestown Shipwreck Museum in Cornwall with his wife Bridget in 1976, had previously established the first Royal Navy sub-aqua group and had organised the expedition that recovered Sir Cloudsley Shovell's fleet, which in 1706 was wrecked off the Isles of Scilly. Richard later became a professional diver, and wrote and published extensive surveys of wrecks in UK waters, while Bridget Larn was also an experienced leisure diver who retrieved many of the objects that later went on display in the Shipwreck Museum (this was before the Protection of Wrecks Act (1973)). At both museums professional and specialist experience informed the museum's subject-matter and exhibition content.

The pattern repeats elsewhere. All the regimental museums that we visited were founded by officers working with a wider cohort of soldiers and employees within the Armed Forces. And a chart on display at the Ingrow Loco steam locomotives museum lists the active members, their occupations, and the roles that they are qualified or willing to undertake. While they include a bank manager, finance director, retired storekeeper, archaeologist, retired GP, factory operative, and lone 'housewife', over half of the volunteers have a background in engineering. They have variously been in electronics, television sound, power plants, the print industry, railway signalling, or worked with print machinery or as aircraft engineers – all bringing their expertise to bear on the restoration and maintenance of engines.

Other members of the groups that founded museums were not trained in the subject of the museum but had skills that could be put to good use. The group that founded Perranzabuloe Museum included a solicitor, John Rabie, who advised them on becoming a charitable trust; Linda Higgins, a secretary who completed the paperwork; and Chris Easton, a carpenter who worked on the restoration of the building. Chris remembered that he and his fellow volunteer Dave 'both knocked it all together really and we made sure the floors were safe'. Some founder members were actively recruited because of their skills, and builders were

Figure 4.2 Tony Brooks talking to visitors at the 2010 Open Day at King Edward Mine, Cornwall

Figure 4.3 Richard Larn wearing diving equipment, Falmouth Docks, Cornwall, 1970

sought-after additions to a team. When Sylvia Murdoch, her husband Morton, and Kay Matheson were setting up Gairloch Museum on the north-west coast of Scotland in 1978, they approached Roy Mcintyre, a local engineer and building contractor, for help. He explained that 'I was a good soft touch to get interested and when Morton wanted to move things like boats he would ask me if I could do it; and, you know, I daren't ask for money because they didn't have any money, so you just did what you could'. Fifty years later, Roy is still one of the trustees.

The founders of the new museums were not generally academic historians or museum professionals. They rarely had or received any training in curating, collections management, or conservation. Nonetheless, it would be a mistake to assume that the founders were amateurs. On the contrary, many of them had lived experience and professional training in the subjects that the museums addressed, or they had professional expertise in the tasks required to establish museums. They were inexperienced with respect to museum practice but subject specialists or professionals in other respects.[4]

Founders and class

Our narrators often mentioned their roles, trades, and professions, and those of their colleagues. This was partly to explain the logistics of establishing a museum, of who did or gave what, and partly as a proxy for class. For example, when we asked Eileen whom she had worked with to establish Nidderdale Museum in the 1970s she mentioned their occupations. She said that 'Geoffrey Townley was the first chairman. He was the headmaster of the school that I was teaching in. Muriel Swires was the treasurer. And at the time that it happened we were all three working together in the same school. My husband was also a teacher. There was Dayne and Heather Swires, a couple, and Muriel's cousin, Joyce Swires.' 'So, the Swires were well represented?' we asked. Eileen laughed and said, 'Oh yes, the thing is in this day, like so many rural communities, people tend to be interrelated. Joyce was the money girl at a department store. Heather and Dayne were both from farming families and they gave a lot of the agricultural machinery. She spent most of her time with her sleeves rolled up, very old clothes, rubbing down rusty old equipment and blackleading it. Whenever I think of blackleading, I think of Heather, who went home with her hands and arms absolutely black.'

Eileen paused to recollect and continued: 'Joanna Dawson brought a wonderful collection of Methodist memorabilia. She was a local preacher. And a pedigree cattle farmer, at a time when that was quite rare. I'm trying to think who else. Oh yes, Elsy Moss, who kept Shaw Mills Post Office and shop with her husband; she did the costume. She had a collection of her own and she prepared it; she was meticulous. She would press a garment six or eight times before it was satisfactory.'

Eileen's rich description gave us a strong sense of the social and family networks that existed within the group, of the personalities involved, and of their roles within the museum. She also strongly implied that setting up the museum was a collective enterprise that cut across professional and class divisions. Teachers, shop owners, shop assistants, famers, and preachers worked alongside one another. The main proviso for membership was that participants had a common interest in the subject-matter, in setting up the museum, or both.

Other narrators made this point more explicitly, commenting on how class had an impact on the roles they adopted within the museum. Sylvia and Morton Murdoch lived in Glasgow but routinely spent their summer holidays in Gairloch, hiring boats to sail along the coastline. After some years they bought a holiday home, and then in the 1970s Morton was appointed Sheriff of Ross and Cromarty, the historic county to which Gairloch belongs, so they moved to the area more permanently (in Scotland, a sheriff is a judge). However, when the couple held meetings to ask residents to donate objects to a new museum their

Figure 4.4 Celebrating the twenty-fifth anniversary of the foundation of Nidderdale Museum, 1999

status proved to be something of a disadvantage. Sylvia said that the local people had to gain 'confidence that we weren't silly creatures from Glasgow making a fool of them, you see', and Karen Buchanan, who is now the curator at Gairloch Museum, underlined the point.[5] 'People were a bit cautious about giving stuff. Sylvia and her husband will have been very well-educated people and well-to-do, and there was a fear that they were mocking people for having these antiquated objects.'[6]

Their collaborator Kay Matheson fared much better in this respect. Kay was a domestic science teacher at the local high school, she also taught Gaelic, and she was famous. In 1950 she had been one of the three students who removed the Stone of Destiny from Westminster Abbey, travelled undercover to Scotland, and left it in Arbroath Abbey. Until 1296 the stone had been used as the seat for the coronation of Scottish kings, so returning it to Scotland was a rebuttal of English rule. It made her a hero, and when she died, Alex Salmond, the first minister of Scotland, described her as one of the giants of Scottish nationalism.[7] As a result of her teaching and her political credentials, Kay had a lot of local respect, and even

Figure 4.5 Kay Matheson with Gavin Vernon (left) and Ian Hamilton (right). The three removed the Stone of Destiny from Westminster Cathedral in 1950

before the idea of a museum had been raised, residents had given her various artefacts, such as spinning wheels, a wooden cradle, and a wooden dresser. Karen remarked, 'Kay was a better collector because she was from the area and knew everyone.' Here, perceptions of local identity and class intersected. As a result, Sylvia and Morton's attempts at collecting did not always meet with success, whereas Kay, the domestic science teacher and nationalist heroine, was given objects without even having to ask.

For many of our narrators, though, working with people from outside their social class was one of the pleasures of setting up a museum. Trevor England and Chris Smyth, who met when they joined the Vintage Carriages Trust in Keighley in the late 1960s and later worked together to launch that collection as the Museum of Rail Travel, which opened in 1990, made the point most clearly. When we asked why they were so interested in railways, Trevor said, 'It's not so much just the trains: it's the fact of the social interaction with people. You got everything from people that are out of work up to doctors and solicitors, so the spectrum of people that you meet up with in preservation's unbelievable.' Indeed, the close lifelong friendship between Trevor, a steelworker, and Chris, a grammar-school boy who went on to become a nuclear scientist, is a case in point.

In some cases, setting up and working in a team that included people from quite different professional backgrounds enabled the founders and later volunteers to shift out of the social roles that they ordinarily occupied. Trevor explained: 'most solicitors think that it's a lot easier to dress down and become a train driver for the day. People that were working in industry were quite happy to take on management roles because it was something different for them to do as opposed to their day job. I was in secondary modern school and started as a fitter in the steelworks, so at the weekend I didn't particularly want to be working with sledgehammers and things that I had been doing in the week.' These shifts were made possible because the 'people that didn't want to do their everyday job were prepared to hand on their experiences.' Trevor taught engineering to the solicitors and accountants so that they could work on the engines, and in turn they helped him with bookkeeping when he became the treasurer of the Vintage Carriages Trust, a position he occupied for sixteen years, later becoming chair for a further twenty-five.[8]

Even if I limit myself to the founders of the museums so far discussed in this chapter, the group members included archaeologists, artists, bank managers, building contractors, caretakers, carpenters, doctors, farmers, funeral directors, judges, heritage workers, labourers, mining engineers, physicists, preachers, retirees, shop-assistants, shopkeepers, secretaries, solicitors, and steelworkers. There were a lot of servicemen and teachers. The professional mix of the groups had implications for social interaction. Museum groups enabled the founders and volunteers to meet people whom they may not have otherwise encountered, something that was repeatedly cited as a pleasure. They often used the skills from their ordinary lives; the builders advised on building and the secretaries did the paperwork, but running museums also provided an opportunity to swap roles and to share skills. Blue-collar workers helped white-collar workers learn the manual and technical skills that were required to build a museum, create infrastructure, construct displays, repair buildings, and restore vehicles and other artefacts. Equally, the white-collar workers supported their colleagues in keeping the museums' accounts, writing guides and interpretation, chairing meetings, and managing the legalities of establishing museums. For some people, this was an expansion of their existing opportunities; for others, it was a chance to step out of the positions prescribed for them by class or education and thus inhabit a different world from the one offered by their usual working or social life. In this respect the founding groups were remarkably fluid with respect to professional and social stratification.

Young founders

Almost everyone we interviewed for this project was elderly, and some people were over eighty or ninety years of age. To make an obvious if easily overlooked point, most of the museums were established years beforehand, when the founders were young. Although retirees and elderly people were involved from the outset, many of the founders were then in their twenties, thirties, or forties. It is less obvious to note that some of the founders were very young indeed, only just into their teens. These young founders arrived at the museums in a variety of ways.

Some founders had school-age children who were invited, encouraged, or co-opted to help. Eileen Burgess, who co-founded Nidderdale Museum, said that 'Heather and Dwayne Swires brought their two daughters, Deborah and Helen, who were about twelve and fourteen. Mark, my son, was very involved in the preparation of things, particularly in the early years of the museum – he and Geoff Townley's son, Richard, that was the same age, about sixteen, and another lad, Richard Jackson, who was a friend of Geoff's son. They did a lot of cleaning of stuff.'

In other cases, children were drafted in by their teachers. One head teacher had his school's woodwork class make the posts for the rope barriers at the Museum of Transport, Greater Manchester, while Kay Matheson's domestic science class laundered the textiles for Gairloch Museum.[9] Di Skilbeck brought

Figure 4.6 Schoolgirls digging out mud from river basin, National Waterways Museum, Cheshire, 1974

her charges on-site. She was head of geography at Wirral Grammar School for Girls and a member of the group working to establish the National Waterways Museum at Ellesmere Port. They had been given a derelict site at the old docks, and volunteers spent months digging out the silt from the huge canal basins. They included girls at Di's school. A photograph from the time shows fifteen children, aged between eleven and thirteen, wearing wellingtons and standing in thick mud, shovels in hand. One has a headband, others are sporting shorts, and most are streaked with mud. They are paused for the moment, waiting for the adults who are pushing wheelbarrows in the background to return and pick up extra loads.

In Northern Ireland, Tony Ragg ran a model railway club at the school where he taught. One summer Tony and his wife, Ena, took the group on a steam train outing, and afterwards invited any interested pupils to come and help at Whitehead, where a group of volunteers were setting up a railway museum. Mark Kennedy, who was eleven or twelve at the time, accepted the offer, and he told us that 'I ended up standing on the roof of a railway carriage, which my mum would have freaked about, helping to paint up the leaks on the roof.' Now in his late fifties and the museum's curator, he jokingly complained that the founding team, most of whom have continued to volunteer, 'still consider me a teenager'.

Figure 4.7 Mark Kennedy at Whitehead Railway Museum, Carrickfergus, County Antrim, circa 1975

Other children arrived of their own volition. Paul Williams was the youngest in a large family. One of his older brothers worked for the Greater Manchester Department of Transport and part of his job was to check that the buses were maintained to standard. In school holidays he took Paul with him to the various garages on his round and the small boy would sit in the car and watch the mechanics working on the buses. Paul found it fascinating, and when a group of enthusiasts, most of whom worked on the buses, decided to set up a transport museum, he was keen to join them. As a fifteen-year-old schoolboy he helped deep-clean the building, which, having been a Post Office garage, was ingrained with decades of oil and dirt, and build a wooden hut to use as a souvenir shop. A photograph taken shortly after the museum opened in 1978 shows him staffing the souvenir shop, and in another photograph two more teenagers await visitors at the ticket desk. Paul was not the only volunteer of that age at the time.

Likewise, Keith Whitmore became involved in steam preservation and museums in 1969, when he was thirteen years old. He had wanted to start the year before, but his parents were concerned about him travelling alone from their home to the Dinting Railway Centre. Keith persisted and his parents agreed to drop him off while they attended a nearby church on Sundays. He mainly worked on the restoration of the Scots Guardsman locomotive, climbing on to or into the boiler to wirebrush it clean. At fifteen he was asked to help with the sales and built up a

Figure 4.8 Reception staffed by young volunteers, Museum of Transport, Greater Manchester, circa 1980

successful business acquiring or buying and then selling model railway sets to raise money for the site. He later went on to co-found Ingrow Loco, the successor museum to Dinting Railway Centre.

The micromuseums boom was cross-generational and enabled in part by the work of children and teenagers. They were not just brought along to play or otherwise amuse themselves. Rather, they came of their own volition, learned new skills, took responsibility for complex tasks, and undertook physically demanding work. For them, the museum was an exciting place to be, and they wanted to be among the museums' founders.[10]

Women founders

The groups that founded micromuseums were inclusive with respect to the class and the age of the participants. There was often a real sense of the museum being a collaborative, community undertaking, with tradespeople and professionals, teenagers, young, middle-aged, and elderly volunteers working together. However, depending on the type of museum, the founding groups were divided along the lines of gender. War and conflict museums and transport museums were predominantly male preserves, whereas local history museums had much more of a gender mix.

It is important to register that a few women did have leading roles in the foundation of war and conflict museums and in transport museums. In 1994 Zena and Peter Scoley worked to establish the Metheringham Airfield Visitor Centre in Lincolnshire. The couple acted in partnership, and after their deaths their contributions were individually and equally commemorated in the museum. Paula Cooper and her partner, Mike, similarly collaborated to launch the Bubblecar Museum in 2004 in Somerset, later relocating the museum to Lincolnshire. Paula now runs it as a solo concern.

In other cases, women, often wives, have supported the male founders. When we met Geoff Burton, who led on the foundation of RAF Ingham Heritage Centre, he mentioned that his wife, Deborah, had helped him prepare the materials for the initial exhibition in the village hall. He also explained that she became secretary to the heritage group, accompanied him on research trips, and that it is likely she will run the museum café once the building is finished. In other instances the help was less direct, such as when women took care of a couple's children, thereby freeing the husband or partner to spend time establishing a museum. Pat Bentley, whose husband, Mick, was one of the founders of the Dinting Railway Centre, said, 'I didn't like being left on a Sunday (which is when he volunteered) but, there again, he'd give me his time during the week.' She acknowledged that 'Mick saw more of his children when they were younger than my father did', but she also said that 'there were times when I would have liked to have got on the footplate and had a go'. Pat facilitated her husband's involvement at the expense of her own.[11]

The museums of war and conflict and of transport that we visited routinely relied on women's input. Many micromuseums owe their existence to coffee mornings and cake sales, and women variously fundraised, worked as administrators, offered intellectual and emotional support, and took care of children. However, their contributions were often less visible than those of the men who acted as project leaders or were identified as the instigator of a museum. If museums are understood as being founded by a group, and indeed by an expanded group rather than by a single individual, then it is correspondingly easier to recognise that women did make a contribution in these ostensibly male spheres.[12]

In contrast to museums of transport and of war and conflict, women often established local history museums, and it is useful to consider the reasons why this was the case. One factor concerns gender divisions within the institution from which a museum emerged. For example, the regimental museums that I have discussed so far were established between the 1960s and 1990s and were set up by retired or semi-retired officers. At that point there were few, if any, women officers of comparable age and seniority.[13]

Another important factor was economic. Buying and maintaining a steam loco-motive or a double-decker bus is a major investment. Some of the men who started Dinting Railway Centre took out loans against their houses to pay for the engines and to build a space in which to store them. At one particularly difficult juncture there was a real risk that the group might lose the site and that the men would forfeit their family homes.[14] The group also paid out of their own pockets for replacement parts for the engines and for building materials. In 1970, there were almost twice as many men as women in employment in the UK; women received lower pay on average, had fewer of the 'top jobs', and were much more likely to work part-time.[15] Given the differences in earning power, it is unlikely that that many married women would have had the same unilateral access to family funds as their husbands, or that women, married or otherwise, would have had compa-rable disposable incomes. In contrast to the expensive star objects on display in transport museums, the exhibits in local history museums generally had low eco-nomic value and were almost invariably donated. The founders of Nidderdale Museum were given everything that went on display, as were those at Perranzabu-loe and Gairloch museums. So long as the founders had the trust and support of local people, it was possible to establish a local history museum with very little expenditure. Women were able to make local history museums with the resources that were available to them.

There are also reasons why women actively wanted to open museums. During the 1970s and 1980s local history museums often used dioramas or recreated rooms to depict aspects of everyday life. Gairloch Museum had recreations of a 1940s village shop, a schoolroom, a stable, and the inside of a lighthouse, with the highlight being a full-size recreation of a croft house. At one end of the room a mannequin of a young woman was positioned at a spindle next to an open hearth, while a mannequin of an older woman sat looking over a doll in a hooded cradle. A large dresser with patterned china on its shelves stood to the side of the room, and there were box beds built into the far wall. When Sylvia Murdoch looked back, she said, 'People were just getting interested in heritage. It seems odd now because it's such a big thing, but then museums were usually very dusty, and contained butterflies on pins, and skeletons and things. Natural history, they were nearly all natural history, they were places you went to on a wet day.'[16] It is important to rec-ognise that community-led micromuseums were relatively new, and in setting up a local history museum and in developing these displays Sylvia, Kay, and the rest of the group were able to foreground the lives of ordinary people, and specifically those of women. The single room of a croft cottage — the place that was the centre of so many women's lives, where they spun flax and wool, sewed, cooked, and

Figure 4.9 Croft house at Gairloch Museum, Ross-shire, Highland, 2018

looked after the children — was made into the centre stage of a museum. It claimed that women crofters' experiences and history were worthy of attention.

The diorama also showcased the skills of the women who made it. As in many other local history museums, the group set-dressed a series of tableaux and crafted objects for use within them. Sylvia made the clothes for the mannequins. 'I did the spinning, and crocheted all the shawls, and made all the mutches (a woman's white cotton cap) and the aprons. And, I may say, I was at pains to do them by hand. Because I thought if anybody inspects that and sees it's done on a machine, that won't do.' Kay stripped down and repainted a pine dresser that she had found in a local farmhouse. And other women participated in the annual living-history events held at the museum. Bella McRae made butter and Margie Russell made oatcakes. Traditionally female skills that were usually confined to the home – arranging interiors, spinning, crochet, sewing, and cooking – all became the means of making museums: they were moved from the private and into the public sphere.[17] Local history museums provided women founders with the opportunity to document and celebrate the lives of other women, to create connections with other women over time, and to display their own often overlooked skills.

Lastly, several of the founders whom we met made a link between local history and family history. Heather, curator at the Museum of North Craven Life, said, 'Women are very communicative, and they have a network of local connections.

Figure 4.10 Margie Russell demonstrating how to make oatcakes to a young visitor, Gairloch Museum, Ross-shire, circa 1980

Your grandmother tells you something or your neighbour tells you something, and you become the holder of a particular history. The women know what goes on in a place and whose families have lived in the town for generations. You can't generalise but I think that's where some of the fascination with local history comes from.' For her, the women residents' stories and knowledge of family history easily translated into an awareness of local history. Elizabeth Cameron, one of the founders of the Laidhay Croft Museum, made an almost identical point in relation to objects. Now in her mid-eighties, she said that keeping old things was drilled into her. 'My mother had stuff belonging to her mother and her granny and you just don't throw anything away: you keep it.' We asked, 'Is that what you're doing here – keeping the women's things?' She laughed and quickly agreed. 'Well, I think so, more or less,' although she added that 'I'm trying to get rid now.' Apparently, her sons were reluctant to keep any of the lustreware that she had personally collected over the decades, and she needed to find it a home. For her, it was women who kept the domestic and everyday objects, and who remembered the people and stories associated with them. Some of those objects were used to furnish local history museums.

Figure 4.11 Criterion Heritage Centre, Blue Town, Isle of Sheppey, Kent

Founders and ethnicity

Our research concentrated on transport, war and conflict, and local history museums founded after 1960. To the best of our knowledge, the only Black or Asian
person to found a museum in those subjects and that period is Jenny Hurkett, who
in 2009 set up the Criterion Heritage Centre in Blue Town on the Isle of Sheppey,
in Kent.

Jenny said that she founded the museums because she was angry that Blue
Town was marginalised and ignored by the local council, and because even the
residents thought that the area was a dump. She wanted to draw attention to its
impressive history – the Regency dockyards, garrison, and townhouses; how
Nelson's body was brought ashore at Blue Town; the Victorian zoos, ferries, and
bowling greens; and how the RAF was launched at its port – and so she began
collecting artefacts. Local residents brought her things they had been keeping in
attics, and the dockyard gave her two beautiful carved ship figureheads. In the
absence of anywhere better she put them on display in the bathroom showroom
that she and her husband owned. 'You can see how it wasn't a plan,' Jenny remarked
when we asked her about the models of sailing ships lined up on the formica units.

The situation changed when Jenny's husband became ill and the couple had to
close the showroom. In an earlier impression the building had been a hotel with a

small music hall, so she decided to take a lump sum out of her pension and convert the building into a combined heritage centre and music hall that would host bands and events. Her children were not enthusiastic and tried to dissuade her, but she said, 'I had become Mrs Angry and I just thought, I'm gonna do this, so that's what I did – started very small and it's just grown over the eleven years.' The Criterion now has dozens of extremely loyal volunteers and has developed new spaces, displays, projects, and events (including another museum focusing on the aviation history of the island).

Later in the conversation Jenny referred to herself as 'Mrs It's Unfair'. When we asked her about where her anger and sense of injustice came from, she started to talk about her family history. Jenny was born in Kolkata to an Anglo-Indian family. She explained that her parents were educated in English, they 'had to do their arithmetic in pounds, shillings and pence', and 'it was all about you coming back to the mother country'. After Independence was declared, the new administration viewed Anglo-Indians as being too British, and many people lost their jobs. The family decided to leave and applied to emigrate to Australia, but her mother was refused entry. Jenny is dark-skinned and she said, 'My mum was my colouring and my dad is a bit fairer, and he was accepted but she wasn't.' Prompted by the sight of our raised eyebrows, she said, 'And then you're talking about my nan and her two

Figure 4.12 Jenny Hurkett, founder of Criterion Heritage Centre

sisters who had different colour skins. Auntie Enid was blonde and had blue eyes and she ended up being the governess to the viceroy's children. My Aunt Nesta was much cleverer; she became a matron, but she was my colouring and could only work with Anglo-Indians – she wasn't allowed to work in White hospitals. People would check your gums and your nails to see [the pigmentation]'. 'So when you're asking me', Jenny continued, 'maybe that is where my "hang on, this isn't fair" comes from.'

Opening a local history museum on the Isle of Sheppey is a long way from experiencing racism in British India and post-war Australia, but, for Jenny, there was a connection between the discrimination that her family had experienced and how the people of Sheppey were looked down upon or marginalised. For her, it was important that everyone could be proud of who they were, where they lived, and where they had come from, irrespective of ethnicity. The museum was a means of making sure that happened in Blue Town.

The Asian Music Circuit Museum, in contrast, was set up to address the lack of coverage of Asian music and dance in the UK. It is to this venue that I now turn, not least because the circumstances of its foundation are markedly different to that of most other small independent museums, as was its eventual demise. Unlike most micromuseums, it developed out of an Arts Council project, and in that sense had official backing and endorsement.[18]

Viram Jasani is an authority on Indian music who taught at King's College London and the London Guildhall School of Music, and is popularly known for playing tabla on the song 'Black Mountain Side' on Led Zeppelin's debut album. In

Figure 4.13 George Harrison, Ravi Shankar, and Viram Jasani in London circa 2000

1984 he was invited to join Arts Council of Great Britain's advisory panel for music, an experience he found demoralising. Senior members of the board were dismissive of him and of Asian culture more generally, Asian music was relegated to the category of 'Other' on the agenda for each meeting, and proposals for Asian music initiatives were routinely turned down due to lack of available funding.[19] Meanwhile, opera houses and national theatres were receiving substantial grants.

Viram lobbied for change and in response the Arts Council commissioned George Pratt, head of music at Keele University, to lead an internal inquiry on 'Afro-Caribbean/South Asian Music'. The ensuing report was hard-hitting, pointing to the lack of South Asian and Afro-Caribbean expertise on Arts Council panels and, given the Black and Asian population in the UK, the lack of funding for the associated arts. It was also critical of Eurocentric decision-making in arts programming and, noting prior inquiries on similar topics, the lack of progress in rectifying inequality. The authors made numerous proposals about tackling various aspects of racism and developing a proactive approach to supporting Afro-Caribbean and South Asian practitioners and culture. More specifically, they recommended that the Arts Council should establish and fund two national touring companies: one promoting African and Caribbean and the other Asian music, and that they should also facilitate training in these areas.[20] The Arts Council accepted the report in its entirety and in 1989 launched the Asian Music Circuit, running it as an in-house company, as it did with other musical networks at that point. Two years later, it was devolved to an independent trust, and Viram, who by now had left the advisory board, was invited to become the first chairperson, heading up a team of six staff.

In the years that followed the Asian Music Circuit organised hundreds of concerts and workshops, bringing some of the best musicians and dancers from India, China, Indonesia, Vietnam, Afghanistan, and other Asian countries to play in venues that varied from a village hall in Cornwall to the Proms at the Albert Hall. They ran schools programmes, held masterclasses, and developed a reputation for excellence and leadership in the field.[21] They also opened a museum. In 2001 Viram secured just over £1 million of capital funding from the Heritage Lottery Fund and Arts Council England, which allowed them to buy a building in Acton, west London. In the course of travelling to research Asian music and to commission new acts, the team had collected numerous musical instruments, and others had been given or bought from performers in the UK. They had also filmed instruments being made and played both in their home locations and in venues in the UK. These objects and audiovisual materials formed the basis of a permanent and free exhibition that opened in 2007. Video footage from the time shows a

Figure 4.14 Asian Music Circuit Museum, London, main gallery with interactive console, circa 2007

professionally fitted-out space with touchpads providing information on each object and a state-of-the-art interactive station that enabled visitors to play ragas by moving within the space.

Then in 2011 their funding was completely cut. The Asian Music Circuit, which incorporated the Asian Music Circuit Museum, had received Arts Council funding from its inception, with grants rising from around £195,000 to around £500,000 per annum as the scale of their activities grew. They appealed, but their complaint was turned down, so they sought and were granted legal permission to take the case to judicial review. Solicitors acting on their behalf noted that the cuts would be fatal to the Asian Music Circuit and were contrary to Arts Council England's stated aim of diversifying the arts.[22] The *Guardian* newspaper also came out in their defence, publishing an editorial that referred to the decision as 'madness' and called upon Arts Council England to reconsider.[23] It was to no avail, and in 2014 the museum display was dismantled, their collection given to York University, and the building sold. The company produced a scaled-down repertoire of exhibitions and concerts in external venues and finally closed in 2018.

Arts Council England's decision to cut funding to the Asian Music Circuit was made in a period of austerity and reduced funding to the arts, but it was still questionable. Moira Sinclair, then executive director, said that the panel had fully 'understood the impact that the Asian Music Circuit could have with regards to the diversity of the portfolio in supporting and showcasing talent and in providing a programme that appealed to audiences that were not so well-served by public investment in the arts'.[24] Nonetheless, she continued, there were stronger applications and the panel had sought to mitigate any negative effects by funding other Asian music organisations in the regions. More specifically, staff at Arts Council England noted that its proposals for multiplying income streams were weak, and that it had no plans for new partnerships. However, as the judicial report made clear, other organisations that were similarly assessed with respect to income did receive funding, and little notice was taken of its track record and extensive network of existing partnerships. And despite Simpson's claim, the closure of the Asian Music Circuit certainly left a gap in provision. Writing at the time of the funding announcement, the news service Minority Perspective anticipated a net loss in expertise, knowledge, and experience, as well as in infrastructural support for Asian music in some regions.[25] Their assessment of the situation was later confirmed in a report called the 'South Asian Dance and Music Mapping Study', commissioned by Arts Council England in 2019, only one year after the Asian Music Circuit had finally closed. The authors, Courtney Consulting, found that there were low numbers of South Asian production companies in the UK, little infrastructure to support South Asian musicians and dancers, a lack of opportunities for professional training, insufficient partnerships between production companies and established venues, and too few leaders – precisely the services that the Asian Music Circuit had provided. No equivalent museum has since opened in its place.

It is likely that the Asian Music Circuit's application for funding could have been stronger, but it is also likely that their expertise and their contribution to UK music and museums were insufficiently valued. As part of their research Courtney Consulting interviewed numerous Asian practitioners and organisations and noted that a common concern emerged, namely how quality was assessed and who was in a position to make that assessment. There was a strong consensus that funders did not have sufficient expertise in this part of the sector and that appraisals were made through a 'White lens'.[26]

Like Viram Jasani, Sandra Shakespeare was concerned about lack of coverage, in this instance of Black history and culture in the UK. While the Black Cultural Archives has a long and important history of collecting documents, photographs, and oral histories, and in 2014 opened an exhibition space, Sandra noted the absence of a dedicated museum of Black history in the UK, a situation that she plans to remedy.[27]

Sandra first started thinking about a museum of Black history when she was working for the National Archives on projects that addressed Caribbean history. At the time she was also a member of Museum Detox, a network for people of colour working in museums, libraries, archives, and heritage. In 2014 they organised a small group visit to the National Museum of African American History and Culture in Washington DC, and Sandra said that she was 'totally and absolutely blown away by the experience'. The sheer scale of the museum and the range of its exhibits opened her eyes to possibilities in the UK. 'I thought what if? What if we dared to just imagine, if we dare to dream? What if we started the conversation with our friends and colleagues who we know across museums and who work in heritage? How could we build a new collection that really speaks to a Black British experience here in the UK?'

A year later she saw a call for sessions at the Museums Association annual conference, submitted a proposal, and was invited to organise a two-hour workshop on the subject of a Black British Museum. Speaking at the conference, she pointed out that Black people feel invisible in museums: 'They cannot see themselves, they're not in the frame, they're not on the plinth, they're not in the big flagship exhibitions'. She called for 'a museum where that representation, that visibility, the complexities, the nuances of our history are there and they are centre stage through the collections'.[28] Reiterating those points when we spoke, she added that it is important for young people to discover how they, their parents, and grandparents came to the UK and became part of the fabric of this society: how 'their history is part of the DNA of our society'. She also pointed out that young people need to see museums being managed and run by people of colour, rather than them mainly working in the canteen or in the cloakrooms, 'which sadly still is the case for lots of the national institutions'. The Black British Museum would provide a space where Black people could tell their own histories, learn about those histories, and feel comfortable and valued.

When we spoke to her she said, 'It was a provocation. I thought there might be people saying, who does she think she is, get her off, but people were really enthusiastic so it was: right, now we've started this, we've got to keep going. I made it my business.' Since then, Sandra has established a Community Interest Company and is aiming at establishing online resources and then a permanent museum over a ten-year period.[29]

Several major museums in the UK have collections of Asian, African, and Caribbean artefacts. However, as Sandra pointed out, apart from the Black Cultural Archives there are no museums in the UK where Black people have established and maintain direction over those narratives, and, as our research suggests, there are comparatively few founded by Asian people or other minority ethnic groups. Public funding enabled the foundation of the Asian Music Circuit, and its director then took the step of opening a museum, but that project was later undercut by the withdrawal of grant aid. When we met, Viram commented that the lack of Asian and Black people in the sphere of publicly funded culture and the lack of attention paid to their cultural forms can be directly attributed to institutional racism. However, that does not account for why so few Asian or Black people opened their own museums. After all, the Arts Council did not provide core funding for any of the other museums discussed so far in this chapter. In this respect, it is important to consider the structural factors that made it easier for White people to open museums than for their Black, Asian, or minority ethnic counterparts. Thus, in the next three sections I look at how exactly the micromuseums boom was established with respect to accommodation, collections, and labour.

Finding accommodation

Very little hard cash changed hands in the opening years of the museums boom. A few museums got substantial sums of money for new buildings and staff, while many received small pots of funding from patrons, charities, the Ministry of Defence, and, perhaps above all, the local authorities. Even so, it is noticeable how much was achieved through help in kind.

Almost all the museums that we visited were housed in repurposed accommodation. When we visited a group of local history museums in a small area of South Wales we found that they occupied a wide range of buildings – a workmen's hall, a miners' institute, the steelworks company office and a pub – all of which are now owned by the local authority. The museums paid a very low rent or just covered the cost of utilities, with the council continuing to maintain the fabric of the building. The Army similarly supported regimental museums, which opened in redundant barracks, depots, and other military buildings. The cost of moving and of refurbishing the spaces was generally met by the Ministry of Defence, which also covered running costs and paid for staff, although this situation has since changed. In 2008, the Bourne-May report recommended that the Ministry of Defence should only fund one museum per serving regiment and that funding was to be phased out for those museums relating to antecedent regiments. The report noted that the changes would result in the number of funded museums dropping from sixty-nine in 2008 to eighteen by 2022 and fifteen by 2035.[30] Yet while fewer regimental museums receive funding directly from the Ministry of Defence, many are still maintained by regimental associations, or they find accommodation in historic homes and castles owned by families with connections to the unit in question. War and conflict museums that are not allied to a regiment may also depend on or benefit from private assistance, particularly from landowners who support the use of wartime sites as museums. Like local authorities and the Ministry of Defence, they give the founding groups space to open a museum, only charging them a nominal rent.

Transport museums were often established on a comparable basis, with parent organisations, landlords, companies, or charities offering space at low cost. For instance, Transport for Greater Manchester owns the huge tram shed that houses the Museum of Transport, Greater Manchester, which opened in 1977; it has never charged rent and looks after the repair of the building. The British Commercial Vehicle Museum was housed in a building previously owned by British Leyland Motors, which had originally established the collection, and given to the museum in trust. Transport museums can also cover the cost of accommodation by renting out space to vehicle owners. It is difficult to find somewhere large and dry enough to house a vintage delivery van, never mind an antique fire engine or tram, and the owners generally need access to workshops so that they can easily repair and restore their vehicles. Transport museums usually rent some of their space to enthusiasts, too, thereby ensuring that they can pay the bills and a mortgage or rent, with the additional vehicles being added to those on exhibition. In many cases they have both subsidised space and rental income that generates revenue to cover other costs.

On the whole, providing free or low-cost space for museums is beneficial for everyone concerned. Many of the civic buildings, airfield sites, barracks, tram sheds, or railway depots did not easily lend themselves to modern working life, or to cheap adaptation. Mel Warrender, who led on the foundation of the Ebbw Vale Works Museum, reported that when the council refurbished the company offices, 'they were left with a lot of empty rooms', which they partly filled by inviting the museum to take up residence. Having a museum on the premises kept the building in public use, covered the insurance and utility bills, and had the potential to bring tourists into an area they may not otherwise visit. Some museums also had the potential to generate additional income or to improve the offer at an existing attraction. It was a win–win arrangement.

Amassing objects

Most of the objects that went on display were also acquired free of charge. Virtually everything given to local history museums was donated, and it was rare for them to purchase anything, although, unusually, Aldbourne Heritage Centre had a small acquisitions budget dating from a fundraising campaign that exceeded its target. Regimental museums generally began with collections of war trophies, silverware, portraits, uniforms, weapons, campaign furniture, instruments, and other objects that had accrued over time in the officers' mess: they had pre-established collections. Once the museum opened, members of the regiment or their families made further gifts, often of kit, medals, and personal objects. The exhibits at military museums, as distinct from regimental museums, comprised a mixture of purchases from eBay and other auctions, donated artefacts, and ord-nance, wrecked planes, and other vehicles that were unearthed by amateur archae-ologists, metal detectorists, and the official bodies responsible for salvage.

Transport museums that started out as part of a company, whether that was British Leyland Motors or Transport for Greater Manchester, resembled regimen-tal museums in that they often inherited a collection, while others accrued objects through a process of salvage and donation. In addition, and unlike the other micromuseums we visited, objects were often purchased at considerable expense. Locomotives, carriages, and other rolling stock was sold at scrap value, calculated per ton, as were redundant buses and trams. These are heavy objects and corre-spondingly expensive, so enthusiasts often clubbed together to make the purchase. In some instances, wealthier supporters or members of the groups would provide the funds, make interest-free loans, or leave bequests to this end, something that we rarely encountered elsewhere. Car museums stand out from other types of transport micromuseums in that they are more likely to be privately owned and the exhibits bought as investments.

Many micromuseums established their collections at no or low cost. However, there are cases where there was very little to collect or display. When we visited the local history museums in the South Wales Valleys, Alyson Tippings, who was destination management officer for Blaenau Gwent Council and part of the team that set up Tŷ Ebbw Fach Heritage Centre in 2010, commented on the active destruction of the local built environment and material culture. She said, 'The Six Bells colliery was the heartbeat of that village and it's why the village was here. And now the pit is gone.' Alyson meant that statement literally. 'They knocked all the buildings down and bulldozed them down the shaft and capped the shaft off, because the government didn't want any legacy of the industry as a reminder in these communities of the miners' strike. It was a serious act of vandalism.' The buildings' contents were also deliberately thrown away. Alyson remembers that the Royal Commission of Ancient and Historic Monuments Wales sent one man down to Six Bells to try to salvage plans, ledgers, and photographs, but he arrived in a Mini, so there was a limit to how much he could take. Everything else went down the shaft with the rubble. Alyson said, 'I am sure if you uncapped that shaft and went down there you would find old dressed stone, you would find the manager's leather chair, and all those things.' As a result, the displays at Tŷ Ebbw Fach mainly consist of photographs and wall texts, an approach that is rare among micromuseums, which tend to be object-focused, even object-heavy.

On the whole, though, there were objects in abundance, and, like the accommodation, they were generally provided without charge. When objects had to be bought they were usually purchased collectively, with numerous founding members, volunteers, and supporters chipping in.

Doing the work

The labour required to set up micromuseums was also generally unpaid, or at least was not paid by the museum. A large proportion of the people who initially launched museums were volunteers, working in their spare time. Some were retired and had the free time to dedicate to setting up museums, although many balanced their museum work alongside paid employment. They worked in their lunch breaks, evenings, weekends, and holidays to repair roofs, replace windows and guttering, install facilities, plaster, decorate, and garden. Geoff Burton at RAF Ingham Heritage Centre said he had learned how to lay bricks. Volunteers at Pewsey Heritage Centre built an education room in its entirety, and even the electrical company that installed the wiring and lights only charged for materials. At Dinting Railway Centre and then at its successor museum, Ingrow Loco, the volunteers did everything for themselves, including the wiring, while the founding group at Nidderdale Museum spent every Thursday evening and weekend designing and building the exhibits. Some volunteers went on to spend decades ensuring the smooth running of the museums that they had worked to establish.

The workforce also came through other routes. During the 1980s the Manpower Services Commission helped set up training programmes as a means of alleviating endemic unemployment, and some small museums applied for and were provided with apprentice builders and tradespeople. Local authorities paid for their buildings to be minimally converted or made sound. In Manchester, the Museum of Transport stipulated that anyone housing a privately owned vehicle on-site must commit to so many hours of voluntary work per year. The Armed Forces provided labour, sending trainees to excavate trenches or lay roads for museums in their area, and existing workforces were drafted in to help establish museums within their own organisation. Just as buildings were repurposed as museums, soldiers,

Figure 4.15 Work in progress at RAF Ingham Heritage Centre

regimental secretaries, company managers, and marketing executives all doubled up as builders, museum curators, collections managers, conservators, tour guides, and assistants. In some cases, they had little choice; in others, they instigated the foundation of the museum, or volunteered to work on it, or both.

Alternatively, people repurposed themselves without their employers' explicit consent; a good example is Purfleet Heritage and Military Centre in Essex. Alan Gosling was the resident caretaker on a post-war estate in Purfleet that had been built on the site of an eighteenth-century army base. The site had included a proof house and five magazines constructed to store gunpowder for the British Army and Navy during the Napoleonic wars. Of these, only one magazine remained, and by the late 1970s it was in a state of near dereliction. The outside of the building was thick with ivy, there was buddleia growing out of the roof, and a spate of vandalism had led to the door being sealed with reinforced concrete. Concerned for its preservation, Alan Gosling, his wife, Sue, and other residents petitioned the council to let them convert it into a museum. They agreed, and Alan and Gil, a fellow caretaker, started to spend much of their time clearing the building. The estates manager lent them professional power tools to help with the project. Alan said, 'Thurrock Council I've got to admit were extremely good to me. I was

Figure 4.16 Purfleet Heritage and Military Centre, Essex

working for them and they knew that some of the working hours I was doing things here. But as long as it didn't interfere with my job, the governors that I had through the years were extremely good, turning a blind eye. So, I've got Thurrock Council to thank for that – well, not just me, everybody.' Alan and Gil used some of their paid time, and their senior managers were either unaware of the situation or, as Alan implied, tacitly allowed them to do so.

As time progressed some of the museums were able to employ paid staff. Notably, though, the governance of the museum generally remained with the volunteers. For instance, Heather Lane, the current director of the Museum of North Craven Life, manages a team of permanent staff, who variously have responsibility for catering, running the café and shop, and for education, exhibitions, and projects. Although it is a part-time and sometimes full-time job, she is a volunteer. Ingrow Loco, also in Yorkshire, pays its front-of-house staff and its cleaners, but training, exhibitions, and management remains in the hands of the volunteers.

The experience of setting up a museum was not identical for everyone. Some founders, particularly women, struggled to find the time to establish or maintain museums. Susan, who co-founded Purfleet Heritage and Military Centre, said that it was hard 'trying to work, and look after family, juggle everything', and Elizabeth Cameron made similar comments. She co-founded the Laidhay Croft Museum and had sole responsibility for issuing tickets, giving guided tours, and otherwise managing the museum. She also had a young family and with her husband ran the family farm, which is where the croft was located. When we asked

Figure 4.17 Elizabeth Cameron outside Laidhay Croft Museum, with family and friends, circa 1972

how she managed, she replied, 'My husband got a big old mirror, which he put on the wall of our house, so from my kitchen sink I could see, ah, there's somebody, and run to meet them – I didn't have to sort of pay attention from the door so much. And that worked perfectly.' Elizabeth's situation became easier when the children were a little bit older and started stepping in to help. She explained that 'one son, Stewart, he used to say, "You can go home now mum, I'll do it", and he could tell the visitors about the croft; he was maybe ten years old'.

A few volunteers left the organisations they had helped found, partly but not entirely as a result of the pressures of time. In the 1970s Tony Lewery was one of a group of four who conceived of and led on the foundation of the North Western Museum of Inland Navigation (later the National Waterways Museum). Although the group managed to secure a large space for the museum at Ellesmere Port, the site was derelict and Tony explained that they held 'weekend work parties, every weekend for a couple of years, actually physically digging out the basin, clearing the mud and then demolishing the roof of the toll-house and repairing that, so that there could be an exhibition in there'. Once the site was functioning they appointed paid staff, but differences in approach began to emerge, particularly about the quantity of boats that were being accepted. Tony said they did not have the

Figure 4.18 National Waterways Museum, June 1976

resources to preserve that number of vessels and many began to fall apart. 'That's one of the reasons I just drifted away: I couldn't bear it really and I had to earn a living.' Tony and his wife, Mary, also had a young family to support, and that was an issue. 'I put in my hours to begin with but really, as time went on, I was doing, for nothing, the sorts of jobs that I ought to be getting paid for, and we weren't very rich, so it was important that I earned a living, rather than spend more and more time on the boat museum.' Having been part of the original founding team of four and having worked intensively to see the museum open, he stepped down.

In terms of the workforce, then, the new museums boom was founded on a wave of voluntary and co-opted labour, family support, favours, and to a lesser extent through employment schemes.

Institutional ethos

There are a few isolated instances where micromuseums had significant start-up funding from government bodies. Tŷ Ebbw Fach was facilitated through grants from the Welsh government's Communities First programme, which attempted to alleviate poverty through regeneration, community development, and tourism. More usually, though, the founders of the new museums gathered their own resources. Experts and non-experts, people from across the class divide, young and old volunteers – all came together around a common interest, pooling their knowledge, skills, and time to found new micromuseums.

The founding groups were well supported by their wider communities. They received a huge amount of in-kind support from any number of organisations and companies. MPs, councillors, local celebrities, and minor aristocracy weighed in and helped the founders secure permissions and accommodation; builders and tradespeople worked for free, providing materials at cost or lending their tools and major pieces to the museums groups; solicitors and secretaries did the paperwork in their spare time; local authorities, regiments, companies, and landowners gave space. Thousands of people and organisations gave objects of all kinds, from steam engines to medals, and taffeta dresses to cribs. In many ways the micromuseums boom was a wonderful history of collaboration and co-operation.

The rising numbers of small independent museums were also a testament to what can be done with relatively few resources. At first sight at least, they were generally low-key operations. They did not require huge financial investment or any kind of official or institutional approval. These new micromuseums were not instigated by local authorities or other major museums, and with only a few very isolated exceptions, they were not core funded by the bodies that are officially responsible for supporting museums in the UK. In principle, anyone could set one up so long as they had access to a space, no matter how modest.

Yet this picture of community activity is a partial one. It is important to recognise that individuals need to have the capacity to volunteer, the financial wherewithal to donate objects, and the contacts and cultural capital to levy support. The pressures of family, juggling workloads, and having to earn a living meant some struggled to find the time to volunteer, or were never able to do so. It was also noticeable that when women were involved in setting up museums they tended to occupy the less visible roles, and that they were more likely to found local history museums, which required a low financial outlay.

Perhaps even more significantly, institutions and organisations support cognate museums. This is partly because the museum may be related to that specific body or site – as is the case with military aviation, regimental, corps, and transport museums. It is also a matter of ethos and perceived fit, whether that is between local history and a local authority, or a castle and a regiment. The same applies in other instances. The museums that focus on Asian religion and the Jewish museums were all supported by the associated temples, gudwaras, and synagogues. Likewise, hospitals and medical associations host medical museums; museums of cricket, golf, football, and rugby are associated with club headquarters or famous pitches; and so on. In all these cases, museum founders were able to build on the existing infrastructure, and there was a wider group of people who were prepared to support a museum financially.

There are instances where museums find accommodation against type, although this is usually when groups buy or rent premises on a commercial basis. For instance, the Scottish Vintage Bus Museum purchased a huge ex-Navy depot in which to operate, and it was able to do so because its previous investment and ventures had been profitable. It is also possible to run museums on a private, commercial basis, as does the Gordon Boswell Romany Museum in Spalding, Leicestershire. Such an approach requires a popular and attractive collection, and in the latter case beautifully painted Romany wagons form the core of the displays. To date, we have not yet encountered a museum being given free accommodation by an unrelated organisation.

To a large extent, the micromuseums boom occurred on the coat-tails of existing institutions. Established institutions and organisations supported micromuseums and founders in their own image, creating self-replicating and normative circuits of value. Conversely, museums that do not relate to specific organisations, companies, or public services will find it harder to leverage support. To put the situation bluntly, established and largely White organisations supported White founders to create museums that were consonant with the funders' values, histories, and aims. This created great opportunities for some, far fewer for others.

Conclusions

The micromuseums boom

Whitehead Railway Museum is in Carrickfergus, a Victorian coastal town some ten miles north east of Belfast. When I visited I was greeted by two of its founding members, Charles Friel, who has written several books on Irish railways, and Mark Kennedy, who was barely into his teens when he first volunteered and is now the curator. They showed me round the site, explaining that the railway was built for day trippers and commuters, and pointing out some of their prized locomotives. As their tour came to an end we were joined by Lisa Adair, the museum manager,

Figure 5.1 Johnny Glendinning, John Friel, and Will Glendinning on the footplate of No. 186 locomotive, Whitehead Railway Museum, Carrickfergus, County Antrim, 1970

and by two other members of that original group, Johnny Glendinning (at one point chair of the Northern Ireland Museums Council) and Tony Ragg, both of whom happened to be in the workshop that day.

The older men were lifelong friends, having joined the Railway Preservation Society of Ireland when it was first founded in 1964, at which point Johnny and Tony were at school together. They were all standing around telling stories, correcting each other's accounts, and teasing one another, when Lisa suggested that they tell me how they met their wives. It transpired that Johnny had married Charles' sister, Mary, and Charles had met and married Johnny's cousin Christine. In 1972 Tony had organised the Three Rivers Railtour, an overnight trip by steam train from Dublin to Waterford and on to Belfast, and Mary invited her friend Ena to help run the dining car. Ena and Tony met, started dating, and were later wed. Seeing my increasing confusion the men promised that there would be no test on which members of the group were related by marriage. Lisa said, 'The railways for these guys – it's life.' The conversation showed how bonds of friendship and marriage connected the group. They shared far more than an interest in railways.

I was told a less complicated but similarly resonant story at the Museum of North Craven Life in Settle. Anne Read, who had co-founded the museum in 1977, and who had stayed in post as the honorary curator until 2019, was leaving. Her successor, Heather Lane, commented that a large group of volunteers had also

Figure 5.2 Ena Ragg and friends, Whitehead Railway Museum, Carrickfergus, 1972

Figure 5.3 Civic Society and trustees of Museum of North Craven Life, North Yorkshire, 1 January 1977

chosen that moment to go. Was there a problem, I asked; was her leaving contentious? 'No,' Heather replied, 'but they all had all started together and most of them are in their eighties now and for some of them it was Anne's museum.' They had been young women when they set out to open a museum and had volunteered for over forty years. It is hard to overstate how close some of these founding groups were, how long they worked together, and the degree to which the museums were a collective endeavour.

For this final chapter I return to my original questions and make some concluding remarks about why the founders initially wanted to open museums and the factors that enabled them to do so, pointing to some commonalities in their experience. I reassess Raphael Samuel's claims about popular engagement and unofficial histories, and close by thinking about the museums' future prospects.

Communities of change

By now, it should be clear that there were multiple reasons why founders wanted to open museums. Individuals and groups may each have had several key motivations, none of them mutually exclusive.

In some cases, museum founders wanted to preserve objects, although what these things signified varied. Some wanted to preserve specific types of object, especially vehicles. They were extremely knowledgeable about the history of each item, and took a great deal of pleasure in its aesthetic or technical specificity, and in the process of its restoration. The founders of local history museums also wanted to preserve artefacts, not because they were important in themselves so much as for their capacity to embody a person, place, or way of life.

A few founders realised that there were gaps in museum coverage and that certain things had no obvious home: wooden, horse-drawn narrowboats and shipwrecks fall into this category. Here, the concern was for the historical record. Other people wanted to open a museum irrespective of the subject-matter or the objects it contained. They thought that every town should have a museum, or they saw it as an amenity for local residents and tourists – a cheap day out when the weather was wet. Alternatively, founders were motivated by the desire to maintain or enliven a community, especially in areas that have been hard hit by de-industrialisation. They regularly commented on the wish to keep a town alive, and for the museum to form a community hub. Or they envisaged museums as a way of raising money for an area, usually by attracting tourists to the town or village as a whole. It was very rare to find museums established as a means of generating income for an individual, and that only occurred in privately owned museums. It was also comparatively rare for people to cite education as a reason for founding a museum, whereas within professional museum circuits this is generally taken as a given, if not their principal purpose.

Remembrance, duty, and supporting bereaved families were all recurrent motivations for founding museums, especially but not exclusively museums of war and conflict. For instance, the Tŷ Ebbw Fach Heritage Centre was established on the fiftieth anniversary of the Six Bells mining disaster in 1960, in which forty-five men were killed in a pit explosion. And a surprising number of founders opened museums by default. Regimental museums evolved from pre-existing collections, becoming public as the security clearance on buildings changed, making them more accessible to the public; and transport museums grew from preservation groups.

The reasons why founders opened museums were often patterned according to subject-matter. Local history museums were opened as a means of documenting place or developing public services within an area; transport museums tended to be object-focused; and war and conflict museums were generally memorial spaces. But in most cases the museum founders had a variety of motivations. They wanted to remember as well as build supportive neighbourly communities, or to preserve an object as well as provide an attraction. Collecting and setting up museums could be a means to many different ends.

It should also be clear there is no single explanation for the museums boom. It had multiple underpinning factors, including but not limited to the industrialisation of farming, the reorganisation of local authority borders, the nationalisation of the railway and bus services and their subsequent modernisation, the denationalisation of industry and utilities, the breakdown of traditional industrial and rural communities, the growth in road haulage, greater car ownership and the rise of commuting, increases in domestic tourism and in-migration, the end of the Second World War and the downsizing of the Armed Forces, the reorganisation of the regiments, and technological advancement. Some of these factors are diametrically opposed – in some respects the growth of museums was tied to investment in technology and in others a lack of investment in technology, and likewise the boom was linked to both nationalisation and privatisation.

Wealth, health, the welfare state, and stable employment also played a part in the micromuseums boom, as did peace. After decades of economic struggle and war, the 1950s saw the beginning of an age of affluence in the UK. In the years that followed there was a substantial rise in people's incomes and purchasing power, with many more people being able to buy their own homes and having a substantially higher disposable income.[1] Although affluence varied depending on location, age, and class, and while it did not continuously increase over the decades, broadly speaking the generation who were opening micromuseums during the 1970s and 1980s were relatively comfortably off. They also worked shorter hours than their parents and grandparents, had longer holidays, and lived longer. They could comfortably retire and still engage in other projects, including setting up and running museums. And they could generally do so without fear of attack. It is noticeable that micromuseums have not proliferated to the same extent in Northern Ireland as in England, Scotland, and Wales, and those that have opened did so largely after the ceasefire in 1994.

Yet despite the heterogeneity of circumstances that enabled the foundation of museums, and the range of subjects they covered, we detected three points of commonality. First, even when their titles may suggest otherwise, micromuseums tend to focus on particular histories and not on overarching categories: steam locomotives and not on the carriages they pulled, or vice versa, or on buses from northwest England, or commercial vehicles produced by British Leyland. They tell the story of a railway, a regiment, or a squadron, a specific airfield, or an event, or they document the history of a single valley, village, or parish. Micromuseums generally bear witness to an interest in the local and the specific, rather than the so-called universal. The boom was driven by a care for the particular: this place, this object, these skills, and these people.

Second, almost all the museums we visited were motivated by some kind of change. What that change was and how museums were construed as a response to it varied, but nonetheless the new wave of small independent museums was a means of managing considerable social and economic upheaval. In salvaging objects, recording histories, or fostering communities of interest, the founders variously hoped to establish a degree of continuity across the generations and within the area as it had been and was now, to retain what was valuable, to mitigate loss, and sometimes to resist or at least protest those alterations. Setting up museums gave the founders a sense of agency with respect to the changes that they had lived through and the consequences for the environment, employment, housing, inter-generational contact, inter-faith contact, social interaction, and happiness.

Third, the museums helped to maintain or establish community. This manifested in several different ways. Many of the founders worked late nights and their weekends to get museums up and running, enjoyed the sense of collaboration, and often made lasting friendships in the course of doing so. That work embedded them within a museum community and within the wider community, whether that was of the place, or a special interest group, or an organisation. They also provided amenities for others. Among other things, the museums were meeting places, man sheds, somewhere for families to visit on a rainy day, depositories for the community's objects, and memorials.

And making museums showed that the founders cared for that community, whatever it might be. The town might have been emptied out or become swamped with tourists and incomers, the regiment might have been amalgamated into a larger unit, factories might have closed, or transport links might have been cut, but in setting up a museum people demonstrated responsibility, civic or organisational pride, and a willingness to work for the common good, as they saw it. Whatever had changed for that group, setting up the museum – working together – demonstrated that community did still exist.

Official and unofficial histories

Raphael Samuel celebrated the growing numbers of small independent museums in the UK, attributing it to ordinary people's engagement in history-making, and not to professional historians or people with specialised training. Making a related point, he maintained that micromuseums were a form of unofficial history. Here, Samuel was not so much talking about exhibition content; rather, he was making a distinction between the new small independent museums and those that received core funding from the government.

To some degree, the micromuseums boom can be construed exactly as Raphael Samuel suggested. Thousands of people set up their own museums. They saw that the objects they cared about and the stories and histories they valued were not being represented in major institutions, or at least not in the ways they recognised, and they decided to rectify that situation. Or they thought their village, town, or area would benefit from a museum and went ahead with founding one. These new micromuseums undoubtedly marked a change in who opened museums. The founders were often real specialists on the subject to hand, either through experience of living in a particular area, or working for a particular organisation or industry, or both. Many pursued their own studies and research to further develop their knowledge, but very few were museum professionals or academic experts. And the founding groups were also very mixed with respect to class and age.

As such, micromuseums were evidence of popular engagement in history and of the democratisation of museum-making. As Eileen Burgess, who co-founded Nidderdale Museum, said, 'We set up ordinary museums, about ordinary people, and for ordinary people'; and that was an extraordinary and radical achievement. In many ways this was undoubtedly a popular engagement in history: history being told from below. None of these museums were made by or for an elite.

There are, however, some substantial caveats to this account. While people from across the social strata worked together in pursuit of a common interest, and teenagers were given opportunities that would more usually be outside their orbit, micromuseums were far less mixed in terms of gender. Although it was common to find women leading on the foundation or management of local history museums, they rarely had comparable roles in establishing museums of war and conflict or transport. And the new museums were even more segregated in terms of the founders' ethnicities. The micromuseums boom was evidence of popular engagement in history, but generally of White engagement in White histories.

Raphael Samuel also celebrated micromuseums as a form of unofficial history-making, and indeed the founders did establish museums without much or any official sanction. They simply went ahead, co-opted spaces, collected artefacts, and opened exhibitions that embodied their concerns, priorities, and values; these projects were not ratified by funding bodies or museum professionals. To that degree, the new micromuseums were an example of unofficial history-making.

Once again, though, some caution is required. Although usually established by non-professionals, many micromuseums still functioned in an official capacity insofar as they represented or publicised an institution. The Army historically supported regimental museums because they were viewed as having a useful role in recruitment, especially in areas such as Cornwall, where there was little or no Army presence. Local history museums are understood to improve, represent, and advocate for their area, while others represent the values, accomplishments, and aims of companies, the Church and other faith groups, not to mention guilds, the police, prison, emergency services, hospitals, and the landed gentry. While micromuseums are independent insofar as they have no core funding from the state, they are not necessarily independent with respect to other institutions.

The notion of micromuseums being a form of unofficial history is also complicated by their connections to major museums and to professional museum bodies. Regimental museums benefit from the input and oversight of both the National Army Museum and the Army Museums Ogilby Trust, while in England and Wales some micromuseums are supported by the Museums Development Network, which has a role in enabling micromuseums to reach professional standards. Major museums also helped their smaller counterparts. Some gave objects on long-term loan. The Jacobs locomotive that was on show at the Dinting Railway Centre belonged to Beamish: Museum of the North, while others gave redundant equipment. The Museum of Rail Travel in Keighley only properly opened to the public when the National Rail Museum gave them a set of raised platforms enabling visitors to walk alongside the collection of carriages rather than being at eye level with their wheels. In short, there was not and is not a strict divide between micro and major museums.

And, perhaps most importantly, organisations change. Although the founders may have initially begged for and borrowed venues, labour, and artefacts, some of these tiny ventures later established themselves on more formal terms, applied for and gained Museum Accreditation, which recognises that they have met professional standards, and began to employ paid staff. The National Waterways Museum began with a conversation around a pub table and its foundation was due to the work of hundreds of volunteers, but it quickly appointed a paid director and other members of staff and went on to attract around 70,000 visitors a year.

In a few cases, museums that were set up within the community are used instrumentally to achieve ends endorsed by national governments and the European Union. Early in the twenty-first century, major funding was made available to boost tourism and economic development in Northern Ireland, and this enabled both the Museum of Free Derry and the Siege Museum, which tells the story of the Apprentice Boys of Derry/Londonderry, to build new purpose-designed accommodation. While these museums are not official in the sense of being established by a professional curator, and indeed the Museum of Free Derry tells a history that has been extremely uncomfortable for the British Army and government, they are strategically funded to achieve particular ends. Their role in regeneration, community building, and boosting the tourist economy is endorsed at the highest levels of state power, although, as the history of the Asian Music Circuit Museum makes clear, that support can be abruptly withdrawn.

The notion of micromuseums being a form of unofficial history is problematic in that many micromuseums advocate for and were supported by established institutions, work with major museums, gradually professionalise, and are instrumentalised. They can be unofficial entities, but they can equally be a manifestation of existing interests. Indeed, the notion of micromuseums as necessarily part of an unofficial history, or as being ad hoc, amateur, or do-it-yourself, can obscure the considerable institutional support and the social networks that often underwrite their foundation.

It is important to recognise that the official and unofficial intersect in complex and varied ways. In this context, celebrating micromuseums as evidence of bottom-up activity, history from below, or unofficial history is too easy and potentially reductive because it ignores the way that different types of knowledge, training, and expertise exist alongside each other, sometimes harmoniously and sometimes in tension. Equally, it overlooks the ways in which community action can function in tandem with council, corporate, and government interests. Thus, instead of thinking in terms of official as opposed to unofficial histories, it is necessary to ask precisely how official and unofficial interests intersect, to what ends, and with what outcomes.

Into the future

The late-twentieth-century heritage debates generally conceived of the museums boom as an over-preoccupation with the past at the expense of the present. In our experience, the founders of micromuseums were generally looking forwards: they wanted to transport particular objects, histories, and values into the future for the use and pleasure of generations to come. The museum operated as a time machine, not so much in that it transported audiences back to previous eras, but because it brought fragments of the past into the present and future.

These suppositions rely on a great deal of faith. The museum is envisaged as preserving objects and histories for posterity, and it is assumed that future generations will find value in its contents. Micromuseums run by special interest and community groups do have fairly low levels of closure (with museums of rural life proving something of an exception), but there is a question as to whether or not that will continue to be the case. Some of the museums we visited had prospered and grown over the years. In 2017 Whitehead Railway Museum opened new galleries, a new interpretative centre, a machine workshop for restoration work, and

Figure 5.4 Whitehead Railway Museum

Figure 5.5 Museum of North Craven Life

a sixty-foot locomotive turntable, while in Settle, Heather had raised around £250,000 for restoration work on the Grade II listed building and to completely rehang the galleries. They and other small museums are changing, growing, and all set to carry on.

Many of the museums we visited were also weathering the COVID pandemic reasonably well. This book was written between 2020 and 2022, and there were often long periods when museums were temporarily closed. We conducted some additional interviews during a break between lockdowns and all the staff we spoke to reported that they were coping. Unlike larger independent museums that have teams of paid staff, their running costs were low, the financial shortfall was small, and volunteers were generally keen to return to work, not least because the museum was the source of considerable social interaction. At the time of writing, very few micromuseums have closed due to the impact of the pandemic.

Yet there are undoubtedly obstacles ahead. Property prices have risen relative to average wages and it is harder for would-be founders to purchase suitable accommodation. Local authorities have been subject to over a decade of budget cuts and some have decided to start charging their tenants commercial rates.[2] The Maritime Museum in Walton-on-the-Naze in Essex closed in 2020 after Tendring District Council increased their rent on the historic lifeboat station that they occupied, and it is entirely possible that the same will happen elsewhere. It is also common for micromuseums to be staffed by elderly volunteers. The founders and volunteers who opened museums in the 1970s and 1980s are now past retirement age, and while some have managed to involve new people, succession is a cause for concern.[3] The difficulty here is that younger generations do not necessarily have the same emotional connection to the histories on display or share the same interests. They are also retiring later, have more caring responsibilities, and do not have the same amount of free time as their predecessors.[4] In some respects, then, it is likely that some or even many micromuseums will close. This does not necessarily mean that they have failed; rather, those museums served a purpose that was important and necessary to the founders, volunteers, and audiences and which then came to an end. Arguably, museums do not have to go on forever.

It is easy to take the plethora of local history museums, railway museums, and war and conflict museums for granted. Some of the micromuseums that were founded in the 1970s and 1980s can now look tired or slightly dull to twentieth-century eyes. Nonetheless, it is important to remember that the micromuseums boom was a radical process. Ordinary people were not simply participants at organised events, far less an audience. Rather, they drew together the resources at their disposal and were the instigators and creators of history-making and museum-making. They interrupted and changed the established museum sector, interposing their concerns and experience, and insisting on the validity of their histories.

Despite the challenges, micromuseums are still opening. Some of these museums address different subject-matter from those of their predecessors and indeed are often responding to the gaps in coverage. They include the East End Women's Museum, the Vagina Museum, and the Museum of Neo-Liberalism. They also take different forms. The Museum of Transology and the Museum of Homelessness both exist as a series of linked exhibitions and events, as does the Museum of Ordinary People, which in many ways encapsulates the intent of so many of its predecessor organisations. The Museum of British Colonialism conducts important archaeological research and produces films that are made available online, while the Museum of Portable Sound exists only as a mobile phone, and visiting the museum is akin to participating in a performance. By creating project-based or online museums, the founders circumvent some of the difficulties and indeed limitations of permanent collections-based museums. The Black British Museum is in the planning stages, as is the Somali Museum.

Like their predecessors, these founders have all questioned and challenged the form of a museum, of what it should contain or represent, and of who can articulate their concerns. The micromuseums boom changed the sector, but the story has not yet ended.

Appendix

List of interviews

Between 2018 and 2019, Toby Butler (TB) conducted interviews with fifty-seven people who were involved in founding over forty museums. Fiona Candlin (FC) conducted follow-up interviews at many of those venues and a further twenty-one interviews at additional museums between 2019 and 2022. Both also conducted interviews with subject specialists.

The interviews listed below are those that are quoted from or whose content is directly referenced within the book. The roles mentioned are those pertinent to the subject of the interview and in some cases are historical. Current post-holders have been specified where necessary for disambiguation.

Unless otherwise specified, the transcripts of the interviews are available on the Mapping Museums website, as are those that we did not directly reference but which informed the study as a whole. The transcripts and the audio recordings are held in the Mapping Museums Oral History Archive at the Bishopsgate Institute, London.

Adjutant General's Corps Museum
Col. Tony Figg, head of Army heritage, Ministry of Defence (2005–14), and co-founder. Interviewer TB 05/12/18.

Aldbourne Heritage Centre
Terry Gilligan, Alan Heasman, John Dymond – trustees and co-founders. Interviewers TB 21/11/18; FC 15/10/20.

Asian Music Circuit Museum
Viram Jasani, founder and director. Interviewer FC 06/01/22.

Black British Museum
Sandra Shakespeare, founder and director. Interviewer FC 03/06/21 (not archived, on request).

174

Black Watch Museum
Col. Hon. David Arbuthnott, regimental secretary. Interviewer FC 05/09/20.
Ronnie Proctor, assistant to regimental secretary. Interviewer FC 24/09/20.

British Commercial Vehicle Museum
John Gilchrist, chair of the trustees, British Commercial Vehicle Museum Trust. Interviewers TB 13/12/19; FC 16/12/19.

Brynmawr and District Museum
Vivienne Williams, company secretary; Sandra Plaister, director; Alan Williams, curator – co-founders. Interviewers TB 07/03/19; FC 21/10/20.

Charlestown Shipwreck and Heritage Centre
Richard Larn, co-founder. Interviewer TB 13/03/19.

Criterion Heritage Centre
Jenny Hurkett, founder and manager. Interviewers TB 19/10/18; FC 16/10/20.

Ebbw Vale Works Museum
Mel Warrender, founder and chair, Ebbw Vale Works Archival Trust. Interviewer TB 07/03/19.

Gairloch Heritage Museum
Roy Macintyre, chair of trustees; Karen Buchanan, curator. Interviewers TB 26/06/19; FC 22/09/20.

HorsePower: The Museum of the King's Royal Hussars
Patrick Beresford, regimental secretary and honorary curator. Interviewer TB 05/12/18.

Ingrow Loco
Keith Whitmore, chair, Bahamas Locomotive Society; Matt Arnold, museum assistant. Interviewer TB 16/12/18.
Steve Allsop, co-founder. Interviewer FC 01/12/19.

Kent and Sharpshooters Yeomanry Museum
Guy Farage, co-founder and chair; Daniel Taylor, curator. Interviewer TB 29/10/18.

Appendix: list of interviews

King Edward Mine Museum
Tony Brooks, founder and chair. Interviewer TB 15/03/19.

Laidhay Croft Museum
Elizabeth Cameron, co-founder, museum manager, and secretary of Laidhay Preservation Trust. Interviewers TB 17/05/19; FC 20/09/20.

Metheringham Airfield Visitor Centre
Andy Marson, committee member from 2006 and chair 2012–16; Rod Sanders, chair. Interviewers TB 04/02/18; FC 29/09/20.

Micro Museum
Carol and Mike Dear, founders. Interviewer TB 05/11/18.

Museum of Free Derry
Adrian Kerr, founder and curator. Interviewer FC 14/06/21.

Museum of North Craven Life
Anne Read, co-founder and curator. Interviewer TB 17/12/18.
Anne Read and Heather Lane, curator. Interviewer FC 28/08/20.

Museum of Rail Travel
Chris Smyth, chair, Vintage Carriages Trust; Trevor England, chair. Interviewers TB 17/12/18; FC 01/12/19.

Museum of Transport, Greater Manchester
Paul Williams, volunteer. Interviewer FC 10/03/21.

National Waterways Museum
Tony Lewery, co-founder. Interviewer TB 13/05/19.

Nidderdale Museum
Eileen Burgess, secretary; Joanna Moody, secretary. Interviewers TB 14/12/18; FC 26/08/20.

Peace Museum
Peter van Dungen, co-founder. Interviewer FC 28/09/20.
Gerald Drewett, co-founder and trustee. Interviewer FC 11/11/20.

Perranzabuloe Museum

Chris Easton, co-founder and trustee; Linda Higgins co-founder, chair, and trustee. Interviewers TB and Jake Watts 14/03/19.

Pewsey Heritage Centre

Paul Cowan, founder and chair. Interviewer TB 21/11/18.

Purfleet Heritage and Military Centre

Susan Gosling, co-founder. Interviewer TB 07/02/19.
Alan Gosling, co-founder; Susan Gosling, co-founder; John Jones, Len Milledge, Brenda Williams, Julie Stonehouse – volunteers. Interviewers TB and FC 05/09/19.

RAF Ingham Heritage Centre

Geoff Burton, founder and chair. Interviewers TB 06/02/19; FC 29/09/20.

Romany Gypsy Museum (Selborne)

Peter Ingham, founder and owner. Interviewer FC 04/01/22 (not archived, on request).

Royal Irish Fusiliers Museum

Caroline Corvan, curator. Interviewer FC 12/06/21.

Scottish Vintage Bus Museum

Jasper Pettie, founder, secretary, and treasurer. Interviewers TB 21/05/19; FC 13/12/19.

Shipwreck Museum

Peter Marsden, founder. Interviewer TB 15/03/19.

Suffolk Regiment Museum

Tony Calder, chair; Claire Wallace, curator; Tony Slater, secretary and trustee. Interviewer FC 01/10/20.

Tŷ Ebbw Fach Heritage Centre

Alyson Tippings, destination management officer, Blaenau Gwent Council. Interviewer TB 06/03/19.
Lucy Harding, volunteer. Interviewer FC 21/10/20.

Whitehead Railway Museum

Charles Friel, founder member; Mark Kennedy, curator; Peter Scott, director and founder member; Johnny Glendinning, founder member; Lisa Adair, general manager; Tony Ragg, founder member. Interviewer FC 09/06/21.

Interviews with specialists

Frank Olding, heritage officer, Blaenau Gwent Council. Interviewer TB 07/03/19.

David Harrigan, manager, Aviation Heritage Lincolnshire. Interviewer TB 05/02/19.

Julian Farrance, Regimental and Corps Museum liaison officer; Kelsey Loveless, assistant Regimental and Corps Museum liaison officer – National Army Museum. Interviewers FC and Jake Watts 06/02/19 (not archived).

Interview material conducted by people external to the research team has been referenced within the text.

Notes

Introduction

1 Patrick Cook, owner and founder of the Bakelite Museum, Somerset. Unpublished interview with Fiona Candlin as part of unpublished DIY Museums research (which predated the Mapping Museums project), 16/07/2015. The Bakelite Museum closed in 2018. The Mapping Museums team made a short film about its closure, which is available at: https://vimeo.com/375988349. Accessed 04/10/21.

2 Kenneth Hudson suggested that three quarters of the museums in Europe were small, although he defined this as having fewer than ten members of staff, which is large in comparison to the museums we discuss. Ron Chew notes that there is no consistent definition of what counts as a small museum but also thinks that 75% of museums in the USA could be considered small. Ron Chew, 'In Praise of the Small Museum', *Museum News*, March/April (2002). On museums in the USA and Europe see: Kenneth Hudson, 'The Museum Refuses to Stand Still', in *Museum Studies: An Anthology of Contexts*, ed. Bettina Messias Carbonell (Malden, MA: Blackwell, 2004), 85–91.

3 For more information on the Bakelite Museum see: Simon Tait, *Palaces of Discovery: The Changing World of Britain's Museums* (Stroud: Quiller Press, 1989), 55–7.

4 On the omission of provincial museums from Museum Studies see: Lianne McTavish, *Defining the Modern Museum: A Case Study of the Challenges of Exchange* (Toronto: University of Toronto, 2014); Kate Hill, *Culture and Class in English Public Museums, 1850–1914* (Aldershot and Burlington, VT: Ashgate, 2005).

5 This work was published as Fiona Candlin, *Micromuseology: An Analysis of Small Independent Museums* (London: Bloomsbury, 2016).

6 For a discussion of surveys, coverage, and the impact of the accreditation process on accounts of the museum sector see: Fiona Candlin et al., 'The Missing Museums: Accreditation, Surveys, and an Alternative Account of the UK Sector', *Cultural Trends* 29, no. 1 (2019): 50–67.

7 The team consisted of myself as principal investigator; Alexandra Poulovassilis as co-investigator; Andrea Ballatore, lecturer in data science, who led on mapping and data integration; Jamie Larkin as researcher with responsibility for data collection; Nick Larson was the computer science researcher and worked on programming; he was followed by Val Katerinchuk; Mark Liebenrood joined the team to help with data entry and, after Jamie left, kept the data updated. For a discussion of how the database was

designed see: Alexandra Poulovassilis et al., 'Creating a Knowledge Base to Research the History of UK Museums through Rapid Application Development', *Journal on Computing and Cultural Heritage* 12, no. 4 (2019): 30:1–30:27. On how we collected data and managed patchy data see: Fiona Candlin and Alexandra Poulovassilis, 'Understanding and Managing Patchy Data in the UK Museum Sector', *Museum Management and Curatorship* 35, no. 4 (2019): 446–59.

8 The database, report, links to publications, and other resources are available via the project website: https://museweb.dcs.bbk.ac.uk/home. Accessed 31/01/22.

9 For a full report on findings see: Fiona Candlin et al., 'Mapping Museums 1960–2020: A Report on the Data' (London: Birkbeck, University of London, March 2020).

10 In later years many local authorities devolved the management of their museums to independent groups. We continued to log those museums as 'local authority' so as not to distort the historical picture. If devolved museums are included in the statistics then there is an even greater shift towards independence.

11 For the definitions and a discussion of their variations see: 'Defining Museums': http://blogs.bbk.ac.uk/mapping-museums/2017/10/30/defining-museums/. Accessed 31/01/22.

12 Vincent Noce, 'What Exactly Is a Museum? ICOM Comes to Blows over New Definition', *The Art Newspaper*, 19/08/19: www.theartnewspaper.com/2019/08/19/what-exactly-is-a-museum-icom-comes-to-blows-over-new-definition. Accessed 27/01/22.

13 On the problems with definitions with regards to museum practice in the Global South see: Bruno Soares Brulon, 'Museum in Colonial Contexts: The Politics of Defining an Imported Definition', in *Defining Museums of the 21st Century: Plural Experiences*, eds Bruno Soares Brulon, Karen Brown, and Olga Nazor (Paris: ICOM International Committee for Museology, 2018), 163–8. On other approaches to definition see: Karen Brown and François Mairesse, 'The Definition of the Museum through Its Social Role', *Curator: The Museum Journal* 61, no. 4 (2018): 525–39; Victor Ginsburch and François Mairesse, 'Defining a Museum: Suggestions for an Alternative Approach', *Museum Management and Curatorship* 16, no. 1 (1 January 1997): 15–33.

14 For a detailed discussion of how our definitions of museums were formulated see: Fiona Candlin and Jamie Larkin, 'What Is a Museum? Difference All the Way Down', *Museums and Society* 18, no. 2 (2020): 115–31.

15 Anna Woodham, 'Museum Studies and Heritage: Independent Museums and the Heritage Debate in the UK', in *A Museum Studies Approach to Heritage*, eds Sheila Watson, Amy Barnes, and Katy Bunning, 1st edn (London: Routledge, 2018), 29–43. Examples of the heritage debates being situated as a baseline for discussion include: Iain J. M. Robertson, 'Heritage from Below: Class, Social Protest and Resistance', in *The Public History Reader*, eds Hilda Kean and Paul Martin (London and New York: Routledge, 2013), 56–67; Robert Lumley, 'The Debate on Heritage Reviewed', in *Heritage, Museums and Galleries: An Introductory Reader*, ed. Gerard Corsane (London: Routledge, 2005), 15–25; Laurajane Smith, *Uses of Heritage* (London and New York: Routledge, 2006), 39–42.

16 For a useful discussion of productive nostalgia see: Laurajane Smith and Gary Campbell, '"Nostalgia for the Future": Memory, Nostalgia and the Politics of Class', *International Journal of Heritage Studies* 23 (2017): 612–27. On rethinking aspects of the heritage debates see: Lara Rutherford-Morrison, 'Playing Victorian', *The Public Historian* 37, no. 3 (01/08/15): 76–101.

17 Robert Hewison, *The Heritage Industry: Britain in a Climate of Decline* (London: Methuen, 1987), 9, 91. The journalist Neal Ascherson followed similar themes in a series of articles. Neal Ascherson, 'A Society That Falls Back on Miming the Creation of Its Wealth Is Sick', *Independent on Sunday*, 19/02/95; Neal Ascherson, 'Why "Heritage" Is Right-Wing', *Observer*, 08/11/87; Neal Ascherson, 'What Should We Preserve?', *Independent*, 16/10/93; Neal Ascherson, 'Reminders from the Past to Suspend Our Disbelief', *Independent*, 26/04/92. See also Paul Reas and Stuart Cosgrove, *Flogging a Dead Horse: Heritage Culture and Its Role in Post-Industrial Britain* (Manchester: Cornerhouse, 1993).

18 John Urry, *The Tourist Gaze*, 2nd edn (London: Sage, 2001), 97

19 Bob West, 'The Making of the English Working Past: A Critical View of the Ironbridge Gorge Museum', in *The Museum Time-Machine: Putting Cultures on Display*, ed. Robert Lumley (London and New York: Routledge, 1988), 35–62. Bella Dicks, *Heritage, Place and Community* (Cardiff: University of Wales Press, 2000).

20 Raphael Samuel, *Theatres of Memory* (London: Verso, 1994).

21 John Corner and Sylvia Harvey, 'Mediating Tradition and Modernity', in *Enterprise and Heritage: Crosscurrents of National Culture,* eds John Corner and Sylvia Harvey (London and New York: Routledge, 1991), 49–75.

22 Gordon Fyfe, 'Sociology and the Social Aspects of Museums', in *A Companion to Museum Studies*, ed. Sharon Macdonald (Chichester: Wiley-Blackwell, 2011), 33–49.

23 Patrick Wright, *On Living in an Old Country: The National Past in Contemporary Britain* (Oxford: Oxford University Press, 2009).

24 A thoughtful and detailed discussion of museum type and distribution in the UK was provided by David Prince and Bernadette Higgins-McLoughlin, *Museums UK: The Findings of the Museums Data-Base Project* (London: Museums Association, 1987).

25 Robert Lumley, *The Museum Time-Machine: Putting Cultures on Display*, Comedia Book (London and New York: Routledge, 1988), 1. Robert Hewison, 'Commerce and Culture', in *Enterprise and Heritage: Crosscurrents of National Culture*, eds John Corner and Sylvia Harvey (London and New York: Routledge, 1991), 162–77. Ascherson, 'Why "Heritage" Is Right-Wing'. All mentioned that a new museum opened every fortnight. A new museum opened every week according to Hewison, *The Heritage Industry*, 9. And three museums opened each week according to Patrick Boylan, 'The Museum Professions', in *A Companion to Museum Studies*, ed. Sharon Macdonald (Malden, MA and Oxford: Blackwell, 2006), 415–30.

26 In 1960 the North West and North East accounted for 15.6% of England's museums, the South East and South West for 36.2%. In 2017, the North West and North East accounted for 13.9% of England's museums, the South East and South West for 36.23%.

27 Samuel, *Theatres of Memory*, 8. Samuel also included the 'under-labourers' in his category of unofficial history – that is, the unacknowledged assistants, archivists, cataloguers, and librarians, as well as the wives who typed manuscripts and who contributed to final, official publications.

28 Samuel, *Theatres of Memory*, 27.

29 Raphael Samuel, 'Theme Parks – Why Not? History Is Everybody's', *Independent on Sunday*, 12/02/95. Samuel aligned the new wave of independent museums with heritage, which he read as being a mass rather than an elite activity. Raphael Samuel, 'Flogging a Dead Horse', in *Theatres of Memory*, 259–314.

30 Cultural capital was originally taken to refer to high-art cultures; it has been largely replaced by the notion of the cultural omnivore – someone who can move across high

and popular cultures. Richard Peterson and Roger Kern, 'Changing "Highbrow" Taste: From Snob to Omnivore', *American Sociological Review* 61, no. 5 (1996): 900–7.

31 Patrick Wright, 'Appendix to the Oxford Edition: Sneering at the Theme Parks: An Encounter with the Heritage Industry', in *On Living in an Old Country: The National Past in Contemporary Britain*, updated edn (Oxford: Oxford University Press, 1989), 238–56. There is a single interview with Robert Opie, who opened the Museum of Brands and Packaging, and an autobiography by Frank Atkinson, who led on the foundation of Beamish: Museum of the North, but not much else. John Elsner and Roger Cardinal, '"Unless You Do These Crazy Things…" An Interview with Robert Opie', in *The Cultures of Collecting*, eds John Elsner and Roger Cardinal (London: Reaktion, 1994), 25–48. Frank Atkinson, *The Man Who Made Beamish: An Autobiography* (Gateshead: Northern Books, 1999).

32 Smith, *Uses of Heritage*, 37.

33 Laurajane Smith, Paul A. Shackel, and Gary Campbell, eds, *Heritage, Labour, and the Working Classes* (London: Routledge, 2011).

34 Andrew Miles and Lisanne Gibson, 'Everyday Participation and Cultural Value', *Cultural Trends* 25, no. 3 (2016): 151–7. By way of clarification, it may be useful to note that the structures for museum funding in the UK are extremely complex. Broadly, the Department for Digital, Culture, Media and Sport (DCMS), which is a department in central government, funds national museums in England and provides funding for Arts Council England, which then distributes grants according to its various portfolios and schemes. These go to organisations of all sizes and types, although museums generally have to be accredited to qualify, and they do not provide core funding to local authority museums. Civic museums are supported by the local city or county council or unified authority, depending on the local administrative structure, which is in turn funded by central government. Central government also allocates funding to the devolved nations, and Northern Ireland, Scotland, and Wales have their own bodies with responsibility for museums.

35 Mark Taylor, 'Nonparticipation or Different Styles of Participation? Alternative Interpretations from Taking Part', *Cultural Trends* 25, no. 3 (02/07/16): 169–81.

36 There are two special journal issues detailing outcomes from the research. Andrew Miles and Lisanne Gibson, 'Everyday Participation and Cultural Value: Special Issue', *Cultural Trends* 25, no. 3 (2016). Andrew Miles and Lisanne Gibson, 'Everyday Participation and Cultural Value in Place: Special Issue', *Cultural Trends* 26, no. 1 (March 2017).

37 Candlin, *Micromuseology*. Popular publications also present micromuseums as an alternative to major institutions. Robin Halstead et al., *Bollocks to Alton Towers: Uncommonly British Days Out* (London: Penguin, 2006). Hunter Davies, *Behind the Scenes at the Museum of Baked Beans: My Search for Britain's Maddest Museums* (London: Virgin Books, 2010). 'Orhan Pamuk's Manifesto for Museums', *The Art Newspaper* – international art news and events (05/07/16): www.theartnewspaper. com/2016/07/06/orhan-pamuks-manifesto-for-museums. Accessed 17/05/19.

38 Helen Gregory and Kirsty Robinson, 'No Small Matter: Micromuseums as Critical Institutions', *Canadian Art Review* 43, no. 2 (2018): 89–101. On academic conceptualisation of micromuseums as removed from government policy and public funding see also: Tammy Stone-Gordon, *Private History in Public: Exhibition and the Settings of Everyday Life* (Lanham, MD: AltaMira Press, 2010). And as eccentric see: Hilde S. Hein, *The Museum in Transition: A Philosophical Perspective* (Washington, DC and London:

Smithsonian Institution Press, 2000), 18. One of the few texts to question the amateur/ professional distinction that lies at the heart of the official/unofficial binary is Mariona Moncunill-Pinas, 'Museum-Making as Serious Leisure', *Digithum*, no. 17 (2015), 20–7.

39 The literature that positions museums in relation to popular activity includes Richard Daniel Altick, *The Shows of London* (Cambridge, MA: Belknap Press of Harvard University Press, 1978); Alison Griffiths, *Shivers down Your Spine: Cinema, Museums, and the Immersive View* (New York and Chichester: Columbia University Press, 2008); Andrea Stulman Dennett, *Weird and Wonderful: The Dime Museum in America* (New York and London: New York University Press, 1997). See also Fiona Candlin, 'Rehabilitating Unauthorised Touch *or* Why Museum Visitors Touch the Exhibits', *The Senses and Society* 12, no. 3 (2017): 251–66. On how India's subaltern population is notoriously unwilling to follow the museum's script see the wonderfully titled Saloni Mathur and Kavita Singh, eds, *No Touching, No Spitting, No Praying: The Museum in South Asia* (New Delhi: Routledge, 2015).

40 Paul Hazell and Kjetil Fallan interestingly argue that sanctioned and unsanctioned knowledge should be brought together in the study of design classics. Their comments on the highly specialised knowledge of enthusiasts are also relevant to this study, as are their comments on oral histories of enthusiasm. Paul Hazell and Kjetil Fallan, 'The Enthusiast's Eye: The Value of Unsanctioned Knowledge in Design Historical Scholarship', *Design and Culture* 7, no. 1 (01/03/15): 107–23.

41 Elizabeth Crooke, 'An Exploration of the Connections among Museums, Community and Heritage', in *The Ashgate Research Companion to Heritage and Identity*, eds B. J. Graham and Peter Howard (Aldershot: Ashgate, 2008), 31.

42 Crooke has written extensively on notions of community in museums and on projects in community museums. See also: Elizabeth Crooke, 'Museums, Communities and the Politics of Heritage in Northern Ireland', in *Museums and Their Communities*, ed. Sheila Watson (London: Routledge, 2007), 300–12; Elizabeth Crooke, *Museums and Community: Ideas, Issues and Challenges* (London and New York: Routledge, 2007); Lianne McTavish, *Voluntary Detours: Small Town and Rural Museums in Alberta* (Montreal: McGill-Queen's University Press, 2021).

43 Individual histories of micromuseums take several forms. An example of a published history is Eileen Burgess, 'The Making of a Museum', in *Traces of Nidderdale in 40 Years and 40 Objects: Stories of the Museum*, ed. Joanna Moody (Pateley Bridge: Nidderdale Museum Society, 2014), 133–47. An example of an unpublished history is the anonymously authored 'Gairloch Heritage Museum: The Past Twenty-One Years' (Gairloch Museum, 1998).

44 On the opening of historic houses to the public see: Peter Mandler, *The Fall and Rise of the Stately Home* (New Haven, CT and London: Yale University Press, 1997).

45 We chose museums in areas from across the spectrum of classifications used in the Output Area Classification schema. This is a geodemographic classification devised by the Office of National Statistics and it describes small areas in the UK based on the characteristics of the population they contain. For example, areas categorised as 'Urban Elites' areas tend to have younger and more educated residents than average, while 'Multi-Ethnic Suburbs' have more non-White minority residents and more social housing than average.

46 Kate Hill, *Women and Museums, 1850–1914: Modernity and the Gendering of Knowledge* (Manchester: Manchester University Press, 2016). See also: Lianne McTavish, 'Strategic Donations: Women and Museums in New Brunswick, 1862–1930', *Journal of Canadian*

Studies 42, no. 2 (2008): 93–116; Anne Whitelaw, 'Women, Museums and the Problem of Biography', in *Museums and Biographies: Stories, Objects, Identities*, ed. Kate Hill (Woodbridge: Boydell Press, 2012), 75–86.

47 Esther Mann, curator of the Army Music Museum, private communication, 10/02/18.

48 A recording of the seminar held to mark the launch of the Mapping Museums Oral History Archive at Bishopsgate Institute is available at: https://museweb.dcs.bbk.ac.uk/films. Accessed 01/11/21.

49 On selection process and its impact on oral histories see: Carla Pascoe Leahy, 'Selection and Sampling Methodologies in Oral Histories of Mothering, Parenting and Family', *Oral History* 47, no. 1 (2019): 105–16.

50 There are a handful of analyses of individual closed museums. These include: Steven Conn, 'The Birth and Death of a Museum', in *Do Museums Still Need Objects?* (Philadelphia: University of Pennsylvania Press, 2010), 20–57; Steven Lubar et al., eds, 'Special Journal Edition: Lost Museums', *Museum History Journal* 10, no. 1 (2017). For an overview of museum closure in the UK see: Mark Liebenrood, 'Museum Closure in the UK, 1960–2010: Contexts and Microhistories' (London, Birkbeck, University of London, 2022).

51 For a useful discussion of how people tell stories, to whom, and what is at stake in the telling (albeit in a very different context) see: Kenneth Plummer, *Telling Sexual Stories: Power, Change, and Social Worlds* (London and New York: Routledge, 1994).

52 Paul Thompson, *Voices from the Past* (Oxford and New York: Oxford University Press, 1988).

53 Speaking in 1999 Stuart Hall commented: 'the explosion of interest in "history from below", the spread of local and family history, of personal memorabilia and the collections of oral histories – activities witnessed to in, for example, Raphael Samuel's memorable celebration of the "popular heritage", *Theatres of Memory*, – have shifted and democratised our conception of value, of what is and is not worth preserving … However, by and large this process has so far stopped short at the frontier defined by that great unspoken British value – "whiteness".' His talk concentrated on what was and was not collected and represented. My emphasis is on who establishes museums. Stuart Hall, 'Whose Heritage? Unsettling the Heritage: Re-Imagining the Post-Nation', in *The Politics of Heritage: The Legacies of 'Race'*, eds Jo Littler and Roshi Naidoo (Abingdon: Routledge, 2005), 21–31.

54 Prince Frederick Duleep Singh (23/01/1868–15/08/1926) was the second surviving son of Maharajah Duleep Singh, last Maharajah of Punjab, and Maharani Bamba, who was of Abyssinian descent. (With thanks to Melissa Hawker from the Ancient House Museum for this information.) The Ancient House Museum is now a local authority museum.

55 For information on the LYC Museum and Art Gallery see: 'Li Yuan-chia Foundation': www.lycfoundation.org/. Accessed 03/09/20.

56 Natubhai Shah founded the Jain Museum in Leicester in 1980 in a large room that forms part of the temple complex. It consists of a series of tiny dioramas imported from Veerayatan, the Jain Institute, in Bihar, India. These depict stories from the Jain scriptures and were intended as an educational resource. The Guru Nanuk Gudwara Sikh Museum opened as part of the Guru Nanak Dev Ji Gudwara in the same town in 1992. The museum consists of artworks and photographs, a large model of the Golden Temple in Amritsar, which is the pre-eminent spiritual site for Sikhism, and a small collection of weaponry, including throwing spears and kirpan, the holy daggers

traditionally worn by Sikhs. The Neasden Temple Museum in London opened with the building in 1995, although its status now remains unclear. It was closed during the pandemic and at the time of writing there were no plans for it to reopen.

57 For information on the Bloomsbury Jewish Museum, Camden Jewish Museum, Museum of Jewish Life in Manor House, and the Jewish Military Museum in Stamford Hill see: Rickie Burman, *The Jewish Museum, London: Introduction and History* (London: Scala, 2006). The fourth Jewish museum in London, the Memorial Scrolls Trust Museum, opened in Westminster in 1988. For the story of the scrolls acquisition see: Philippa Bernard, *Out of the Midst of the Fire* (London: Westminster Synagogue, 2005). On the foundation of the museum see: https://memorialscrollstrust.org/index. php/our-history/london-new. Accessed 07/01/2022.

58 For a discussion of the Gordon Boswell Romany Museum see: Candlin, *Micromuseology*, 162–3. For more on the South East Romany Museums, see 'A Romany Museum in Marden', BBC Kent: www.bbc.co.uk/kent/voices/museum.shtml. Accessed 23/11/21. There have been a number of other Romany museums in the UK, but they have not usually been founded by Romanys.

59 For a detailed account of the Black Cultural Archives see: Hannah J. M. Ishmael, 'The Development of Black-Led Archives in London' (Ph.D., UCL (University College London), 2020).

60 There are also museums that directly address particular cultures, ethnic groups, or the movement of peoples, such as the Gurkha Museum in Winchester, the Palestinian Museum and Cultural Centre in Bristol, and the Asian Arts Museum in Bath, but their founders were not Gurkhas, Palestinians, or Asians.

61 T. J. Barringer and Tom Flynn, *Colonialism and the Object: Empire, Material Culture and the Museum* (London: Routledge, 1998); Tony Bennett, *Pasts beyond Memory: Evolution, Museums, Colonialism* (London and New York: Routledge, 2004).

62 Sara Wajid and Rachael Minott, 'Detoxing and Decolonising Museums', in *Museum Activism*, eds Robert R. Janes and Richard Sandell (London and New York: Routledge, 2019), 25–35.

63 Fath Davis Ruffins, 'Building Homes for Black History: Museum Founders, Founding Directors, and Pioneers, 1915—95', *The Public Historian* 40 (2018): 13–43.

64 Daniel James, 'Listening in the Cold: The Practice of Oral History in an Argentinian Working-Class Community', in *The Oral History Reader*, eds Robert Perks and Alistair Thomson, 3rd edn (London and New York: Routledge, 2016), 73–91.

65 McTavish, *Voluntary Detours*.

66 Andrew Flinn, 'Archival Activism: Independent and Community-Led Archives, Radical Public History and the Heritage Professions', *InterActions: UCLA Journal of Education and Information Studies* 7, no. 2 (31/05/11).

67 On community archives see: Andrew Flinn and Anne Gilliland, 'Community Archives: What Are We Really Talking About?', ed. Larry Stillman (CIRN Prato Community Informatics Conference, Centre for Community Networking Research, Centre for Social Informatics, Monash University, 2013).

68 For instance, see: Laurajane Smith, *Emotional Heritage: Visitor Engagement at Museums and Heritage Sites* (Abingdon and New York: Routledge, 2020); Sheila Watson, 'Emotions in the History Museum', in *The International Handbooks of Museum Studies, Volume 1*, eds Andrea Whitcomb and Kylie Message (Hoboken, NJ: John Wiley & Sons, 2015); Andrea Witcomb, 'Remembering the Dead by Affecting the Living: The Case of a Miniature Model of Treblinka', in *Museum Materialities: Objects, Engagements,*

Interpretations, ed. Sandra Dudley (New York: Routledge, 2010), 39–52. For a discussion of how the museum staff emotionally engage with objects see: Anna Woodham, Rhianedd Smith, and Alison Hess, *Exploring Emotion, Care and Enthusiasm in 'Unloved' Museum Collections* (Amsterdam: ARC Humanities Press, 2020).

1 Transport museums

1   For a detailed discussion of the increasing numbers of museums in the UK see: Candlin et al., 'Mapping Museums 1960–2020'.

2   Philip Sidney Bagwell, *Transport in Britain from Canal Lock to Gridlock* (London: Hambledon and London, 2002). T. R. Gourvish, *British Railways 1948–73: A Business History* (Cambridge: Cambridge University Press, 2011).

3   Gerald Crompton, 'The Railway Companies and the Nationalisation Issue 1920–50', in *The Political Economy of Nationalisation in Britain 1920–50*, eds Robert Milton and John Singleton (Cambridge: Cambridge University Press, 2005), 116–43.

4   Bagwell, *Transport in Britain from Canal Lock to Gridlock*.

5   Richard Beeching, *The Reshaping of British Railways* (London: HMSO, 1963); Richard Beeching, *The Development of the Major Railway Trunk Routes* (London: British Railways Board, 1965).

6   Leighton Buzzard Light Railway was built after the First World War to serve quarries in the region and closed after quarries switched to using road transport because of its greater cost-effectiveness and the rationalisation of the wider rail network. It was taken over by railway enthusiasts and opened as a museum in the 1960s. Likewise, the Scottish Industrial Railway Centre focuses on the steam railway built to serve the local colliery and which was in operation until the late 1970s when the colliery closed. On industrial railways and their use as heritage attractions see: Abhishek Bhati, Josephine Pryce, and Taha Chaiechi, 'Industrial Railway Heritage Trains: The Evolution of a Heritage Tourism Genre and Its Attributes', *Journal of Heritage Tourism* 9, no. 2 (3 April 2014): 114–33.

7   The Stockport prefix was dropped when the Society's base of operation changed.

8   'Andrew Barclay Works No 2258 Tiny 0-4-0ST', Preserved British Steam Locomotives, 14/03/18: https://preservedbritishsteamlocomotives.com/andrew-barclay-works-no-2258-tiny-0-4-0st/. Accessed 04/03/20.

9   The enthusiasts who worked to save the Bluebell Railway similarly wanted it to be a viable railway rather than a purely heritage concern. Richard Sykes et al., 'Steam Attraction: Railways in Britain's National Heritage', *Journal of Transport History* 18, no. 2 (01/08/16): 156–75.

10 T. C. Barker, *An Economic History of Transport in Britain*, 3rd edn (London: Hutchinson, 1974), 160–85.

11 The Scottish Vintage Bus Museum was registered as a charity in 1985 but did not regularly open as a museum until they moved to the Lathalmond site in 1993.

12 For information on the collection see: *The Lathalmond Guide Book* (Lathalmond: The Scottish Vintage Bus Museum, 2007).

13 Interview with Mike Bentley. Transcript from the Steam in Our Soul project, 2002 (London: Micromuseums Archive, Bishopsgate Institute).

14 For information on the collections at Ingrow Loco and the Museum of Rail Travel see: Paul Brunt, *Keighley and Worth Valley Railway Stockbook: A History of the Collection* (Keighley: Keighley and Worth Valley Railway Preservation Society, 2013).

15 George West, Graham Allen, and Pete Skellon, 'Steam in Our Soul: A Story of Railway Enthusiasm and the Rise and Fall of the Dinting Railway Centre' (Keighley: Bahamas Locomotive Society (Ingrow Loco), 2002). Steam in Our Soul followed the example of Ewan MacColl, the English folk singer who in 1957 worked with the producer Charles Parker to write 'The Ballad of John Axon', a documentary for BBC radio. Axon was a locomotive driver who had been based at the Edgeley Sheds in Stockport and who had died the previous year when the supply pipe broke away from the steam brake on his engine. He was travelling on the line between Manchester and Buxton, which crosses the high peaks of Derbyshire, and banking engines were used to push the trains up the steep inclines. Unaware that the brakes had failed, the crew continued to stoke the rear engine, driving the train onwards. Knowing that there would be no way to slow the locomotive once they reached the summit, Axon instructed the fireman to jump clear while he stayed with the engine, hoping to mitigate the consequences of any collision. Axon was awarded the George Cross for his bravery. In preparing for the documentary, MacColl visited Axon's widow and workmates. He used their stories as the basis for his lyrics, but rather than delivering a conventional performance, the documentary inter-wove his songs with the voices of Axon's community and the sounds of that environ-ment. 'The Ballad of John Axon' clearly had resonance for the group at Ingrow, not least because many of the volunteers had originally worked at the Edgeley Sheds. 'The Ballad of John Axon' (London: BBC, 1958).

16 On the camaraderie of restoring vintage locomotives and how volunteers are trained see: Terry Wallace, '"Working of the Train Gang": Alienation, Liminality and Commu-nitas in the UK Preserved Railway Sector', *International Journal of Heritage Studies* 12, no. 3 (15 March 2006): 218–33.

17 Tomasso Pardi, 'Industrial Policy and the British Automotive Industry under Margaret Thatcher', *Business History* 59, no. 1 (2017): 75–100.

18 'The Politics of Building Cars', 01/04/05: http://news.bbc.co.uk/1/hi/uk_politics/ 4294709.stm. Accessed 07/07/21.

19 Andrew McLaughlin and William Maroney, 'Privatization as Industrial Policy: State Withdrawal from the British Motor Industry', *Public Administration* 74, no. 3 (1996): 435–52.

20 John Gilchrist kindly provided the following timeline.

  1) In 1975 the British Leyland Motor Corporation set up a new division to manage and preserve the corporation's collection of historic vehicles.

  2) In 1979 that division became BL Heritage Ltd and was headquartered at Studley in Warwickshire. The manager was given responsibility over the collections. Those collections were used for company events and hospitality and were funded by their respective divisions.

  3) In 1983 British Leyland formed four independent charitable trusts to preserve its historic collections:

   3.1 British Motor Industry Heritage Trust (BMIHT), the Managing Trust;

   3.2 Austin Rover Heritage Trust, now the Heritage Motor Centre at Gaydon;

   3.3 Jaguar Daimler Heritage Trust, closed down and incorporated into Gaydon;

   3.4 British Commercial Vehicle Trust, which opened the British Commercial Vehicle Museum (BCVM) to the public in 1983.

  Following the privatisation of British Leyland through the mid-1980s, the trusts went their own separate ways, although the retiring management of BMIHT ensured BCVM fully complied with the requirements of a professional museum.

21 Emily Boyle, 'Creating an Organizational Network out of the Ashes of Despair', *Leader-ship and Organizational Development Journal* 15, no. 7 (1994): 11–14.

22 The purchase of the Truck and Bus Division included the intellectual property rights to the light trucks, which the group carried on making and sold on to DAF, who had re-floated the company in Europe. The group continued to run Leyland Trucks on a profitable basis until 1998, when they sold it to the US conglomerate PACCAR.

23 John Gilchrist, private communication, 11/11/21.

24 Alan Warren, *Barry Scrapyard: The Preservation Miracle* (Newton Abbot: David & Charles, 1988). Dai Woodham Interview: www.youtube.com/watch?v=UMMeZnLTj7Q. Accessed 21/09/19.

25 A point also made by Chris Gosden, Frances Larson, and Alison Petch, *Knowing Things: Exploring the Collections at the Pitt Rivers Museum, 1884–1945* (Oxford and New York: Oxford University Press, 2007), 5–7.

2 War and conflict museums

1 Armies are formed of corps, corps are made up of divisions, divisions comprise bri-gades, and brigades are made up of battalions (infantry), batteries (artillery), and squadrons (armour and support arms).

2 'Life And Death In Bomber Command', Imperial War Museums: www.iwm.org.uk/ history/life-and-death-in-bomber-command. Accessed 10/10/21.

3 Ronald Blake, 'Airfield Closures and Air Defence Reorientation in Britain during the Cold War and Its Immediate Aftermath', *Area* 41, no. 3 (01/09/09): 285–99.

4 On Polish settlement in the UK see: Wieslaw Rogalski, *The Polish Resettlement Corps 1946–1949: Britain's Polish Forces* (Warwick: Helion and Company, 2019).

5 'The Regimental System', National Army Museum: www.nam.ac.uk/explore/ regimental-system. Accessed 30/03/20.

6 Up until the 1970s there was a greater degree of affiliation to specific ports. Royal Navy squadrons and ship types were allocated to specific ports. After their training, Navy sailors were sent to a home port and usually spent their entire career working out of that location, even if on different ships, thereby enabling families to put down roots.

7 Jeremy A. Crang, *The British Army and the People's War 1939–1945* (Manchester: Manchester University Press, 2000). Simon Rogers, 'Army Cuts: How Have UK Armed Forces Personnel Numbers Changed over Time?', *Guardian*, 2011: www.theguardian. com/news/datablog/2011/sep/01/military-service-personnel-total. Accessed 23/11/20.

8 Duncan Sandys, 'Defence: Outline of Future Policy' (London: Her Majesty's Stationery Office, 1957).

9 Dan Keohane, *Security in British Politics, 1945–99* (Basingstoke: Macmillan Press, 2000).

10 Rogers, 'Army Cuts'.

11 The 1965 Healey review gave an economic rationale for continuing to reduce the size of the Armed Forces, and the 1975 Mason review set out to further reduce defence expenditure and deepen the commitment to nuclear deterrence. The 1981 Defence Review reduced the size of the surface fleet, saw the closure of the Chatham dockyard, and placed an increased reliance on reservists. The 1991 paper *Options for Change* announced that manpower would be cut by 18%; the 1998 Strategic Defence Review led

on the reduction of surface and submarine fleet, and of RAF aircraft; and in 2003 'Delivering Security in a Changing World' reduced army numbers by a further 1,000, and cut RAF and Navy personnel. Roy Mason, 'Defence Review' (London: Her Majesty's Stationery Office, 1975). John Roy Nott, 'Defence Review' (London: Her Majesty's Stationery Office, 1981). Richard Ware, *UK Defence Policy: Options for Change* (Great Britain, Parliament, House of Commons, Library, Research Division, 1991). Tom Dodd, *The Strategic Defence Review White Paper* (Great Britain, Parliament, House of Commons, Library, 1998). Geoff Hoon, 'Delivering Security in a Changing World: Defence White Paper' (London: Ministry of Defence, 2003).

12 Wyn Rees, 'The 1957 Sandys White Paper: New Priorities in British Defence Policy?', *Journal of Strategic Studies* 12, no. 2 (1999): 215–29.

13 For an account of collections on show throughout an officers' mess see: Charles Kirke and Nicole M. Hartwell, 'The Officers' Mess: An Anthropology and History of the Military Interior', in *Dividing the Spoils: Perspectives on Military Collections and the British Empire*, eds Henrietta Lidchi and Stuart Allan (Manchester: Manchester University Press, 2020), 106–27.

14 'Regimental Headquarters', *The Red Hackle*, April (1962): 6.

15 C. B. Otley, 'The Educational Background of British Army Officers', *Sociology* 7, no. 2 (1973): 191–209. On these points see also: Geoffrey Field, '"Civilians in Uniform": Class and Politics in the British Armed Forces, 1939–1945', *International Labor and Working-Class History*, no. 80 (2011): 121–47; C. B. Otley, 'The Social Origins of British Army Officers', *Sociological Review* 18, no. 2 (01/07/70): 213–39.

16 David French, *Military Identities the Regimental System, the British Army, and the British People, c. 1870–2000* (Oxford and New York: Oxford University Press, 2005), 128.

17 The Women's Royal Army Corps had largely been disbanded by this point as women were being recruited across the regiments. The WRAC collection was deposited with the National Army Museum.

18 Britain includes England, Scotland, and Wales but not Northern Ireland. The UK includes Northern Ireland.

19 For a comprehensive account of the Troubles see: David McKittrick and David McVea, *Making Sense of the Troubles*, 2nd edn (London: Penguin Books, 2012).

20 Anon, 'The Regimental Museum', *The Faugh-A-Ballagh*, January (1932): 11–12. Anon, 'The Regimental Museum', *The Faugh-A-Ballagh*, October (1932): 168–70.

21 L. E. Buckell, 'Regimental Museums: Museums in Northern Ireland', *Journal of the Society for Army Historical Research*, Museum Supplement no. 1, Autumn (1949): 1–4.

22 'Re-Opening of the Regimental Museum', *The Faugh-A-Ballagh*, Spring (1963): 81–4.

23 'Re-Opening of the Regimental Museum', 84.

24 The founders' aims for military museums do not quite chime with those stated by the Ministry of Defence. See Justine Reilly, Kate Vigurs, and Joanne Boardman, 'Scoping the Army Museums Sector' (Salisbury: Army Museums Ogilby Trust, 2016).

25 On the sanitisation of war museums see: Ralf Raths, 'From Technical Showroom to Full-Fledged Museum: The German Tank Museum Munster', *Museum and Society* 10, no. 3 (2012): 174–82.

26 On questions of balance in museums in Northern Ireland see: Fiona Candlin, 'Partisans Reviewed: The Problematic Ethics of Multi-Perspectival Exhibitions', in *Micromuseology: An Analysis of Small Independent Museums* (London: Bloomsbury, 2016), 75–92; Shawn Reming, 'Sharing the Past in a Divided City: Belfast's Ulster Museum', *International Journal of the Inclusive Museum* 4, no. 2 (2011): 1–12.

27 Elizabeth Crooke has considered the life history of the objects in the Museum of Free Derry and their use as agents in the collective processes of public remembering. Elizabeth Crooke, 'Memory Politics and Material Culture: Display in the Memorial Museum', *Memory Studies* 12, no. 6 (01/12/19): 617–29,

28 The conference proceedings were published as 'Bringing Peace to People: Meeting of Directors and Staff of Peace and Anti-War Museums and Related Institutions Worldwide' (Bradford: Give Peace a Chance Trust, n.d.).On peace museums see: Peter van Dungen, 'The Peace Museum in Bradford and Peace Museums Worldwide', in *City of Peace – Bradford's Story*, ed. Carol Rank (Bradford: Bradford Libraries, 1997); Peter van Dungen, 'Peace Museums: Recent Developments', *Medicine and War* 10, no. 3 (2003): 218–29.

29 The Peace Museum remains in Bradford, although it has since found new, more accessible premises.

30 This situation changed after the Bourne-May report of 2008 (see p. 152). Jonathan Bourne-May, 'Army Museums Study' (London: Ministry of Defence, 2011).

3 Local history museums

1 The exception is Northern Ireland, where there are very few independent local history museums.

2 Lianne McTavish admits to initially finding settler museums in Canada somewhat homogeneous and hence boring. Like us, she then revised that initial judgement. McTavish, *Voluntary Detours*.

3 Bernard Jennings, ed., *A History of Nidderdale* (Huddersfield: Advertiser Press Limited, 1967). The process of producing the history was described by the course tutor. Bernard Jennings, 'Group Work in Local History: Adult Education and the Study of History', *Victorian Studies* 15, no. 1 (1971): 81–6.

4 W. Harwood Long, 'The Development of Mechanization in English Farming', *Agricultural History Review*, 11, no. 1 (1963): 15–26.

5 Robert A. Robinson and William J. Sutherland, 'Post-War Changes in Arable Farming and Biodiversity in Great Britain', *Journal of Applied Ecology* 39, no. 1 (2002): 157–76.

6 John Dearlove, *The Reorganization of British Local Government: Old Orthodoxies and a Political Perspective* (Cambridge: Cambridge University Press, 1979). Gerry Stoker, 'The Struggle to Reform Local Government: 1970–95', *Public Money & Management* 16, no. 1 (January 1996): 17–22.

7 Burgess, 'The Making of a Museum', 135.

8 Burgess, 'The Making of a Museum'.

9 As such, the rise of local history museums can be viewed as part of a general decline in deference, which the historian Florence Sutcliffe-Braithwaite has linked to the social changes of the period. She cites a veritable list of factors that all began to erode cultural norms, including the end of empire, the Suez crisis, consumer consciousness emphasising choice and entitlement, the churches' decreasing confidence that they could speak for and shape national values, the satire boom, youth cultures, and the 1960s and 1970s social movements relating to gender, race, sexuality, peace, and the environment. Their collective impact meant that fewer people were willing to accept or defer to traditional class hierarchies, and what had once seemed fixed and enduring was open to question

and critique. Florence Sutcliffe-Braithwaite, *Class, Politics, and the Decline of Deference in England, 1968–2000* (Oxford: Oxford University Press, 2018).

10 Edwin Jones, 'The Rise and Fall of Dunlop Semtex' (Blaenau Gwent Heritage, June 1996).

11 'Coal Towns "Still Feeling" Job Cuts', *BBC News*, 19/06/14: www.bbc.com/news/uk-wales-27920610. Accessed 09/08/21. Huw Beynon and Ray Hudson, *The Shadow of the Mine: Coal and the End of Industrial Britain* (London: Verso, 2021).

12 Priyanka Shankar, 'The Ebbw Vale Steelworks – A Lost Legacy', *Cardiff News Plus*, 23/05/16: https://jomec.co.uk/cjsnewsmaij/news/the-ebbw-vale-steelworks-a-lost-legacy/. Accessed 23/11/20.

13 Mike Foden, Steve Fothergill, and Tony Gore, 'The State of the Coalfields: Economic and Social Conditions in the Former Mining Communities of England, Scotland and Wales' (Sheffield Hallam University, Centre for Regional Economic and Social Research, 2014): www4.shu.ac.uk/mediacentre/state-coalfields-new-research. Accessed 21/11/20.

14 Frank's description finds an echo in a series of portrait photographs taken by Joseph Murray of the last employees at Ebbw Vale Steelworks, which were placed alongside the men's moving descriptions of how they felt when the works closed. 'The Last Shift at Ebbw Vale', *BBC News*, 03/02/17: www.bbc.com/news/in-pictures-38826361. Accessed 17/09/20.

15 Mary Wiliam, Eurwyn Wiliam, and Dafydd Wiliam, *The Brynmawr Furniture Makers: A Quaker Initiative 1929–40* (Orsaf: Gwasg Carreg Gwalch, 2012). Roger Smith, 'Utopian Designer: Paul Matt and the Brynmawr Experiment', *Furniture History* 23 (1987): 88–97.

16 Bella Dicks makes a similar point in her analysis of Rhondda Heritage Park, also in the Welsh Valleys. She sees the site as limited in that it constructs a unitary model of community, which is not the case at Brynmawr Museum, but also points out that the values of mining culture are upheld as part of a wider valuation of working-class labour and forms of organisation. The Heritage Park forms a resource for collective action and shows the communal potential of the valley's working class. It is both constraining and utopian. Bella Dicks, 'The Life and Times of Community: Spectacles of Collective Identity at the Rhondda Heritage Park', *Time & Society* 6, nos 2–3 (01/07/97): 195–212.

17 The scheme was notorious for being a means of massaging high unemployment figures, for the scant training it offered, and for financially exploiting the trainees, who were paid around £55 per week.

18 Malcolm Williams, 'Why Is Cornwall Poor? Poverty and In-Migration since the 1960s', *Contemporary British History* 17, no. 3 (2003): 55–70.

19 Allan Williams and Gareth Shaw, 'The Age of Mass Tourism', in *Cornwall since the War: The Contemporary History of a European Region*, ed. Philip Payton (Redruth: Institute of Cornish Studies, 1993), 84–97. 'Cornwall Council Annual Report 2018 – 2019' (Truro: Cornwall Council, 2019): www.cornwall.gov.uk/media/vx5jsxga/annual-report-2018-to-2019.pdf. Accessed 14/03/21.

20 Williams, 'Why Is Cornwall Poor?'

21 Malcolm Williams, 'Housing the Cornish', in *Cornwall since the War: The Contemporary History of a European Region*, ed. Philip Payton (Redruth: Institute of Cornish Studies, 1993), 157–80.

22 The geographer David Harvey has explored instances where communities insist on the specificity of place as a means of resisting the forces of capitalism or global change. He

refs to this as 'militant particularism'. David Harvey, *Justice, Nature and the Geography of Difference* (Oxford: Blackwell, 1996).

23 For a discussion on concepts of place see: Tim Cresswell, *Place: A Short Introduction* (Oxford: Blackwell, 2004).

4 The museum founders

1 Samuel, *Theatres of Memory*, 8.
2 Arts Council England, Museums Galleries Scotland, Museums Association, and Association of Independent Museums, 'Character Matters: Attitudes, Behaviours and Skills in the UK Museum Workforce' (London, 2016).
3 The notion of uneven development derives from Mary Poovey's book of that name. Mary Poovey, *Uneven Developments: The Ideological Work of Gender in Mid-Victorian England*, Women in Culture and Society (Chicago, IL: University of Chicago Press, 1988).
4 Workers' expertise in their own history is a central theme in Sven Lindqvist, 'Dig Where You Stand', *Oral History* 7, no. 2 (1979): 24–30.
5 Sylvia Murdoch, founder of Gairloch Museum. Interview by Karen Buchanan, curator of Gairloch Museum, 21/07/2017.
6 Isabel Grant, who established the Highland Folk Museum, wrote that country people were often skeptical of her motivations and reasons for collecting, fearing that she was condescending to them. Sylvia Morton was briefly taught by Grant, admired her work, and sought to emulate her example. It is possible that in telling this anecdote Sylvia is consciously or unconsciously echoing her predecessor. Isabel Grant, *The Making of Am Fasgadh: An Account of the Origins of the Highland Folk Museum by Its Founder* (Edinburgh: National Museums Scotland, 2007).
7 Nick Jedrzejewski and Mike Merritt, 'Kay Matheson, Stone of Destiny Raider, Dies at 84', *The Scotsman*, 09/07/13: www.scotsman.com/arts-and-culture/kay-matheson-stone-destiny-raider-dies-84-1568561. Accessed 07/12/21.
8 Terry Wallace argues that in belonging to a group of train enthusiasts the external identities of the volunteers on heritage railways were diluted: they became a community of equal individuals. Our work certainly echoes his comment but with some caveats. We did not observe the dilution of external identities in railway museums or those that covered other subjects. On the contrary, our narrators usually stressed their disparate identities and drew attention to the fact that solicitors worked alongside quarrymen. In doing so they reinforced the point about collectivity. The museum group superseded rather than eradicated any social stratification. Wallace, '"Working of the Train Gang"'.
9 Anon, 'Gairloch Heritage Museum'.
10 Our research suggested that children and teenagers were less involved as the museums boom progressed. This is consonant with findings about children's freedom being increasingly restricted in the later part of the twentieth century. Mathew Thomson, *Lost Freedom: The Landscape of the Child and the British Post-War Settlement* (Oxford: Oxford University Press, 2013).
11 Pat Bentley, interviewed by Graham Allen and Pete Skellon, undated (between 2000 and 2002), Ingrow Loco archive.
12 On expanded notions of museum founders see: Gosden, Larson, and Petch, *Knowing Things* and Hill, *Women and Museums, 1850–1914*.

13 Women have been eligible to apply for all roles in the Army since 2018, other than in the Gurkhas, and have a very low presence among senior officers. 'Protecting Those Who Protect Us: Women in the Armed Forces from Recruitment to Civilian Life: Second Report of Session 2021–22' (London: House of Commons Defence Committee, 2021). On gender in regimental museums see Reilly, Vigurs, and Boardman, 'Scoping the Army Museums Sector'.

14 West, Allen, and Skellon, 'Steam in Our Soul'.

15 Sara Connolly and Mary Gregory, 'Women and Work since 1970', in *Work and Pay in Twentieth-Century Britain*, eds Nicholas Crafts, Ian Gazeley, and Andrew Newell (Oxford: Oxford University Press, 2007).

16 Sylvia Murdoch, founder of Gairloch Museum. Interview by Karen Buchanan, curator of Gairloch Museum, 21/07/2017.

17 On showcasing women's skills in early- and mid-twentieth-century folk museums see: Laura Carter, *Histories of Everyday Life: The Making of Popular Social History in Britain, 1918–1979* (Oxford: Oxford University Press, 2021).

18 In 1994 the Arts Council of Great Britain was replaced with the National Arts Councils, so England, Northern Ireland, Scotland, and Wales each had their own governing body. In 2002 the Arts Council of England merged with the ten English regional arts boards, and in 2003 the new organisation was rebranded as Arts Council England. This discussion crosses that time period and so refers to either 'the Arts Council' or Arts Council England as appropriate.

19 Nicholas Kenyon was then chair of the advisory board. In 2021 he stepped down from his post as director of the Barbican amid an investigation into institutional racism. Lanre Bakare, 'Barbican Boss to Step down after "Institutional Racism" Row', *Guardian*, 23/06/21: www.theguardian.com/culture/2021/jun/23/barbican-boss-to-step-down-after-institutional-racism-row. Accessed 06/01/22.

20 George Pratt, 'Afro-Caribbean/South Asian Music Inquiry Report' (London: Arts Council of Great Britain, 1986), CRER/MAA/REP/1/19, Modern Records Centre, University of Warwick.

21 On the profile of the Asian Music Circuit see: Asjad Nazir, 'Bringing Music to the Three Worlds', *Eastern Eye*, 20/06/18: www.easterneye.biz/bringing-music-to-the-three-worlds/. Accessed 08/01/22.

22 'Asian Music Circuit ("AMC") – National Music Touring Company Promoting Pan-Asian Music Refused Funding by Arts Council England ("ACE"), Challenges Decision Making Process', Bindmans LLP, 01/05/12: www.bindmans.com/news/asian-music-circuit-amc-national-music-touring-company-promoting-pan-asian-. Accessed 08/01/22. For a list of the South Asian organisations that were funded, and for a discussion of the value of South Asian arts, see: Jasjit Singh, 'What "Value" South Asian Arts in Britain?', *South Asian Popular Culture* 14, no. 3 (2016): 155–65.

23 'In Praise of … the Asian Music Circuit', *Guardian*, 26/04/11.

24 David Foskett, The Queen on the Application of Asian Music Circuit and Arts Council England, No. CO/5702/2011 (Manchester Civil Justice Centre 01/06/12).

25 'Save the Asian Music Circuit', *Minority Perspective* (blog), 22/04/11: https://minorityperspective.co.uk/2011/04/22/save-the-asian-music-circuit/. Accessed 09/01/22.

26 Arts Council England, 'South Asian Dance & Music Mapping Study' (London: 2020). For a useful commentary on the report and the question of the 'White lens' see: Shivaangee Agrawal, Sanjeevini Dutta, and Magdalen Gorringe, 'Pulse: Response to the

Notes

ACE South Asian Dance and Music Mapping Study': www.pulseconnects.com/pulse-response-ace-south-asian-dance-and-music-mapping-study. Accessed 17/01/22.

27 See also the Somali Museum, which is in planning and is led by Kinsi Abdulleh.

28 Sandra Shakespeare, 'The Black British Museum' (Museum Association Annual Conference, 2020).

29 Sandra Shakespeare subsequently co-edited a takeover issue of the *Museums Journal*, addressing Blackness, equality, and change in the UK museum sector. Sandra Shakespeare, Cherly Bowen, and Tola Dabiri, eds, 'Creating a Black British Museum: The Museum X Takeover Issue', *Museums Journal*, no. October (2021).

30 Bourne-May, 'Army Museums Study'.

Conclusions

1 John Benson, *Affluence and Authority: A Social History of Twentieth-Century Britain* (London: Hodder Arnold, 2005). A. Holmans, 'Housing', in *Twentieth-Century British Social Trends*, eds A. H. Halsey and Josephine Webb (Basingstoke and New York: Macmillan and St Martin's Press, 1999), 487–8.

2 Mia Gray and Anna Barford, 'The Depths of the Cuts: The Uneven Geography of Local Government Austerity', *Cambridge Journal of Regions, Economy and Society* 11, no. 3 (29/10/18): 541–63.

3 Issues of succession in small museums were also raised in 'Rebuilding Volunteering Capacity in the Heritage Sector: A Briefing Note from the Heritage Sector to Covid-19 – Draft at 15 April 2020' (London: Department for Digital, Culture, Media and Sport, April 2020).

4 Geraldine Kendall Adams, 'Volunteering in Museums Finds Itself at a Crossroads', *Museums Journal*, no. July (2019): www.museumsassociation.org/museums-journal/analysis/2019/07/01072019-volunteering-museums-at-a-crossroads/. Accessed 23/06/20.

Selected bibliography

Agrawal, Shivaangee, Sanjeevini Dutta, and Magdalen Gorringe. 'Pulse: Response to the ACE South Asian Dance and Music Mapping Study', 2021. www.pulseconnects.com/pulse-response-ace-south-asian-dance-and-music-mapping-study. Accessed 17/01/22.

Altick, Richard Daniel. *The Shows of London*. Cambridge, MA: Belknap Press of Harvard University Press, 1978.

Anon. 'The Regimental Museum'. *The Faugh-A-Ballagh*, January (1932): 11–12.

———. 'The Regimental Museum'. *The Faugh-A-Ballagh*, October (1932): 168–70.

———. 'Re-Opening of the Regimental Museum'. *The Faugh-A-Ballagh*, Spring (1963): 81–4.

Arts Council England. 'South Asian Dance & Music Mapping Study'. London, 2020.

Arts Council England, Museums Galleries Scotland, Museums Association, and Association of Independent Museums. 'Character Matters: Attitudes, Behaviours and Skills in the UK Museum Workforce'. London, 2016.

Ascherson, Neal. 'A Society That Falls Back on Miming the Creation of Its Wealth Is Sick'. *Independent On Sunday*. 19/02/95.

———. 'What Should We Preserve?' *Independent*. 16/10/93.

———. 'Reminders from the Past to Suspend Our Disbelief'. *Independent*. 26/04/92.

———. 'Why "Heritage" Is Right-Wing'. *Observer*. 08/11/87.

Atkinson, Frank. *The Man Who Made Beamish: An Autobiography*. Gateshead: Northern Books, 1999.

Bagwell, Philip Sidney. *Transport in Britain from Canal Lock to Gridlock*. London: Hambledon Continuum, 2002.

Barker, T. C. *An Economic History of Transport in Britain*. 3rd edn. London: Hutchinson, 1974.

Barringer, T. J., and Tom Flynn. *Colonialism and the Object: Empire, Material Culture and the Museum*. London: Routledge, 1998.

Bennett, Tony. *Pasts beyond Memory: Evolution, Museums, Colonialism*. London and New York: Routledge, 2004.

Benson, John. *Affluence and Authority: A Social History of Twentieth-Century Britain*. London: Hodder Arnold, 2005.

Bernard, Philippa. *Out of the Midst of the Fire*. London: Westminster Synagogue, 2005.

Beynon, Huw, and Ray Hudson. *The Shadow of the Mine: Coal and the End of Industrial Britain*. London: Verso, 2021.

Selected bibliography

Bhati, Abhishek, Josephine Pryce, and Taha Chaiechi. 'Industrial Railway Heritage Trains: The Evolution of a Heritage Tourism Genre and Its Attributes'. *Journal of Heritage Tourism* 9, no. 2 (03/04/14): 114–33.

Blake, Ronald. 'Airfield Closures and Air Defence Reorientation in Britain during the Cold War and Its Immediate Aftermath'. *Area* 41, no. 3 (01/09/09): 285–99.

Bourne-May, Jonathan. 'Army Museums Study'. London: Ministry of Defence, 2011.

Boylan, Patrick. 'The Museum Professions'. In *A Companion to Museum Studies*, edited by Sharon Macdonald, 415–30. Malden, MA and Oxford: Blackwell, 2006.

Boyle, Emily. 'Creating an Organizational Network out of the Ashes of Despair'. *Leadership and Organizational Development Journal* 15, no. 7 (1994): 11–14.

Brown, Karen, and François Mairesse. 'The Definition of the Museum through Its Social Role'. *Curator: The Museum Journal* 61, no. 4 (2018): 525–39.

Brulon, Bruno Soares. 'Museum in Colonial Contexts: The Politics of Defining an Imported Definition'. In *Defining Museums of the 21st Century: Plural Experiences*, edited by Bruno Soares Brulon, Karen Brown, and Olga Nazor, 163–8. Paris: ICOM International Committee for Museology, 2018.

Buckell, L. E. 'Regimental Museums: Museums in Northern Ireland'. *Journal of the Society for Army Historical Research*, Museum Supplement no. 1, Autumn (1949): 1–4.

Burgess, Eileen. 'The Making of a Museum'. In *Traces of Nidderdale in 40 Years and 40 Objects: Stories of the Museum*, edited by Joanna Moody, 133–47. Pateley Bridge: Nidderdale Museum Society, 2014.

Burman, Rickie. *The Jewish Museum, London: Introduction and History*. London: Scala, 2006.

Candlin, Fiona. 'Rehabilitating Unauthorised Touch or Why Museum Visitors Touch the Exhibits'. *The Senses and Society* 12, no. 3 (2017): 251–66.

———. *Micromuseology: An Analysis of Small Independent Museums*. London: Bloomsbury, 2016.

Candlin, Fiona, and Jamie Larkin. 'What Is a Museum? Difference All the Way Down'. *Museums and Society* 18, no. 2 (2020): 115–31.

Candlin, Fiona, and Alexandra Poulovassilis. 'Understanding and Managing Patchy Data in the UK Museum Sector'. *Museum Management and Curatorship* 35, no. 4 (2019): 446–59.

Candlin, Fiona, Jamie Larkin, Andrea Ballatore, and Alexandra Poulovassilis. 'Mapping Museums 1960–2020: A Report on the Data'. London: Birkbeck, University of London, March 2020.

Candlin, Fiona, Jamie Larkin, Andrea Ballatore, and Alexandra Poulovassilis. 'The Missing Museums: Accreditation, Surveys, and an Alternative Account of the UK Sector'. *Cultural Trends* 29, no. 1 (2019): 50–67.

Carter, Laura. *Histories of Everyday Life: The Making of Popular Social History in Britain, 1918-1979*. Oxford: Oxford University Press, 2021.

Chew, Ron. 'In Praise of the Small Museum'. *Museum News*, March/April (2002).

Conn, Steven. 'The Birth and Death of a Museum'. In *Do Museums Still Need Objects?* 20–57. Philadelphia: University of Pennsylvania Press, 2010.

Connolly, Sara, and Mary Gregory. 'Women and Work since 1970'. In *Work and Pay in Twentieth-Century Britain*, edited by Nicholas Crafts, Ian Gazeley, and Andrew Newell, 142–77. Oxford: University Press, 2007.

Corner, John, and Sylvia Harvey. 'Mediating Tradition and Modernity'. In *Enterprise and Heritage: Crosscurrents of National Culture*, edited by John Corner and Sylvia Harvey, 49–75. London and New York: Routledge, 1991.

Selected bibliography

Crang, Jeremy A. *The British Army and the People's War 1939–1945*. Manchester: Manchester University Press, 2000.

Cresswell, Tim. *Place: A Short Introduction*. Oxford: Blackwell, 2004.

Crompton, Gerald. 'The Railway Companies and the Nationalisation Issue 1920–50'. In *The Political Economy of Nationalisation in Britain 1920–50*, edited by Robert Milton and John Singleton, 116–43. Cambridge: Cambridge University Press, 2005.

Crooke, Elizabeth. 'Memory Politics and Material Culture: Display in the Memorial Museum'. *Memory Studies* 12, no. 6 (01/12/19): 617–29.

———. 'An Exploration of the Connections among Museums, Community and Heritage'. In *The Ashgate Research Companion to Heritage and Identity*, edited by B. J. Graham and Peter Howard, 415–24. Aldershot: Ashgate, 2008.

———. 'Museums, Communities and the Politics of Heritage in Northern Ireland'. In *Museums and Their Communities*, edited by Sheila Watson, 300–12. London: Routledge, 2007.

———. *Museums and Community: Ideas, Issues and Challenges*. London and New York: Routledge, 2007.

Davies, Hunter. *Behind the Scenes at the Museum of Baked Beans: My Search for Britain's Maddest Museums*. London: Virgin Books, 2010.

Dearlove, John, *The Reorganization of British Local Government: Old Orthodoxies and a Political Perspective*. Cambridge: Cambridge University Press, 1979.

Dennett, Andrea Stulman. *Weird and Wonderful: The Dime Museum in America*. New York and London: New York University Press, 1997.

Dicks, Bella. *Heritage, Place and Community*. Cardiff: University of Wales Press, 2000.

———. 'The Life and Times of Community: Spectacles of Collective Identity at the Rhondda Heritage Park'. *Time & Society* 6, nos 2–3 (01/07/97): 195–212.

Dodd, Tom. *The Strategic Defence Review White Paper*. Great Britain, Parliament, House of Commons, Library, 1998.

Dungen, Peter van. 'The Peace Museum in Bradford and Peace Museums Worldwide'. In *City of Peace – Bradford's Story*, edited by Carol Rank. Bradford: Bradford Libraries, 1997.

———. 'Peace Museums: Recent Developments'. *Medicine and War* 10, no. 3 (1994): 218–29.

Elsner, John, and Roger Cardinal. '"Unless You Do These Crazy Things…" An Interview with Robert Opie'. In *The Cultures of Collecting*, edited by John Elsner and Roger Cardinal, 25–48. London: Reaktion, 1994.

Field, Geoffrey. '"Civilians in Uniform": Class and Politics in the British Armed Forces, 1939–1945'. *International Labor and Working-Class History*, no. 80 (2011): 121–47.

Flinn, Andrew. 'Archival Activism: Independent and Community-Led Archives, Radical Public History and the Heritage Professions'. *InterActions: UCLA Journal of Education and Information Studies* 7, no. 2 (31/05/11).

Flinn, Andrew, and Anne Gilliland. 'Community Archives: What Are We Really Talking About?', edited by Larry Stillman. Centre for Community Networking Research, Centre for Social Informatics, Monash University, 2013.

Foden, Mike, Steve Fothergill, and Tony Gore. 'The State of the Coalfields: Economic and Social Conditions in the Former Mining Communities of England, Scotland and Wales'. Sheffield Hallam University, Centre for Regional Economic and Social Research, 2014.

French, David. *Military Identities: The Regimental System, the British Army, and the British People, c. 1870–2000*. Oxford and New York: Oxford University Press, 2005.

Fyfe, Gordon. 'Sociology and the Social Aspects of Museums'. In *A Companion to Museum Studies*, edited by Sharon Macdonald, 33–49. Chichester: Wiley-Blackwell, 2011.

Selected bibliography

Ginsburch, Victor, and François Mairesse. 'Defining a Museum: Suggestions for an Alternative Approach'. *Museum Management and Curatorship* 16, no. 1 (01/01/97): 15–33.

Gosden, Chris, Frances Larson, and Alison Petch. *Knowing Things: Exploring the Collections at the Pitt Rivers Museum, 1884–1945*. Oxford and New York: Oxford University Press, 2007.

Gourvish, T. R. *British Railways 1948–73: A Business History*. Cambridge: Cambridge University Press, 2011.

Grant, Isabel. *The Making of Am Fasgadh: An Account of the Origins of the Highland Folk Museum by Its Founder*. Edinburgh: National Museums Scotland, 2007.

Gray, Mia, and Anna Barford. 'The Depths of the Cuts: The Uneven Geography of Local Government Austerity'. *Cambridge Journal of Regions, Economy and Society* 11, no. 3 (29/10/18): 541–63.

Gregory, Helen, and Kirsty Robinson. 'No Small Matter: Micromuseums as Critical Institutions'. *Canadian Art Review* 43, no. 2 (2018): 89–101.

Griffiths, Alison. *Shivers down Your Spine: Cinema, Museums, and the Immersive View*. New York and Chichester: Columbia University Press, 2008.

Hall, Stuart. 'Whose Heritage? Unsettling the Heritage: Re-Imagining the Post-Nation'. In *The Politics of Heritage: The Legacies of 'Race'*, edited by Jo Littler and Roshi Naidoo, 21–31. Abingdon: Routledge, 2005.

Halstead, Robin, Jason Hazeley, Alex Morris, and Joel Morris. *Bollocks to Alton Towers: Uncommonly British Days Out*. London: Penguin, 2006.

Harvey, David. *Justice, Nature and the Geography of Difference*. Oxford: Blackwell, 1996.

Hazell, Paul, and Kjetil Fallan. 'The Enthusiast's Eye: The Value of Unsanctioned Knowledge in Design Historical Scholarship'. *Design and Culture* 7, no. 1 (01/03/15): 107–23.

Hein, Hilde S. *The Museum in Transition: A Philosophical Perspective*. Washington, DC and London: Smithsonian Institution Press, 2000.

Hewison, Robert. 'Commerce and Culture'. In *Enterprise and Heritage: Crosscurrents of National Culture*, edited by John Corner and Sylvia Harvey, 162–77. London and New York: Routledge, 1991.

———. *The Heritage Industry: Britain in a Climate of Decline*. London: Methuen, 1987.

Hill, Kate. *Women and Museums, 1850–1914: Modernity and the Gendering of Knowledge*. Manchester: Manchester University Press, 2016.

———. *Culture and Class in English Public Museums, 1850–1914*. Aldershot and Burlington, VT: Ashgate, 2005.

Holmans, A. 'Housing'. In *Twentieth-Century British Social Trends*, edited by A. H. Halsey and Josephine Webb, 487–8. Basingstoke and New York: Macmillan and St Martin's Press, 1999.

Hoon, Geoff. 'Delivering Security in a Changing World: Defence White Paper'. London: Ministry of Defence, 2003.

Hudson, Kenneth. 'The Museum Refuses to Stand Still'. In *Museum Studies: An Anthology of Contexts*, edited by Bettina Messias Carbonell, 85–91. Malden, MA: Blackwell, 2004.

Ishmael, Hannah J. M. 'The Development of Black-Led Archives in London'. Ph.D., UCL (University College London), 2020.

James, Daniel. 'Listening in the Cold: The Practice of Oral History in an Argentinian Working-Class Community'. In *The Oral History Reader*, edited by Robert Perks and Alistair Thomson, 3rd edn, 73–91. London and New York: Routledge, 2016.

Jennings, Bernard. 'Group Work in Local History: Adult Education and the Study of History'. *Victorian Studies* 15, no. 1 (1971): 81–6.

Selected bibliography

Jennings, Bernard. ed. *A History of Nidderdale*. Huddersfield: Advertiser Press Limited, 1967.

Jones, Edwin. 'The Rise and Fall of Dunlop Semtex'. Blaenau Gwent Heritage, June 1996.

Kendall Adams, Geraldine. 'Volunteering in Museums Finds Itself at a Crossroads'. *Museums Journal*, no. July (2019). www.museumsassociation.org/museums-journal/analysis/2019/07/01072019-volunteering-museums-at-a-crossroads/. Accessed 23/06/20.

Keohane, Dan. *Security in British Politics, 1945–99*. Basingstoke: Macmillan Press, 2000.

Kirke, Charles, and Nicole M. Hartwell. 'The Officers' Mess: An Anthropology and History of the Military Interior'. In *Dividing the Spoils: Perspectives on Military Collections and the British Empire*, edited by Henrietta Lidchi and Stuart Allan, 106–27. Manchester: Manchester University Press, 2020.

Liebenrood, Mark. 'Museum Closure in the UK, 1960–2010: Contexts and Microhistories'. Ph.D., Birkbeck, University of London, 2022.

Lindqvist, Sven. 'Dig Where You Stand'. *Oral History* 7, no. 2 (1979): 24–30.

Long, W. Harwood. 'The Development of Mechanization in English Farming'. *Agricultural History Review*, 11, no. 1 (1963): 15–26.

Lubar, Steven, Lukas Rieppel, Ann Daly, and Kathrinne Duffy, eds. 'Special Journal Edition: Lost Museums'. *Museum History Journal* 10, no. 1 (2017).

Lumley, Robert. 'The Debate on Heritage Reviewed'. In *Heritage, Museums and Galleries: An Introductory Reader*, edited by Gerard Corsane, 15–25. London: Routledge, 2005.

————. *The Museum Time-Machine: Putting Cultures on Display*. London and New York: Routledge, 1988.

Mandler, Peter. *The Fall and Rise of the Stately Home*. New Haven, CT and London: Yale University Press, 1997.

Mason, Roy. 'Defence Review'. London: Her Majesty's Stationery Office, 1975.

Mathur, Saloni, and Kavita Singh, eds. *No Touching, No Spitting, No Praying: The Museum in South Asia*. New Delhi: Routledge, 2015.

McKittrick, David, and David McVea. *Making Sense of the Troubles*. 2nd edn. London: Penguin Books, 2012.

McLaughlin, Andrew, and William Maroney. 'Privatization as Industrial Policy: State Withdrawal from the British Motor Industry'. *Public Administration* 74, no. 3 (1996): 435–52.

McTavish, Lianne. *Voluntary Detours: Small Town and Rural Museums in Alberta*. Montreal: McGill-Queen's University Press, 2021.

————. *Defining the Modern Museum: A Case Study of the Challenges of Exchange*. Toronto: University of Toronto, 2014.

————. 'Strategic Donations: Women and Museums in New Brunswick, 1862–1930'. *Journal of Canadian Studies* 42, no. 2 (2008): 93–116.

Miles, Andrew, and Lisanne Gibson. 'Everyday Participation and Cultural Value in Place: Special Issue'. *Cultural Trends* 26, no. 1 (March 2017).

————. 'Everyday Participation and Cultural Value'. *Cultural Trends* 25, no. 3 (2016): 151–7.

Moncunill-Pinas, Mariona. 'Museum-Making as Serious Leisure'. *Digithum*, no. 17 (2015): 20–7.

Nott, John Roy. 'Defence Review'. London: Her Majesty's Stationery Office, 1981.

Otley, C. B. 'The Educational Background of British Army Officers'. *Sociology* 7, no. 2 (1973): 191–209.

————. 'The Social Origins of British Army Officers'. *Sociological Review* 18, no. 2 (01/07/70): 213–39.

Selected bibliography

Pascoe Leahy, Carla. 'Selection and Sampling Methodologies in Oral Histories of Mothering, Parenting and Family'. *Oral History* 47, no. 1 (2019): 105–16.

Peterson, Richard, and Roger Kern. 'Changing "Highbrow" Taste: From Snob to Omnivore'. *American Sociological Review* 61, no. 5 (1996): 900–7.

Plummer, Kenneth. *Telling Sexual Stories: Power, Change, and Social Worlds*. London and New York: Routledge, 1994.

Poovey, Mary. *Uneven Developments: The Ideological Work of Gender in Mid-Victorian England*. Chicago, IL: University of Chicago Press, 1988.

Poulovassilis, Alexandra, Nick Larsson, Fiona Candlin, Jamie Larkin, and Andrea Ballatore. 'Creating a Knowledge Base to Research the History of UK Museums through Rapid Application Development'. *Journal on Computing and Cultural Heritage* 12, no. 4 (2019): 30:1–30:27.

Pratt, George. 'Afro-Caribbean/South Asian Music Inquiry Report'. London: Arts Council of Great Britain, 1986. CRER/MAA/REP/1/19. Modern Records Centre, University of Warwick.

Prince, David, and Bernadette Higgins-McLoughlin. *Museums UK: The Findings of the Museums Data-Base Project*. London: Museums Association, 1987.

'Protecting Those Who Protect Us: Women in the Armed Forces from Recruitment to Civilian Life: Second Report of Session 2021–22'. London: House of Commons Defence Committee, 2021.

Raths, Ralf. 'From Technical Showroom to Full-Fledged Museum: The German Tank Museum Munster'. *Museum and Society* 10, no. 3 (2012): 174–82.

Reas, Paul, and Stuart Cosgrove. *Flogging a Dead Horse: Heritage Culture and Its Role in Post-Industrial Britain*. Manchester: Cornerhouse, 1993.

'Rebuilding Volunteering Capacity in the Heritage Sector: A Briefing Note from the Heritage Sector to Covid-19 Draft at 15 April 2020'. London: Department of Digital, Culture, Media and Sport, April 2020.

Reilly, Justine, Kate Vigurs, and Joanne Boardman. 'Scoping the Army Museums Sector'. Salisbury: Army Museums Ogilby Trust, 2016.

Reming, Shawn. 'Sharing the Past in a Divided City: Belfast's Ulster Museum'. *International Journal of the Inclusive Museum* 4, no. 2 (2011): 1–12.

Robertson, Iain J. M. 'Heritage from Below: Class, Social Protest and Resistance'. In *The Public History Reader*, edited by Hilda Kean and Paul Martin, 56–67. London and New York: Routledge, 2013.

Robinson, Robert A., and William J. Sutherland. 'Post-War Changes in Arable Farming and Biodiversity in Great Britain'. *Journal of Applied Ecology* 39, no. 1 (2002): 157–76.

Rogalski, Wieslaw. *The Polish Resettlement Corps 1946–1949: Britain's Polish Forces*. Warwick: Helion and Company, 2019.

Ruffins, Fath Davis. 'Building Homes for Black History: Museum Founders, Founding Directors, and Pioneers, 1915–95'. *The Public Historian* 40 (2018): 13–43.

Rutherford-Morrison, Lara. 'Playing Victorian'. *The Public Historian* 37, no. 3 (01/08/15): 76–101.

Samuel, Raphael. 'Theme Parks – Why Not? History Is Everybody's'. *Independent on Sunday*. 12/02/95.

———. 'Flogging a Dead Horse'. In *Theatres of Memory*, 259–314. London: Verso, 1994.

———. *Theatres of Memory*. London: Verso, 1994.

Sandys, Duncan. 'Defence: Outline of Future Policy'. London: Her Majesty's Stationery Office, 1957.

Shakespeare, Sandra, Cherly Bowen, and Tola Dabiri, eds. 'Creating a Black British Museum: The Museum X Takeover Issue'. *Museums Journal*, October (2021).

Singh, Jasjit. 'What "Value" South Asian Arts in Britain?' *South Asian Popular Culture* 14, no. 3 (2016): 155–65.

Smith, Laurajane. *Emotional Heritage: Visitor Engagement at Museums and Heritage Sites*. Abingdon and New York: Routledge, 2020.

———. *Uses of Heritage*. London and New York: Routledge, 2006.

Smith, Laurajane, and Gary Campbell. '"Nostalgia for the Future": Memory, Nostalgia and the Politics of Class'. *International Journal of Heritage Studies* 23 (2017): 612–27.

Smith, Laurajane, Paul A. Shackel, and Gary Campbell, eds. *Heritage, Labour, and the Working Classes*. London: Routledge, 2011.

Smith, Roger. 'Utopian Designer: Paul Matt and the Brynmawr Experiment'. *Furniture History* 23 (1987): 88–97.

Stoker, Gerry. 'The Struggle to Reform Local Government: 1970–95'. *Public Money & Management* 16, no. 1 (January 1996): 17–22.

Stone-Gordon, Tammy. *Private History in Public: Exhibition and the Settings of Everyday Life*. Lanham, MD: AltaMira Press, 2010.

Sutcliffe-Braithwaite, Florence. *Class, Politics, and the Decline of Deference in England, 1968–2000*. Oxford: Oxford University Press, 2018.

Sykes, Richard, Alastair Austin, Mark Fuller, Taki Kinoshita, and Andrew Shrimpton. 'Steam Attraction: Railways in Britain's National Heritage'. *Journal of Transport History* 18, no. 2 (01/08/16): 156–75.

Tait, Simon. *Palaces of Discovery: The Changing World of Britain's Museums*. Stroud: Quiller Press, 1989.

Taylor, Mark. 'Nonparticipation or Different Styles of Participation? Alternative Interpretations from Taking Part'. *Cultural Trends* 25, no. 3 (02/07/16): 169–81.

Thompson, Paul. *Voices from the Past*. Oxford and New York: Oxford University Press, 1988.

Thomson, Mathew. *Lost Freedom: The Landscape of the Child and the British Post-War Settlement*. Oxford: Oxford University Press, 2013.

Wajid, Sara, and Rachael Minott. 'Detoxing and Decolonising Museums'. In *Museum Activism*, edited by Robert R. Janes and Richard Sandell, 25–35. London and New York: Routledge, 2019.

Wallace, Terry. '"Working of the Train Gang": Alienation, Liminality and Communitas in the UK Preserved Railway Sector'. *International Journal of Heritage Studies* 12, no. 3 (15/03/06): 218–33.

Ware, Richard. *UK Defence Policy: Options for Change*. Great Britain, Parliament, House of Commons, Library, Research Division, 1991.

Warren, Alan. *Barry Scrapyard: The Preservation Miracle*. Newton Abbot: David & Charles, 1988.

Watson, Sheila. 'Emotions in the History Museum'. In *Museum Theory: An Expanded Field. The International Handbooks of Museum Studies, Volume 1*, edited by Andrea Witcomb and Kylie Message (volume edited by Sharon Macdonald and Helen Rees Leahy), 283–301. Hoboken, NJ: John Wiley & Sons, 2015.

West, Bob. 'The Making of the English Working Past: A Critical View of the Ironbridge Gorge Museum'. In *The Museum Time-Machine: Putting Cultures on Display*, edited by Robert Lumley, 35–62. London and New York: Routledge, 1988.

West, George, Graham Allen, and Pete Skellon. 'Steam in Our Soul: A Story of Railway Enthusiasm and the Rise and Fall of the Dinting Railway Centre'. Keighley: Bahamas Locomotive Society (Ingrow Loco), 2002.

Whitelaw, Anne. 'Women, Museums and the Problem of Biography'. In *Museums and Biographies: Stories, Objects, Identities*, edited by Kate Hill, 75–86. Woodbridge: Boydell Press, 2012.

Wiliam, Mary, Wiliam, Eurwyn, and Wiliam, Dafydd. *The Brynmawr Furniture Makers: A Quaker Initiative 1929–40*. Orsaf: Gwasg Carreg Gwalch, 2012.

Williams, Allan, and Gareth Shaw. 'The Age of Mass Tourism'. In *Cornwall since the War: The Contemporary History of a European Region*, edited by Philip Payton, 84–97. Redruth: Institute of Cornish Studies, 1993.

Williams, Malcolm. 'Why Is Cornwall Poor? Poverty and In-Migration since the 1960s'. *Contemporary British History* 17, no. 3 (2003): 55–70.

———. 'Housing the Cornish'. In *Cornwall since the War: The Contemporary History of a European Region*, edited by Philip Payton, 157–80. Redruth: Institute of Cornish Studies, 1993.

Witcomb, Andrea. 'Remembering the Dead by Affecting the Living: The Case of a Miniature Model of Treblinka'. In *Museum Materialities: Objects, Engagements, Interpretations*, edited by Sandra Dudley, 39–52. New York: Routledge, 2010.

Woodham, Anna. 'Museum Studies and Heritage: Independent Museums and the Heritage Debate in the UK'. In *A Museum Studies Approach to Heritage*, edited by Sheila Watson, Amy Barnes, and Katy Bunning, 1st edn, 29–43. London: Routledge, 2018.

Woodham, Anna, Rhianedd Smith, and Alison Hess. *Exploring Emotion, Care and Enthusiasm in 'Unloved' Museum Collections*. Amsterdam: ARC Humanities Press, 2020.

Wright, Patrick. *On Living in an Old Country: The National Past in Contemporary Britain*. Oxford: Oxford University Press, 2009.

———. 'Appendix to the Oxford Edition: Sneering at the Theme Parks: An Encounter with the Heritage Industry'. In *On Living in an Old Country: The National Past in Contemporary Britain*, updated edn, 238–56. Oxford: Oxford University Press, 1989.

Index

Page numbers in *italic* refer to illustrations.